THE PHILOSOPHY OF SPIKE LEE

The Philosophy of Popular Culture

The books published in the Philosophy of Popular Culture series will illuminate and explore philosophical themes and ideas that occur in popular culture. The goal of this series is to demonstrate how philosophical inquiry has been reinvigorated by increased scholarly interest in the intersection of popular culture and philosophy, as well as to explore through philosophical analysis beloved modes of entertainment, such as movies, TV shows, and music. Philosophical concepts will be made accessible to the general reader through examples in popular culture. This series seeks to publish both established and emerging scholars who will engage a major area of popular culture for philosophical interpretation and examine the philosophical underpinnings of its themes. Eschewing ephemeral trends of philosophical and cultural theory, authors will establish and elaborate on connections between traditional philosophical ideas from important thinkers and the ever-expanding world of popular culture.

SERIES EDITOR

Mark T. Conard, Marymount Manhattan College, NY

BOOKS IN THE SERIES

The Philosophy of Stanley Kubrick, edited by Jerold J. Abrams
Football and Philosophy, edited by Michael W. Austin
Tennis and Philosophy, edited by David Baggett
The Philosophy of the Coen Brothers, edited by Mark T. Conard
The Philosophy of Film Noir, edited by Mark T. Conard
The Philosophy of Martin Scorsese, edited by Mark T. Conard
The Philosophy of Neo-Noir, edited by Mark T. Conard
The Philosophy of David Lynch, edited by William J. Devlin and Shai Biderman
The Philosophy of Horror, edited by Thomas Fahy
The Philosophy of The X-Files, edited by Dean A. Kowalski
Steven Spielberg and Philosophy, edited by Dean A. Kowalski
The Philosophy of Charlie Kaufman, edited by David LaRocca
The Philosophy of the Western, edited by Jennifer L. McMahon and B. Steve Csaki
The Philosophy of Steven Soderbergh, edited by R. Barton Palmer and Steven M. Sanders
The Philosophy of Science Fiction Film, edited by Steven M. Sanders
The Philosophy of TV Noir, edited by Steven M. Sanders and Aeon J. Skoble
Basketball and Philosophy, edited by Jerry L. Walls and Gregory Bassham
Golf and Philosophy, edited by Andy Wible

THE PHILOSOPHY OF SPIKE LEE

Edited by Mark T. Conard

THE UNIVERSITY PRESS OF KENTUCKY

Scholarly publisher for the Commonwealth,
serving Bellarmine University, Berea College, Centre
College of Kentucky, Eastern Kentucky University,
The Filson Historical Society, Georgetown College,
Kentucky Historical Society, Kentucky State University,
Morehead State University, Murray State University,
Northern Kentucky University, Transylvania University,
University of Kentucky, University of Louisville,
and Western Kentucky University.

Editorial and Sales Offices: The University Press of Kentucky
663 South Limestone Street, Lexington, Kentucky 40508-4008
www.kentuckypress.com

15 14 13 12 11 5 4 3 2 1

Library of Congress Cataloging-in-Publication Data

The philosophy of Spike Lee / edited by Mark T. Conard.
p. cm. — (The philosophy of popular culture)
Includes bibliographical references and index.
ISBN 978-0-8131-3380-5 (hardcover : alk. paper) — ISBN 978-0-8131-3381-2 (ebook)
1. Lee, Spike—Criticism and interpretation. I. Conard, Mark T., 1965–
PN1998.3.L44P45 2011
791.4302'33092—dc22
2011007258

This book is printed on acid-free paper meeting
the requirements of the American National Standard
for Permanence in Paper for Printed Library Materials.

Manufactured in the United States of America.

Member of the Association of
American University Presses

Contents

Preface

Mark T. Conard

One of the most significant developments in U.S. cinema during the last thirty years has been the rise of the new black film wave. Filmmakers who grew up and matured in the wake of the civil rights movement and its aftermath began to break through to mainstream audiences with their films and place before those audiences distinctly African American views about life, liberty, and pursuit of the American dream. At the forefront of this development has been Spike Lee, whose films are by turn daring, funny, angry, empathetic, alienating, confrontational, entertaining, and thought-provoking. I chose Lee as the subject of this volume because I think his work is important and worthy of study. It's important cinematically because he is obviously a talented auteur making significant contributions to the history of cinema (in fact, some of his efforts are remarkable achievements), but it's also important because of the themes and issues he takes on and the ideas he expresses through film. He obviously has much to say about race and racism and problems endemic to the black (usually urban) community, but there are a number of other philosophically rich ideas being pondered in his movies. Indeed, Lee is most often striving to say something important, something significant that's controversial and worthy of consideration. Because of that, he engenders strong feelings; one could argue that he's simultaneously one of the most loved and hated filmmakers. He often makes audience members uncomfortable—particularly white audience members, I should think—so it's no wonder that people like me are sometimes ambivalent about his work. If I were to hazard a guess, I'd say that Lee really doesn't want to be loved, so much as listened to and confronted.

The current volume is the result of our having listened closely to what he has to say. The first part, "Justice, Value, and the Nature of Evil," opens with Douglas McFarland's "The Symbolism of Blood in *Clockers*," in which he explores the "relationship between defilement and guilt, the efficacy of law in the cleansing of spilt blood, and the role of children and hence families in a culture of violence." Next, Jason Holt and Robert Pitter, in "The Prostitution Trap of Elite Sport in *He Got Game*," discuss the pressures placed on young athletes and their exploitation at the hands of coaches, family members, and agents, such that their bodies and their talents are commodified in a way akin to prostitution. Then I use one of Lee's more mainstream films to discuss the Aristotelian conception of justice and the nature of community that such a conception requires in "Aristotle and MacIntyre on Justice in *25th Hour*." In "We Can't Get Off the Bus: A Commentary on Spike Lee and Moral Motivation," Gabriella Beckles-Raymond examines Lee's faux documentary of the Million Man March and the relation between identity and moral commitment. Last, R. Barton Palmer uses Lee's retelling of the infamous Son of Sam case to argue in "Monsters and Moralism in *Summer of Sam*" that evil doesn't come only in the form of a murderous psychopath; it also takes the more insidious form of social pressure to cast someone or some group in the role of the undesirable other.

Part II is titled "Race, Sexuality, and Community," and it begins with Elizabeth Hope Finnegan's "(Still) Fighting the Power: Public Space and the Unspeakable Privacy of the Other in *Do the Right Thing*." She claims that Lee's 1989 film challenges the notion that racism can be cured through better individual awareness and knowledge of the hated other and that the only real solution is a complete and systemic reconfiguration of the structure of societal power. In "Coworking in the Kingdom of Culture: Identity and Community in the Films of Spike Lee," Charles F. Peterson claims that "Lee's films show that the formation of a truly inclusive U.S. character is not a smooth linear path . . . rather, it is one fueled by contradictions, conflicts, misunderstandings, and the birth pangs of a new society." Karen D. Hoffman examines, from a feminist perspective, whether Lee's lead female characters are truly liberated in "Feminists and 'Freaks': *She's Gotta Have It* and *Girl 6*." In "The Dialectic of King and X in *Do the Right Thing*," Michael Silberstein uses Lee's controversial film to examine two contrasting approaches to the problem of racism. Next, Ronald R. Sundstrom examines Lee's take on interracial relationships and their effects on the black community in "Fevered Desires and Interracial Intimacies in *Jungle Fever*." And Dan Flory, in "*Bamboozled:* Philosophy through Blackface," argues that the legacy of minstrelsy still influences our thinking and our actions with regard to race today.

The third part, "Time, the Subject, and Transcendence," starts with Jerold J. Abrams's "Transcendence and Sublimity in Spike Lee's Signature Shot," which examines the notion of transcendence as exemplified in Lee's distinctive "floating man" camera shot. Richard Gilmore discusses the commodification of time and the violence inherent in capitalism in "Economies of Time in *Clockers.*" Last, in "Rethinking the First Person: Autobiography, Authorship, and the Contested Self in *Malcolm X,*" David LaRocca uses Lee's biopic to discuss the constitution of the self in biography and autobiography.

These essays are written in nontechnical, jargon-free prose and presuppose no background in philosophy or film studies. Whether you're a die-hard fan (or even a detractor!) of Spike Lee, a film buff generally, or someone with an interest in philosophy, the following essays will help enrich your understanding of and appreciation for this iconic American filmmaker.

Acknowledgments

First, I want to thank the contributors to this volume heartily. Some of them I've worked with many times, and others are contributing to the series for the first time. They all did a truly excellent job, and I appreciate all the time and hard work they devoted to this project. I also want to thank the good people at the University Press of Kentucky for their continued diligence, interest, and enthusiasm. Last, I want to thank my family and friends for their love and support, especially Nayia Frangouli, Chris Landis, John and Linda Pappas, and Aeon Skoble.

Part I

Justice, Value, and the Nature of Evil

The Symbolism of Blood in *Clockers*

Douglas McFarland

Spike Lee dramatically announces the tone and perspective of his adaptation of Richard Price's novel of urban decay, *Clockers* (1995), in the opening credits of the film. Since the silent era, opening credits have served a variety of functions. As David Bordwell points out, they are "highly self-conscious and explicitly addressed to the audience."[1] Not only do titles and names provide a context for the narrative, but still and moving images often "anticipate a motif" or "establish the space of upcoming action." Credits, Bordewell argues, accumulate significance as "memory is amplified by the ongoing story."[2] In *Clockers,* Lee goes much further. He uses the opening credits rhetorically to shock, to repulse, perhaps even to shame the audience with graphic images of the self-destructive violence of African American urban culture. This staging of slain bodies in varying degrees of decay powerfully immerses the audience in blood. It concurrently, and perhaps more importantly, situates that violence within a particular philosophical context of evil: the stain of spilt blood signifies a transgression that defies narrative containment and legal resolution.

There Is a Place

The lyrical and plaintive voice of Stevie Wonder, hopefully musing "there is a place so far away," floats over the Universal corporate logo and immediately draws the audience into the imaginative space of *Clockers.* But it quickly becomes apparent that the voice has deceived us, leaving us unprepared for the initial image of the film. The dulcet tone of the music clashes violently with the first image of the opening credits: a close-up of what at first appears to be a darkened eye surrounded by red. As the camera slowly pulls back, it becomes clear that the dark spot is a fatal bullet wound in the victim's head. The high contrast and heavily saturated colors give the blood a darkened brightness and lurid intensity that suggest contamination and toxic contagion. What follows is a montage of the slain bodies of African American men, often sprawled or twisted in grotesque shapes. Intercut are reaction shots of those sequestered behind crime scene tape, the faces of children, newspaper headlines, video game landscapes, and graffiti. The controlling images, however, are those of the decaying corpses. Their presence makes it clear that the words of the music speak to the need to find refuge in a place "far away" from the urban violence made manifest in the opening credits.

Helpful in understanding how Spike Lee employs these images is Paul Ricoeur's conception of defilement as a symbolic category of evil and how it is dramatized in Attic tragedy. Ricoeur argues that the defilement caused by the violent spilling of blood is essentially irrational and has the power to harm our "psychic and corporeal existence." Perhaps most importantly, this category of evil resists verbal articulation. Formal confessions of fault, the contextualized space of storytelling, and legal codes assessing degrees of transgression are impeded by fear and repulsion over the sight of blood.[3] The Latin word for a sin against divine law reflects this understanding of evil. *Nefas* literally means "that which cannot be spoken"— hence an unspeakable transgression. For Ricoeur, in its visceral form, defilement through blood constitutes an evil that defies verbal expression.

The harm violence generates is communal as well as personal and familial. In his work on images of defilement in Greek tragedy, Jean-Pierre Vernant argues that contagion can spread to an entire city: "It is in the case of death, especially violent death and in particular homicide, that the community feels threatened by defilement and manifests a deep fear of contagion."[4] It is in the context of the civically produced tragic drama of fifth-century Athens that we can see this category of fault move from the unspeakable to that which is represented in a ritualized narrative context. The site of theatrical representation provides a space where the unspoken can be spoken, a space where the polis might contain defilement within a specific narrative form. In Attic tragedy, figures from a collective mythology are staged as imagined embodiments of an evil contagion. Oedipus has spilled family blood and defiled the link between generations by impregnating his mother. In so doing, he has contaminated the city itself. At the climactic moment of the play, when the doors of the house of Oedipus swing open, the unclean source of the plague that threatens Thebes stands before the audience with blood and gore dripping down his face, a literal representation of moral pollution.

It needs to be noted, however, that no explanation of evil, no containment within rational categories of understanding, is offered in Sophocles' staging of evil. Responsibility for the double crime remains intentionally muddled. There is no attempt to disentangle guilt and victimization. Oedipus both acts and is acted upon, the target of fate and a perpetrator of crime. It was not his intention to father his mother's children, but in fact he has done so. Necessity, responsibility, accident, and intention remain hopelessly confused in the crimes of Oedipus. And this is precisely the point of the play. Sophocles means to accomplish nothing more than to maximize the paradox of the guilty victim.[5] In this ambiguous condition, Oedipus cannot be cleansed and returned to the city; he can only be driven away from its boundaries.

In *Oedipus at Colonus,* after years of wandering, Oedipus arrives in a district of Athens where he defends himself to a chorus of citizens. He argues his case as if he were addressing jurors in a court of law, asserting that he unknowingly and without intention committed his crimes and that this should mitigate his responsibility. He demands, in short, that the crimes he has committed be judged according to rationally established degrees of guilt rather than by the absolutism of evil. He insists that his crime be staged not in the theater but in a court of law, a civic space where transgressions are judged according to a legal code. The dramatization of this movement from one category of evil to another is not unique to Sophocles. Aeschylus stages the final play of the *Oresteia* at the Aeropagus, the site of the Athenian law court, where the crimes of Orestes come before a jury of citizens.

Let me now return to the opening credits of *Clockers* and consider how the issues raised by Ricoeur and expressed in Attic drama inform the beginning of the film and prepare the audience for the narrative that will follow. *Clockers* opens with the unspeakable image of a decomposing body. The corpse is depersonalized, a freestanding symbol used rhetorically to expose the audience to contagion, to taint its collective imagination. It is not a factor in the narrative of the film. But the lyric of the song playing over the image, "there is a place so far away," provides the initial steps in creating a context for that body. The words, the tone, and the pace of the music speak movingly to the need to find a refuge unmarked by blood. The audience should immediately sense that the film will address the threat to communal culture the corpse poses. What follows are more photographs of bodies caked in blood. As I pointed out earlier, interspersed amid the decomposing bodies are images of graffiti, street art, newspaper headlines, and electronic games, all of which localize the violence in African American urban culture. Moreover, the crime scene tape, which conspicuously sequesters the slain body, makes it clear that the spilling of blood has come under the auspices of the law. The body of the victim is set apart so that a narrative of guilt and responsibility might be established. The corpse is now categorized not as an unspeakable evil but as a case to be solved.

Lee introduces another critical element in the opening credits: the contamination of children through violence. Headlines in newspapers report murders committed by children with access to guns. This is linked to video games in which violence is carried out in electronic landscapes. And this is connected to graffiti whose cartooning quality is emphasized. The title credits themselves resemble a cartoon. "Clockers" comes from right to left across the screen in bright red and yellow letters childishly askew. The film raises the question of how the contagion of blood that plagues the city infects children and how those children, in turn, become the carriers and spreaders of infection.

The opening credits of *Clockers* immerse the audience in blood and raise questions about the relationship between defilement and guilt, the efficacy of law in the cleansing of spilt blood, and the role of children and hence families in a culture of violence. In a much more subtle and pervasive manner, the credits set up the expectation, perhaps the hope, that the narrative that follows will provide a site for cleansing and purification. Communal storytelling does not simply speak the unspeakable. Nor does it simply eliminate, as E. R. Dodds puts it, "unwanted feelings through contemplating their projection in a work of art."[6] Instead, it offers a shared space in which the issues of cultural identity can be fully engaged. More specifically, *Clockers* situates the stain of urban violence within the context of a public narrative.

The Unclean

The film opens with a young African American male striding toward the camera and then pausing to survey the territory around him. Strike (Mekhi Phifer) is the central character of the film, and it is fitting that he appears in the first and last scenes. He runs a gang of clockers, on-the-street crack dealers, from the benches in a park situated in the Nelson Mandela Housing Project in Brooklyn. His two salient characteristics are his almost obsessive need to be physically clean and a stomach ulcer that afflicts him throughout the film. His clothing and his body bear no outward marks of soiling, but Strike habitually carries with him a vanilla Yoo-Hoo drink to soothe the pain in his stomach. He frequently bends over in discomfort and periodically spits up blood. At one point, the internal bleeding becomes so pronounced that paramedics must be called, and he spends an unspecified amount of time in the hospital. His condition generates little sympathy, however. He is concurrently a source of mockery and repulsion. Darryl Adams (Steve White) mercilessly ridicules him, linking his medical condition to unmanliness: "he got no pussy-Bismo . . . we need more Mylanta for this girl." Strike's condition marks him as one who is unclean. His counterpart in tragic drama is Philoctetes, whose ulcerous wound condemns him to exile on a deserted coastline. The contagion and sins of the community are localized within the body of Strike, in the ulcer that never heals and in the blood his body expels.

Strike's response to the ulcer is a compulsion to keep his outer body clean. The relationship among physical, moral, and sexual defilement, as well as his obsession with outer cleanliness, is dramatically rendered in the first scene of the film. A swarm of police quickly descends on the benches in the housing project to shake down Strike and his clockers for drugs. Although the scene is in part meant to suggest a slave market at which African American men are evaluated with regard to their physical worth, greater emphasis is placed on Strike's stake in the cleanliness of his body.[7] The police force him to pull down his pants and bend over so they can look for hidden drugs. When they don't find any, the police mock him for his unsanitary condition. "Where's your hygiene?" one derisively asks as he turns his head in feigned disgust. Strike vehemently asserts that he changes his clothes every day. In Richard Price's novel, Strike's reaction is even stronger: "Nothing sickened Strike more than filth, any kind of filth. He was clean, cleaner than any of them."[8] While Strike is bent over, holding up his backside, he looks over his shoulder and sees his mother looking down from an upper-story window. His public nakedness in front of his mother, the violation of his body by the police, almost as if they were sexually violating him, and the derisive claim that he has dirtied himself deeply humiliate him. Strike does not carry drugs on his body and is, in this respect, "clean." He is dirty, however, in the eyes of his mother, a spectacle of shameful degradation.

Haunting the neighborhood and shadowing Strike almost as his double is Errol Barnes (Thomas Jefferson Byrd). When Strike asks Rodney (Delroy Lindo) why he doesn't order Errol to kill Darryl Adams, Rodney responds that Errol is on the "A train" and suffers from the "virus." Because he has AIDS, Errol is a pariah who must not be touched—repulsive both physically and morally. Later, in a telling encounter with Strike, Errol asserts that he "ain't no homosexual," meaning that his disease was not sexually transmitted. Instead, the "needle" infected him, and he warns Strike, as if there were some affinity between them, "you gonna pay for using that shit." Errol used an "unclean" needle, shot "shit" into his arm, and consequently defiled his body. He is the unclean specter that haunts the neighborhood. But he also haunts Strike, who has taken Errol's place in Rodney's hierarchy and whose ulcer already suggests physical corruption.

Family Blood

In *Clockers,* defilement is literally and symbolically centralized within Strike's body, but it also circulates through a spectrum of family and quasi-family relationships: Strike and his mother, Strike and Tyrone, Strike and Andre, Strike and Victor, Strike and Rodney, and, to a certain extent, Strike and Rocco. Aeschylus provides the model in the *Oresteia* for this kind of dramatization of blood. Before he can leave for the Trojan War, Agamemnon, the head of the House of Atreus, must sacrifice his daughter, staining himself and the entire enterprise with her blood. Upon his return from the war, he is slain by his wife, Clytemnestra. The murder takes place offstage, behind the façade of the House of Atreus. At the climax of the play, the doors of the house open and the bloody body of Agamemnon is rolled out on stage, the grim embodiment of the defilement that pollutes the family. In the next play in the series, *The Libation Bearers,* the son of Agamemnon is hounded by the Furies, chthonic goddesses who thirst for family blood. They demand that Orestes take revenge by killing Clytemnestra, who has polluted herself by killing his father. The blood, in other words, seeps down from parent to child. In a startlingly lurid version of this generational defilement in Statius's *Thebaid,* Oedipus, in a moment of almost psychotic perversity, calls on those same Furies to spread among his own sons the contagion that has befouled him. In describing one of these Furies, Statius employs a cluster of graphic images that effectively convey the dread her evil embodies: "She was suffused with spreading pestilence. / Corrupt blood puffed her skin. Her black mouth spewed / hot vapors, which spread famine and diseases / and distant drought and epidemic death."[9]

Defilement in a variety of forms is similarly passed between generations in *Clockers.* Strike is a source of shame and contagion to his mother and to his brother Victor. During the police raid in the park, Strike is humiliated by the public exposure of his body and the derision of his "hygiene." He passes that shame on to his mother, who is sullied by the degradation of her son. Near the end of the film, she hurls his "filthy lucre" back in his face to prevent him from further contaminating the family. As she embraces Victor and his children, she casts out Strike.

Strike himself has been stained by Rodney, who figuratively adopted Strike as his son. Although Andre (Keith David), the public housing police officer, has attempted to establish himself as the male authority figure in the projects, particularly in his earlier relationship with Strike and then with Tyrone, Rodney stands out as the principal father figure in the neighborhood. He has sired what seems to be a raft of children, and his infant child occupies a conspicuous place in his store. Rodney also serves as the patriarch to a family of teenagers he has recruited as clockers, acting as a Fagin to a gang of Artful Dodgers. The key moment in his relationship with Strike occurs when Rodney orders Strike to kill Darryl Adams. Rodney asserts that Adams has "got to be got" because he has infringed on Rodney's market, but Rodney also wants to draw Strike irrevocably into his family. Rodney calls Strike his "staff" and his "son," and he requires that Strike become "bloody." He wants to pass on the stain of blood by which he himself was contaminated years earlier. In a flashback, we see Errol Barnes initiate Rodney into "blood," insisting that he shoot a rival drug dealer point-blank in the head. The miasma of blood—figurative and literal blood—spreads through the families of *Clockers,* its source buried somewhere in the violence of the past.

Now Strike is poised to pass this stain on to a younger generation. He takes Tyrone (Pee Wee Love) under his wing, teaching him how to cut cocaine and handle a gun. Clearly Strike is conflicted, since he also admonishes Tyrone about his "gangsta" video game and warns him to stay clean of drugs. Tyrone's mother, however, sees this relationship differently. She is determined to keep Tyrone from being contaminated by Strike and his clockers. When she discovers that Strike has taken Tyrone for a haircut, she physically attacks him, demanding that he stay away from her son. She takes the haircut as a visual sign of the contagion Strike has passed on. And indeed, near the end of the film, Tyrone shoots Errol Barnes with Strike's gun. Unknowingly, Strike ushers Tyrone across the boundary separating the violence of the video game and the violence of the streets.

Strike's brother also struggles to prevent the violence from infecting himself and his children. Victor dresses impeccably in a white shirt and blazer for his job in an upscale Asian jewelry store. At one point in the film, however, he is confronted by a street person who mocks him and spits on him, literally befouling his face. In an earlier scene, he sits in a bar too sick to complete his shift at a second job. His battle to stay clean has exhausted him, so when Strike tells him a story about Darryl Adams's sexual perversions, Victor succumbs and finally dirties himself by killing Adams. Ironically, his need to purge the neighborhood of contagion leads him to be stained with blood. After the shooting, Victor returns to his mother's apartment and vomits repeatedly in the toilet, as if trying to purge his system of the poison he has ingested.

The Law

The shift from the theatrical staging of evil to its assessment in the context of a set of legal codes thematically informs the narrative of *Clockers*. Ricoeur argues that a specified, precise, and reasoned punishment can cleanse the community of the miasma of evil.[10] Although catharsis is usually associated with Aristotle's notion that tragic drama has a therapeutic purging effect, it has other meanings pertinent to the relationship between evil and the law. Catharsis can signify quite simply a clarity of language and the elimination of ambiguity in the words of the oracle, a purging of the equivocations and uncertainties of the gods. Similarly, the law achieves catharsis by advancing evil from a quasi-religious and dramatic context to one in which transgression can be precisely measured and categorized. This is pointed out by Vernant, who argues that in Greek tragic drama, "We find an imprecision in the terms used, shifts of meaning, incoherencies and contradictions, all of which reveal the disagreements within legal thought itself and also betray its conflicts with a religious tradition and moral thought from which the law is already distinct but whose domains are still not clearly differentiated from its own."[11] In tragedy, the clarity the law ultimately demands has not yet fully asserted itself over religious impurity.

Like the family, the law is a ubiquitous presence in *Clockers*, a constant force striving to maintain civic and familial order. But although the legal system is fully established, with a strict code for assessing criminal conduct and an apparatus for detection and enforcement, the law seems incapable of purging the African American world depicted in the film of the defilement brought on by the spilling of blood. The examination of the body of Darryl Adams at the site of the killing strikingly dramatizes this failure. When the officers arrive at the scene, the corpse has already begun the process of putrefaction, clearly invoking images of the slain bodies in the opening credits. Detectives surround the corpse, following forensic procedures to determine the number of shots, the trajectories of bullets, the presence of defensive wounds, and the time of death. The body has been cordoned off by crime scene tape to preserve the integrity of the evidence. In this closed off space, the agents of the law work to solve the crime, to identify the perpetrator and determine his motives. But as the detectives stand over the body, they simultaneously snicker and make crude jokes about its state of decay. Their mockery relegates the body to something less than human. Derision is a gesture of protection, separating the police officers from the horrific sight they have encountered and placing the decaying corpse into a primitive category of evil. The detectives stand caught between forensic science and the ritualistic casting out of the unclean Other. Paradoxically, the plastic gloves they wear function both to prevent contamination of the evidence and to protect themselves from the contamination of the body. And of course, the detectives' mockery is informed by race. The white police officers enter the neighborhood from the outside, alien and hostile to its environment. And although they represent the law, they demonstrate a visceral reluctance to place African American violence into the category of evil that the law requires. In this scene, Lee powerfully portrays a civic institution that would "cleanse" the blood staining the sidewalk beneath the body of Darryl Adams but that, without hesitation, would also classify that stain as an indelible mark of evil.

The driving force behind the enforcement of the law is Rocco (Harvey Keitel), one of two officers who have been assigned to the case. Although Victor has come forward and confessed to the crime, Rocco believes he fabricated the story and relentlessly interrogates him to get at the truth. Under the law, confession provides an explanation of crime and a basis for its punishment. In Ricoeur's terms, confession offers a narrative context for "fault." Rocco's partner, Detective Larry Mazilli (John Turturro), is content with Victor's narrative of events and is ready to close the case without ascertaining its validity. His attitude does not emanate from any sense of despair and resignation but rather from a cynicism directed at the African American world he polices and condescendingly perceives as hopelessly tainted. Rocco, however, demands an accurate narrative held together by a logically connected series of events. Unlike Price's fully developed portrayal of Rocco in the novel, Lee does not probe deeply into the character of the detective, leaving it to the audience to infer what Rocco perceives to be at stake. He is certainly angry over being played, and as a police detective, he certainly desires to solve the crime, but he also seems deeply and personally invested in containing evil within a rational narrative of cause and effect.

Regardless of his reasons, Rocco's skepticism about Victor's confession entangles him with Strike and his family. Rocco believes that Victor has lied to protect his younger brother. Because Victor is a model citizen with a "clean" record and works two jobs to support his family, his plea of self-defense might very well be believed by a jury. Strike, in contrast, because he is an "unclean" dealer of drugs, would be easily convicted and harshly punished. Rocco has identified Strike as the source of contagion in the family and the community and is frustrated that the law cannot eradicate him. When it becomes clear to Rocco that Victor is actually the killer, he seems unable to assimilate the truth into a narrative that separates good and evil. At the very least, he is confounded by the ambiguity of right and wrong and frustrated by the inability of the law to purify the world he oversees.

Rocco's crisis becomes even more pronounced when he must deal with the shooting of Errol Barnes by Tyrone. There is absolutely no question who committed the crime. It happened in broad daylight in front of a host of witnesses. But for a second time, Rocco has become entangled in a family. Tyrone's mother and Andre, who functions as a surrogate father to Tyrone, plead with Rocco to save the boy, arguing that his conviction will irrevocably taint him. Rocco agrees to instruct Tyrone in how to shape his confession in such a way as to mitigate his fault. Tyrone's official explanation is a scripted narrative intended to circumvent the law and manipulate the judgment of a jury. The ritual site of confession in the context of the legal system is the interrogation room. If the courtroom functions as a theatrical space, the interrogation room is a confessional. For Rocco, the purity of that site is defiled by a falsified confession. Distaste is written on his face when he coaches Tyrone. Rather than cleansing the world, Rocco himself is tainted by its ambiguities and contradictions. All the while, Strike lurks in the background as a source of contagion beyond Rocco's reach. It was, after all, Strike's gun that Tyrone used to kill Errol Barnes. It was Strike who facilitated Tyrone's crossing over from the imagined violence of a video game to the actual spilling of blood.

You Must Take the A Train

The final act of *Clockers* suggests a particular narrative typology: the movement from an urban to a pastoral landscape. But as Strike makes his way out of Brooklyn, there is little of the pastoral in the arid southwestern landscape he surveys from his seat on the train. The tension between escape and expulsion remains unresolved at the end of the film. Strike eludes the wrath of Rodney, who believes his protégé has betrayed him to the police. But he is also exiled from everything he knows. For better or for worse, the city constitutes his cultural grounding, but that world has purged itself of his presence. Strike is conspicuously absent at the reunion between Victor and his family upon his release from prison. When Rocco and Strike arrive at Penn Station, Strike awkwardly thanks the detective for helping him escape, but Rocco almost disgustedly tells him to get out of town and stay out. Rocco seems morally and even physically repulsed by Strike's presence. He is unable to situate Strike within his schema of good and evil. By all reason and logic, Strike should have been the killer of Darryl Adams and Errol Barnes, thereby bearing the weight of evil. Perhaps it is Strikes's ambiguous nature, the muddied confluence of guilt and victimization, that Rocco cannot abide. The uncleanliness of Strike is finally just this: he embodies the contradictions inherent in a more primitive and less rational representation of "fault."

In the final shot of the film, Strike silently looks out from the train, thinking to himself, as travelers often do. Perhaps he is contemplating a new beginning in a new world. But one could not imagine a landscape more alien to someone born and raised in a Brooklyn housing project than the desert through which the train passes. His trek is not one out of Egypt and into the promised land of milk and honey; rather, it is more like the wanderings of Oedipus, who is exiled from Thebes and condemned to occupy no permanent place. Perhaps an even better comparison is to Sophocles' other tragic figure, Piloctetes, who, like Strike, is plagued by an ulcer that refuses to heal. He is banished to a remote, uncultivated island and finds himself "far from houses . . . in an alien and hostile space."[12] Odysseus refers to him as a "man without friends, without city, a corpse among the living."[13] Strike may not be a corpse, but he is certainly far from his family and city. It is difficult to imagine that this journey will bring him the refuge he first sought in his miniature train set. That the film should end with equivocation and ambivalence speaks to the sophistication and honesty of Lee's meditation on the evil of violence and the attempts of human culture to cleanse its stain and explicate its senselessness.

Notes

1. David Bordwell, Janet Staiger, and Kristin Thompson, *The Classical Hollywood Cinema* (New York: Columbia University Press, 1985), 26.

2. Ibid., 43–44.

3. Paul Ricoeur, *The Symbolism of Evil,* trans. Emerson Buchanan (Boston: Beacon Press, 1969), 25.

4. Jean-Pierre Vernant, "The Pure and the Impure," in *Myth and Society in Ancient Greece,* trans. Janet Lloyd (New York: Zone Books, 1988), 124.

5. Jean-Pierre Vernant, "Tensions and Ambiguities in Greek Tragedy," in *Myth and Tragedy in Ancient Greece,* trans. Janet Lloyd (New York: Zone Books, 1990), 37–38.

6. E. R. Dodds, *The Greeks and the Irrational* (Berkeley: University of California Press, 1951), 48.

7. In Richard Price's novel, the scene is explicitly compared to a slave market. See Richard Price, *Clockers* (New York: Picador, 1992), 11.

8. Ibid., 12.

9. Statius, *The Thebaid,* trans. Charles Stanley Ross (Baltimore: Johns Hopkins University Press, 2007), 1.105–8. See also Ruth Padel, *In and Out of the Mind: Greek Images of the Tragic Self* (Princeton, N.J.: Princeton University Press, 1992), 172–79.

10. Ricoeur, *Symbolism of Evil,* 43.

11. Jean-Pierre Vernant, "The Historical Moment of Tragedy in Greece," in *Myth and Tragedy in Ancient Greece,* 25.

12. Jean-Pierre Vernant, "Sophocles' Philoctetes and the Ephebeia," in *Myth and Tragedy in Ancient Greece,* 166.

13. Ibid., 166–67.

The Prostitution Trap of Elite Sport in *He Got Game*

Jason Holt and Robert Pitter

Spike Lee is an accomplished filmmaker who drew much public attention following the release of his first feature films in the late 1980s. *School Daze* (1988), *Do the Right Thing* (1989), and *Jungle Fever* (1991), which he both wrote and directed, tell stories involving complex social, political, and philosophical issues. And they do this so effectively and provocatively that they generated significant controversy when they were first released, illustrating Lee's skill at portraying the complexities of contemporary life on the big screen in a way that provokes serious and sometimes harmful misinterpretation. For example, several American media outlets opposed the release of *Do the Right Thing*, calling it incendiary and claiming it was likely to provoke riots if it were shown. The feared riots never occurred, perhaps because, as Roger Ebert notes, Lee "made a movie about race in America that empathized with all the participants. He didn't draw lines or take sides but simply looked with sadness at one racial flashpoint that stood for many others."[1]

He Got Game (1998) is another Lee film that depicts the complexities of social life not only generally but also in elite sport, specifically basketball. In this film the two protagonists, Jake Shuttlesworth (Denzel Washington) and his son Jesus (Ray Allen), reconnect after a prolonged estrangement due to Jake's incarceration for the murder of his wife, Jesus' mother. Jesus has become an outstanding high school basketball player whose talents are coveted by college and professional teams all over the country. The warden temporarily releases Jake from prison for one reason: to convince Jesus to sign with the governor's alma mater, Big State University. "If you persuade your son to do this," says Warden Wyatt (Ned Beatty), "the governor's given me his word he'll do everything in his power to cut your time here short, considerably."

Through this rather unconventional and somewhat improbable scenario, Lee's film explores significant contemporary social, moral, and political issues in and around sport, primarily through the depiction of Jesus' various relationships with his girlfriend, his family (particularly his father, uncle, and sister), people within the commodified system of intercollegiate and professional basketball, and residents of his own inner-city neighborhood. The development of Jake's relationship with prostitute Dakota Burns (Milla Jovovich) is also given extensive, and seemingly excessive, screen time. Some critics have described the Jake-Dakota relationship as one of several elements that "diffuse the story and drag it down,"[2] or as "a subplot that goes nowhere."[3] As Ray Didinger and Glen Macnow complain, "we still can't figure out what she [Dakota] had to do with the story."[4] On first viewing, one might agree: relative to the main story—Jake's attempt to reconnect with his son and Jesus' decision on the next step in his career—the scenes with the prostitute seem unimportant and inessential, serving as mere filler in the main narrative, if not outright distraction from it. However, subsequent viewings suggest a more charitable reading: the prostitute scenes are integral to the film, revealing precisely the common ground between Jake and Jesus that the characters themselves find so difficult to discover.

The reading of the film we present here may challenge other readings. Michael Giardina and Cameron McCarthy, for instance, discuss the film as an "example and a symptom of popular racial representation that is compatible with the politics of a conservative (Black) middle class."[5] Instead, we examine the film from the point of view of the main characters. While we recognize that these characters are the creation of an individual with a particular personal biography influenced by the "revitalized neo-conservative agenda" of America described by Giardina and McCarthy, we argue that the film is insightful in other ways. It presents an astute perspective on the dilemma faced by people who are, or are in danger of being, treated as commodities, as commodified bodies. In honor of Dakota's often unacknowledged significance in the film, we refer to this dilemma as the *prostitution trap* of elite sport. Before adopting a philosophical perspective on the prostitution trap, we examine in some detail what it means to speak of commodified bodies in the parallel domains of elite sport and prostitution.

Commodified Bodies

It has become quite common for people, especially males living in disadvantaged communities, to see sport not merely as a form of play—as a self-expressing, fulfilling, joyous activity—but also as a means of transcending their class- and race-determined life chances.[6] The elements of play often associated with sport (at least unorganized sport) have been described in idealist terms that focus on notions of subjectivity, spontaneity, and freedom from necessity. Commodified sport, in which a person exchanges his or her abilities for money or other material gains, significantly alters such idealized notions of sport. The commodified sporting self is not so free; it is constrained and objectified as physical capital through the rules of current socioeconomic systems.[7] Consequently, the elite athlete tends to be treated as a commodified body, as is the prostitute, and both are subject to a sense of alienation from themselves.[8] Understanding the body as a commodity challenges the sense of self and others as people, as subjects in their own right, because idealized notions of self (as a free and creative being) are confronted with the undeniable fact that people are often treated as objects to be bought, sold, manipulated, or exploited.

Elite sport and prostitution are perhaps inevitably destined to commodify bodies. Lee illustrates these challenges through subtle yet important parallels between these two social worlds that have much in common. The essence of Lee's depiction of elite sport resembles the social world of prostitution as discussed in several academic studies. Writing about pimp-controlled prostitution, Celia Williamson and Terry Cluse-Tolar note, "Pimps involved in prostitution activities refer to this sector of the underground economy as 'the game.'"[9] In this context, the expression *to have game* describes those pimps who "possess a certain amount of charisma and smooth talking, persuasive conversation toward women." The game is all about getting money by controlling and manipulating others' actions: "pimps believe all capitalistic pursuits are parallel to pimping." There are rules that every pimp must follow to be successful, the most significant of which is getting paid "without shame." Another rule demands that a pimp "sell it to a prospective prostitute . . . without revealing his game plan." To do so, the pimp must develop "his rap," a series of persuasive conversations "that are philosophical in nature and ideological about life and making money." Two recruiting methods frequently used by pimps are so-called seduction and stratagem.[10] Seduction involves promises of love and emotional attachment, while stratagem employs images of grandeur, money ("sitting on a gold mine"), and a romanticized career.

He Got Game suggests that "the game" is everywhere, in one form or another. Lee focuses our attention on it in elite basketball, yet he does so only implicitly in scenes involving overt prostitution. "The game" is explicitly played by almost everyone who comes into contact with Jesus; one character after another brandishes his or her game or rap in front of Jesus.

Jesus knows the game is on, and throughout the film he tries to avoid falling victim to it. The first rap we see comes from Jesus' girlfriend Lala (Rosario Dawson), as she tries to convince Jesus to see a sports agent (which, given his status, is forbidden by the rules). Lala's rap employs seduction. Moments later, Jesus confides in his coach, and we are presented with a generalized coach's rap. Jesus' conversation with Coach Cincotta (Arthur J. Nascarella) unfolds like this:

> JESUS: I'll be so happy when this stuff is over with.
> COACH: It won't be long now. What do you got? A Monday morning 10:00 A.M. press conference, right?
> JESUS: Yeah.
> COACH: Have you made a decision yet?
> JESUS: You know what? That's the thing that's bothering me. And you know what? You're my coach, right? I mean, I don't mind. Every time I walk down the hallways, "Where you goin'? Where you goin'? Have you chosen a school yet? Are you going to the NBA?" I'm tired of hearing that.
> COACH: I can understand that. Look, maybe it's in your best interest to take it as a compliment. People really do care about you.
> JESUS: People don't care about me. They care about themselves. They're just tryin' to get over, tryin' to get a piece of Jesus, that's all.[11]

Coach Cincotta then delivers his rap, which includes lines such as "You can call me anytime" and "Jesus, I have always thought of you as a son." The exchange ends with the coach asking, "Do you remember what I told you?" and Jesus responding, as though fed up with this bromide, "This is going to be the most important decision in your life." This rap lyric is repeated over and over again by a montage of recognizable college basketball coaches. Jesus is seen as an object, a commodified body, sought after by numerous coaches and many others (read pimps).

The Trap Itself

Although an atmosphere of prostitution permeates the film, it is most easily recognizable in the scenes involving Dakota, who lives next door to Jake. These scenes illustrate the banal grittiness of Jake's existence, which for him is the lucky situation of being a temporary "non-con" who must, however, return to prison as soon as his mission is done. The juxtaposition of the mean streets of Jake's temporary reprieve—for him, a step up from normal prison life—with the hype and glitz of Jesus' exceptional situation reflects how far Jake must go to reach his son and anticipates how hard it will be for father and son to find any common ground.

Jake wants Jesus to have a life better than his own and has pushed Jesus hard to "get him to that next level," to be the "first Shuttlesworth that's even gonna make it out these projects." A flashback to Jesus' childhood shows Jake using intimidation and battery to toughen up his son, to help him learn not to let anything interfere with his game. Jesus, however, is merely a child who is too young to understand the lesson, much less the morally suspect method being used. Jake, obsessed with his own vision of what Jesus' future should be, ignores his son's call for compassion (with which we, as viewers, sympathize) and instead continues to treat Jesus as an object—a means to an end—rather than as a person and as the vulnerable child he is. Frustrated by Jesus' reluctance to continue "playing," Jake follows Jesus back home and eventually redirects his anger toward his wife Martha (Lonette McKee), accidentally killing her and further alienating himself from his son.

The scenes with Dakota triangulate the common ground between Jake and Jesus by showing that they are suffering the same misfortune in different guises, the same abuse in different forms. Jake's attempt to reconnect with Jesus is fraught by the coercive pressure of his mission to get his son to accept Big State's offer (and without this mission, Jake would not have had the opportunity to interact with Jesus). Jesus' love of basketball is now fraught by coercive pressure of many kinds from those vying for his services. Dakota's love for her pimp, Sweetness (Thomas Jefferson Byrd), is fraught by his coercing her to turn tricks. The added incentives (money for Dakota; a reduced sentence for Jake; money, sex, and fame for Jesus) strengthen the analogy among the three situations. Dakota's situation is the literal equivalent of the metaphorical—but no less apt—situation in which Jake and Jesus find themselves. They all face the very same trap: prostitution.

It is not simply that all three face a similar kind of trap. The compelling thing is that the trap seems *inevitable,* at least as the film presents it initially; it is the result of what appears to be an unavoidable dichotomy. The film's opening slow-motion montage shows people from different regions and of different ages, classes, and sexes playing basketball with idyllic Aaron Copland music as accompaniment. In it, we find a sense of the beauty of basketball and an appreciation of players' and spectators' love of the sport.[12] In a montage of close-ups later in the film, players from Lincoln High express this idealism verbally: "The game brings me love, peace and happiness," says Lonnie "Dubs" Dukes (John Wallace). "Basketball is poetry in motion," declares Jesus. "Basketball is the birthplace of my dreams, of everything I wanna accomplish in life," states Mance Little (Walter McCarty).

But soon enough the slow, idyllic scenes are replaced by fast-paced, gritty scenes of the mean streets Jake must navigate on his mission, and the sound track here, by contrast, is an unignorable blast of Public Enemy. In this juxtaposition alone—the sweet idealism suggested by Copland versus the unapologetic realism of Public Enemy—we have the musical form of the film's dichotomy: the idealism of love (Jesus' for basketball, Jake's for Jesus, Dakota's for Sweetness) appears hopelessly unrealistic and untenable, given how the world is. Whether inducing Jesus to play for a particular squad, offering Jake a reduced sentence, or convincing Dakota to walk the streets for money, what seems operative throughout the film is the cynical pragmatism of pimps and the plight of their victims, who are made vulnerable precisely by their love (for a game, a son, a lover) in a domain where the pimps or would-be pimps see them as marketable, as having cash value. Such influences, moreover, cannot be ignored; they are out there and determine much of what goes on in the real world. The dichotomy, then, is between a sympathetic, if naïve, and ultimately untenable idealism and an immoral but seemingly unavoidable, cynical pragmatism—as if everyone has their price, and the only thing to do is carve out the best deal possible when prostituting oneself. Stated another way, one must either remain a frustrated idealist or give in and sell out. It is this dichotomy that sets up the prostitution trap: an unrealistic, naïve idealism won't work, and an immoral, cynical pragmatism won't do. This recurring theme is evident in both Jake and Jesus, who demonstrate that there are limits on how much they will allow their cynicism to corrupt or displace their idealized sense of self.

Most of the characters Jesus encounters in the film try to draw him into the trap with a rap of seduction or stratagem. However, and somewhat ironically, it is Big Time Willie (Roger Guenveur Smith), one of the local cognoscenti of the mean streets, who delivers a counter-rap, warning Jesus of the temptations and vicissitudes he will face as a rising basketball star:

> First thing that's gonna take you out is these drugs they got for you. . . . You got the cocaine, heroin, crack cocaine. You got the uppers, the downers, the chiva, crystal meth, acid. We got the nicotine for you. Huh? You don't want none of that? And don't forget about the alcohol, baby. Yeah, we got that malt liquor, a.k.a. liquid crack. . . .
>
> Oh, and they got the other thing for you, man. Yeah, I almost forgot. They got that pussy. I know you know how to spell that. . . .

> H-I-V. . . . He think 'cause he got that ball skill, he goin' up in the NBA, he gonna be immune. How you gonna be immune to pussy? . . . Come on, man. Be real. . . .
>
> And I didn't even mention the bloodsucking leeches. Oh yeah, the newfound family. Pygmy buzzards be hoverin' over you, tryin' to get that loose change. You know what I'm sayin'? They talk about "I love you. Oh, I love you. Oh, I love you, Jesus. Oh, I love you. . . . *Te amo. Jesús, te amo. Aye, qué fiebre.*"[13]

The counter-rap advises Jesus to beware of not only the sensual pleasures on offer because of his status as a star athlete but also the duplicitous and parasitic character of many who will claim to care about him. In each case the appeal is understandable, but so too is the looming threat of wasted talent, squandered resources, and compromised integrity. A pleasing guise sets the trap, and a natural response springs it.

Big Time's lecture consolidates all of what Jesus faces throughout the film. Jesus' physical capital is a valuable commodity, and everyone wants a piece of the action: Jesus becomes an object to be bought, sold, manipulated, exploited. But Jesus is wise to what's going on; he doesn't want to be beholden to anyone—not his high school coach, his girlfriend, or his uncle and legal guardian, all of whom accuse Jesus of "holding out" on them. Each pressures Jesus to take the money and share it with the people who "love" him and have always "been there" for him, or so their raps go.

The prostitution trap arises specifically from the interplay between distinct kinds of rewards—intrinsic and extrinsic—and how these different values intersect with social relations. The distinction between intrinsic and extrinsic value is familiar. A thing has intrinsic value when it is valuable for what it is, for its own sake, whereas something has extrinsic or instrumental value when it is valued for what it leads to, for its consequences, irrespective of whether it has intrinsic value. Activities are intrinsically rewarding when valued for their own sake, for the sheer fun or pleasure or enjoyment derived from engaging in them, whereas activities are extrinsically rewarding when they are valued for their consequences. Leisure and work are typically characterized as intrinsically and instrumentally rewarding, respectively: leisure for its own sake, work for the income it earns. Naturally, leisure activities might have extrinsic value as well (e.g., health benefits from walking), and work may be intrinsically rewarding (for those who like their chosen profession), but it is also possible to engage in activities in which these different types of values diverge (e.g., taking bitter-tasting medicine for one's health, or enjoying smoking despite its adverse effects). In a world where human agents spend much of their time bound to social relationships, the intrinsic-extrinsic dichotomy becomes complicated by social structures: the rules and resources that govern daily life. One would think that, all else being equal, an activity that is both intrinsically *and* instrumentally rewarding would be better than one with only intrinsic or extrinsic value. It is on this reasonable, but in some respects misguided, assumption that the prostitution trap gains its foothold.

From an abstract point of view, the greater the value attached to an activity, the more one should be motivated to engage in it and the more rewarding it should be. In this sense, we tend to view reasons as *aggregative:* add one good reason to another, and the result is the simple sum of the values—or, to put it loosely, a doubly good reason. Often enough, this is what happens. If one enjoys academic research, for instance, and happens to hold a job that pays one to do it, the salary may be seen as an extra reward, an added incentive for doing something intrinsically rewarding. But just as threats and punishment can provide disincentives (e.g., Sweetness's abuse of Dakota, which she is anxious to minimize), so too can extrinsic rewards when these are taken as attempts to control or coerce the person in question.[14] In this case, extrinsic rewards can *compromise* intrinsic rewards, despite their desirability: Jesus' love of basketball is thus threatened by various desirable extrinsic rewards. No matter which college or professional offer he selects, he will get to play elite basketball, but both the circumstances (which team he plays for) and the reasons for choosing them are poised to undermine the very attitude (his love of the game) that makes the trap possible. In this way, the film presents a challenge not only to naïve idealism about love (for a game, a lover, or a son) but also to unreflectively idealistic views of the nature of rationality: in a superficial sense, perhaps, more should always be more, but as it turns out, it isn't.

Avoiding the Trap

If *He Got Game* merely helped to reveal the complexities of the prostitution trap in an entertaining and engaging way, that would be no small service. But the film does more. In addition to showing many facets of the problem while diagnosing it, Lee turns prescriptive and points the way to a solution. The dichotomy between naïve idealism and cynical pragmatism, though compellingly presented, is, in the final analysis, rejected. For those facing the dichotomy, there is a way out, a way to avoid being or becoming complicit in the prostitution trap. Extrinsic rewards have coercive or controlling potential only when they are attached to outcomes not freely chosen, that is, when they function as temptations that undermine rather than express a person's autonomy. It should be noted that the extrinsic rewards offered to Jesus for choosing one school over another or one pro contract over another are either rule-bending or illegal, morally suspect or immoral. If Jesus did not care about his love of basketball and his motivations for choosing among the various options, his values would not be threatened. But he does care—rightly—so they are threatened. Dakota's relationship with Jake appears to be genuine because the usual extrinsic reward confounding her sexual relationships is not in effect: the money-for-sex motivation is suspended. Jake, in contrast, abandons the opportunity to truly reconnect with his son by focusing more and more desperately on convincing him to sign with Big State. Jesus ends up opting for Big State, not so that Jake's sentence will be reduced but because getting a college education and remaining close to his younger sister are important to him.

By the skillful management of details shown and omitted, Lee allows the viewer to imagine that Jesus has beaten the trap on his own terms. Despite his underdog, exploited (but nonetheless fortunate) position, Jesus exerts his autonomy and escapes the trap by rejecting the many seductive and grandiose pitches thrown his way. Although he chooses Big State, Jesus does not sign the contract delivered to him on the school's behalf by his father. We are meant to imagine that Jesus has negotiated an alternative agreement on his own terms. Furthermore, Jesus' prominent absence from the press conference where his decision is announced suggests that he regards the event with a degree of skepticism and so has distanced himself from the proceedings, preserving an idealized sense of self from at least one part of "the game" of elite sport.

Where Jesus succeeds, Jake fails by turning proxy, would-be pimp for Jesus at the governor's behest, even going so far as to challenge his son to a game of one-on-one for the fate of the Big State letter of intent. Jake's failure is tragic, although he partly redeems himself by finally reconnecting with his son through one last heartfelt letter without ulterior motive. By the film's end, Jesus, Dakota, and Jake have managed to free themselves from the prostitution trap. We see Dakota leaving the city on a bus. A reincarcerated Jake walks "out of bounds" in the prison yard, and despite the threat of being shot by the guard, he throws his basketball over the prison wall, defying those with the authority to contain but not control him (a scene that echoes the earlier flashback in which Jesus as a child throws a basketball over the playground fence, defying his father's bullying). In the next moment, as Jesus practices in the empty stadium at Big State, Jake's basketball symbolically arcs down into the court. Jesus puts down his ball and picks up Jake's to the accompaniment, once more, of Aaron Copland music. Jesus has preserved his love of the game and has reconnected with his father in mutual recognition of their individual autonomy.

Refusing to be swayed by extrinsic motivations that threaten to undermine his integrity, Jesus retains it by finding a niche between an unworkable idealism and an immoral pragmatism: he has achieved what might be called an *authentic realism,* neither hypocritical nor blind to his nature or his situation. He has remained true to himself and his values without ignoring his susceptibility to the very real temptations of the prostitution trap. If there is any message here, it is this: walking the fine line between an objectified and a subjective notion of self, between a cynical pragmatism and a naïve idealism, is what it ultimately means to "have game."

Notes

1. Roger Ebert, review of *Do the Right Thing* DVD, *Chicago Sun Times,* May 27, 2001.
2. Emanuel Levy, review of *He Got Game, Variety,* April 27, 1998.
3. Stephen Hunter, review of *He Got Game, Washington Post,* May 1, 1998.
4. Ray Didinger and Glen Macnow, *The Ultimate Book of Sports Movies: Featuring the 100 Greatest Sports Films of All Time* (Philadelphia: Running Press, 2009), 135.
5. Michael D. Giardina and Cameron McCarthy, "Screening Race in America: Sport, Cinema, and the Politics of Urban Youth Culture," in *Youth Culture and Sport: Identity, Power, and Politics,* ed. Michael D. Giardina and Michele K. Donnelly (New York: Routledge, 2008), 36. See also Michael D. Giardina and Cameron McCarthy, "The Popular Racial Order of Urban America: Sport, Identity, and the Politics of Culture," *Cultural Studies <=> Critical Methodologies* 5, 2 (2005): 145–73.
6. See Stanley Aronowitz, *False Promises* (Toronto: McGraw-Hill, 1974).
7. This might simply reflect a deeper problem with institutions generally: "Institutions are characteristically and necessarily concerned with . . . external goods. They are involved in acquiring money and other material goods; they are structured in terms of power and status, and they distribute money, power and status as rewards. . . . [T]he ideals and the creativity of the practice are always vulnerable to the acquisitiveness of the institution, in which the cooperative care for common goods of the practice is always vulnerable to the competitiveness of the institution." Alasdair MacIntyre, *After Virtue: A Study in Moral Theory,* 2nd ed. (Notre Dame, Ind.: University of Notre Dame Press, 1984), 194.
8. Research illustrating this tension includes Martin Roderick, *The Work of Professional Football: A Labour of Love?* (New York: Routledge, 2006); Paul Hoch, *Rip off the Big Game* (Garden City, N.Y.: Anchor, 1972); and Joanna Phoenix, *Making Sense of Prostitution* (Basingstoke: Palgrave, 2001).

9. Celia Williamson and Terry Cluse-Tolar, "Pimp-Controlled Prostitution: Still an Integral Part of Street Life," *Violence against Women* 8 (2002): 1079. Subsequent quotations are from the same page.

10. See James F. Hodgson, *Games Pimps Play* (Toronto: Canadian Scholar's Press, 1997), 43–68.

11. Spike Lee (writ./dir.), *He Got Game,* prod. Jon Kilik and Spike Lee (Touchstone, 1998).

12. For a detailed discussion of how Lee uses Copland's music, see Krin Gabbard, "Race and Reappropriation: Spike Lee Meets Aaron Copland," *American Music* 18, 4 (2000): 370–90.

13. Lee, *He Got Game.*

14. For a useful discussion, see Robert Butcher and Angela Schneider, "Fair Play as Respect for the Game," in *Sports Ethics: An Anthology,* ed. Jan Boxill (Oxford: Blackwell, 2003), 163–64. References cited in Butcher and Schneider are Edward Deci and Richard Ryan, *Intrinsic Motivation and Self-Determination in Human Behavior* (New York: Plenum, 1985), and R. J. Valerand, E. L. Deci, and R. M. Ryan, "Intrinsic Motivation in Sport," in *Exercise and Sport Sciences Reviews 15,* ed. K. Pandoff (New York: Macmillan, 1987), 398–425.

Aristotle and MacIntyre on Justice in *25th Hour*

Mark T. Conard

Spike Lee's *25th Hour* (2002) is the story of a convicted drug dealer's last free day before having to report to prison. The protagonist, Monty (Edward Norton), uses the day to say good-bye to friends and his widower father, and he wraps up some loose business ends. Further, he has a suspicion, encouraged by others, that his girlfriend might have turned him in to the police to save herself from prosecution, so he also uses the time to investigate. All seem to agree that Monty will be easy prey for the hardened cons in prison, such that the seven-year sentence will mean the end of his life as he knows it.[1] His friends and father feel like they're saying good-bye for the last time.

The film was released in 2002, and Lee incorporates the events and aftermath of 9/11 into the story: the terrorist attacks and the damaged collective psyche of New York City form the background and setting in which the events unfold. In doing so, Lee invites us to compare Monty's transgressions (about which he shows no moral compunction) with those of the terrorists and also with those of the Russian mobsters for whom Monty was working. Consequently, certain questions arise: In comparison with the horrors of mass murder, is Monty's drug dealing really so bad? Is drug dealing immoral? Does Monty deserve his seven-year sentence? Is this justice?

Aristotle claims that justice is the most important virtue and argues that eudaimonia, or flourishing (the highest good for human beings), is impossible without justice. Further, justice is closely tied to the nature of the community in which one lives and the values shared by those living in that community.

In this essay, I use Lee's film to explore the nature of justice and the role it plays in our prospects for happiness and flourishing. I examine the actions and lives of Monty and his friends to see in what way and to what degree they exhibit (or fail to exhibit) the virtue of justice as conceived by Aristotle.

I also explore the question of whether their community, New York City, is the kind of place where one can flourish in an Aristotelian sense.

Aristotelian Ethics: Eudaimonia and the Virtues

Aristotle espouses a version of what is known as virtue ethics, which is an ethical theory centered around the development of the virtues as part of one's character. Consequently, he argues that we ought to develop character traits such as wisdom, courage, moderation, and justice.

But why should we develop our characters in this way? Because, says Aristotle, it's the only way to achieve eudaimonia, or human flourishing: the good life. Aristotle's thinking here is distinctly teleological. That is, he argues that things have a function or purpose that they tend toward achieving. This includes living creatures, whose end is dictated by their characteristic activity. For human beings, this characteristic activity is reason; it's reason that distinguishes us from other living things. So eudaimonia, or the best life for human beings, is a life in which our capacity for reason is actualized, in which it's embodied in our actions, decisions, and characters.

This is where the virtues come into play. In addition to the faculty of reason, human beings have desires (for food, drink, and sex, for example) and emotions (such as fear, joy, and disgust). However, we're not simply subject to these desires and emotions. As we're reared and taught by our families and others, we learn to respond to these desires and emotions in more or less healthy ways—that is, in ways that are more or less conducive to our overall well-being. We learn, for example, the right types of foods to consume, and in what quantities, to be healthy and enjoy ourselves. We also learn the appropriate objects of fear and in what situations we ought to stand our ground against danger and in what situations we ought to flee to preserve our safety.

It is reason that helps us determine such things. When we've ingrained in ourselves a propensity to act in accordance with reason, we've acquired a virtue: a disposition or state of character that is acquired by habit or practice. Courage, for example, is an acquired disposition to act appropriately in the face of fear. If we act inappropriately in dangerous situations, we've acquired a vice—either cowardice (a propensity to fear that which needn't be feared) or foolhardiness (a tendency to risk one's life unnecessarily).[2] In either case, we're embodying irrationality in our lives and actions.

Now, the world isn't simply divided into virtuous and vicious people. Human character and behavior are much more complicated than that. An important and fascinating part of Aristotle's ethics, then, concerns *akrasia*, which is sometimes translated as "weakness of will" and sometimes as "incontinence." Incontinence is similar to the vice of intemperance, because they're concerned with the same thing: pleasure and pain. But incontinence is not the same thing as intemperance, says Aristotle; intemperance is worse. The intemperate person doesn't know what the right thing to do is. He takes himself to be acting correctly when he pursues harmful pleasures, even though he is acting against reason and against his own best interests. The incontinent person, in contrast, knows what the right thing to do is; he understands the harmfulness of the pleasures in question, but owing to either weakness or impetuosity, he fails to act correctly.[3] A sign of this difference is that the incontinent person suffers conflict and regret, whereas the intemperate person doesn't.[4]

Incontinence, and thus the conflict between reason and appetite, is nicely illustrated in the film by Jacob's (Philip Seymour Hoffman) struggle with his desire for Mary (Anna Paquin). She acts in a coquettish, interested way toward him, but she is underage and a student in his high school English class. After Monty invites Mary to come into the nightclub with them, we see Jacob struggling with his desire, until he acts against his better judgment and kisses her. This is a clear example of someone who knows what the right thing is, who knows that his desires are bad, but he's conflicted. Jacob isn't the kind of person to act impetuously; he ruminates about—indeed, obsesses over—his desire for Mary, so his problem is one of weakness rather than impetuosity.[5] Jacob isn't a vicious person. He knows what's right and rational, but he's just too weak to do it.

To sum up, then, eudaimonia, or flourishing, will have something essentially to do with our distinctly human capacity for reason. It is, says Aristotle, a life of excellent activity guided by reason (along with material comforts, good friends and family, and a lack of terrible misfortune), and it's via the virtues that we actualize our capacity for reason and embody reason in our lives. Hence, eudaimonia is impossible without cultivating the virtues, and for Aristotle, justice is the most important virtue.

Aristotle's Conception of Justice

In examining Aristotle's conception of justice, there are several questions we need to keep in mind: What exactly is justice? How is justice related to law? What's the relationship between justice and morality? And what's the role of justice in human flourishing?

As to the definition of justice, Aristotle says: "Both the lawless person and the overreaching and unfair person seem to be unjust; and so, clearly, both the lawful and the fair person will be just. Hence the just will be both the lawful and what is fair, and the unjust will be both the lawless and the unfair."[6] So Aristotle conceives of and defines justice in terms of both lawfulness and fairness. Here, he thinks of fairness in terms of the distribution of goods. Injustice in this sense arises from what he calls *pleonexia,* or greed, the desire to get more than one's fair share of things.[7]

Justice as fairness is what Aristotle calls "special justice," whereas justice as lawfulness is "general justice." Regarding the latter, he says: "Since, as we saw, the lawless person is unjust and the lawful person is just, it clearly follows that whatever is lawful is in some way just; for the provisions of legislative science are lawful, and we say that each of them is just."[8] One might be tempted to read this as saying that every law is just, that any law a ruler creates is the right one; that laws, by their very institution, create justice. This would be a relativistic view (there is no independent standard of justice; whoever is in power decides what's right) and would leave no room for the possibility of unjust laws.[9]

But this reading is mistaken. Aristotle is no relativist. In this passage he's referring only to correct laws, those that follow properly from "legislative science." It's possible (and indeed, happens quite often) that lawmakers will create laws that are incorrect and therefore unjust. How, then, are we to understand correctness and thus justice in the creation of laws? Aristotle says: "In every matter that they deal with, the laws aim either at the common benefit of all, or at the benefit of those in control, whose control rests on virtue or on some other such basis. And so in one way what we call just is whatever produces and maintains happiness and its parts for a political community."[10] The first sentence here lays out the two possibilities: a law can correctly aim at the common benefit of everyone in the community, or it can incorrectly aim at the benefit of those in power. So correctness and justice in the creation of laws are determined by the aim and effect of those laws in promoting the common good. Terence Irwin explains: "Justice aims at the common interest of a community. Rational agency requires concern for members of a community aiming at the common good; it therefore requires a just community."[11] What Irwin is saying here is that the flourishing of an individual is impossible outside of his or her community. The community provides the context within which an individual's talents can be developed and utilized, whatever they might be. Whether a person is an athlete, a carpenter, a farmer, or a college professor, society provides—indeed, consists in—the institutions and social networks that make individual fulfillment possible and provide the means for an individual's material support.

Of course, it's only in a community that an individual can develop the kinds of social relations with others that are an essential component of his or her well-being. If the common good deriving from those relations is absent, there's no shared sense of what each of us ought to be pursuing, and there's no common understanding of what the virtues are and for what pursuits they ought to be employed; thus there can be no way to achieve eudaimonia, or flourishing. In such a situation, each person is left to his or her own devices to pursue whatever good seems best and to decide what means are justifiable in those pursuits.

As a corollary to all this, the likelihood of individual success is lessened in proportion to the level of corruption and injustice in the community. The more unjust (and the less unified) a society is, the less possible it is for an individual to flourish. Consequently, as Irwin notes, rational concern for, and interest in, one's own flourishing requires a related concern for the overall well-being and justice of the community. Thus, for Aristotle, justice and law are intimately intertwined with morality and with flourishing.

Frank, Monty, and Aristotelian Justice

As I noted earlier, Lee invites us to raise the issue of justice, and toward this end, it's particularly instructive to compare the lives of Frank (Barry Pepper) and Monty. Indeed, Lee seems to invite us to make this comparison, since Frank is critical and morally condemnatory of Monty's business (behind Monty's back, anyway), telling Jacob that Monty acquired his possessions through "the misery of other people" and that Monty deserves his prison sentence. He says something similar to Naturelle (Rosario Dawson) later in the film, telling her that her clothes and jewelry were "paid in full by the addictions of other people."

However, despite the fact that Frank lives within the letter of the law and Monty is a drug dealer, Monty fares better in the comparison with regard to justice. First, as a Wall Street player, Frank is an Aristotelian overreacher driven by *pleonexia,* or greed. As Irwin notes, "The desire to win at other people's expense is characteristic of special injustice."[12] This characterizes Frank very well, not only in his professional life (where, as a broker, one could say he too lives off the misery of other people) but also in his relations with his friends. He's perfectly willing to denigrate those he supposedly cares about to affirm his belief in his own superiority.[13]

Strictly speaking, then, Frank plays by the rules, insofar as he doesn't break the law; but this doesn't mean he's a virtuous person. Because in Western society there is less and less concern for virtue and the common good, there's an attenuation or loss of general justice, understood as virtue as a whole (more about this later). Because of this, a person like Frank—a more or less typical American—is sorely lacking in individual, special justice (justice as fairness). That is, because our society has no shared or common values beyond the notion that each individual ought to be free to pursue his or her own interests, someone like Frank can easily become selfish and greedy. And note that Frank displays actual vices such as boorishness and greed; he is not merely incontinent like Jacob.

Second, Monty certainly doesn't display complete virtue, but he isn't the greedy overreacher that Frank is. He treats others decently and fairly. We can't imagine him running down his friends the way Frank does, and he's willing to give Naturelle the benefit of the doubt when others accuse her of turning him in to the police. We see him give money to a homeless person. And of course, at the beginning of the film he saves the life of Doyle, his dog. He tells Jacob, somewhat sentimentally, that this is the best thing he's ever done, because every day Doyle has been alive since then has been because of him.

What's more, in regard to Monty's conviction, Lee makes it clear that the law under which Monty was convicted and sentenced is unjust. As Roger Ebert notes in his review: "The movie criticizes the harsh Rockefeller drug laws, which make drugs more profitable and therefore increase crime."[14] The draconian Rockefeller laws impose unusually stiff sentences for drug offenses, leading us to wonder whether Monty is being treated justly.[15] One might also wonder whether drugs ought to be illegal at all. It's certainly not far-fetched to suggest that, historically, drugs other than nicotine and alcohol were made illegal precisely because doing so kept poor minorities disproportionately incarcerated and, in many cases, disenfranchised, and because keeping drugs illegal made a lot of money for some powerful people; one could further argue that there's no defensible reason to continue to legally ban drugs. Nor is it so far-fetched to suggest that mind-altering substances might actually contribute to the good of the society, insofar as they allow some people to expand their imaginations and see the world in more creative, contemplative, and philosophical ways; thus, Monty's drug dealing might be seen as providing a useful and productive service to his community.[16]

Last, and perhaps relatedly, Lee portrays the DEA agents who bust Monty, the representatives of the law, as transgressors who are little concerned with justice or the common good. They encourage Monty's suspicions about Naturelle, and they take a kind of perverse delight in his predicament, trying to use it to get Monty to turn in his Russian boss.[17] This is what motivates them, rather than, say, a desire to keep hard drugs out of the hands of schoolchildren.

So Monty seems to possess at least a degree of justice as fairness, and although he does violate the law, one wonders whether that law and his sentence are fair and thus just. Consequently, to put it in the negative, and in comparison to Frank, Monty doesn't seem to be an unjust person. But does this mean that Monty has achieved eudaimonia, or flourishing, or that he at least had the possibility of achieving it had he not been arrested and convicted of drug dealing?

New York City: A Community with a Common Good?

Aristotle conceives of general justice (justice as lawfulness) as equivalent to virtue as a whole because of its concern for the common good.[18] This raises important questions regarding contemporary (Western, liberal) society and leads to some doubts about an analysis of *25th Hour* on Aristotelian grounds.

First, Aristotle conceived of the ideal community as the ancient Greek city-state, or polis. It was in such an arena, he believed, that one found like-minded citizens engaged in similar projects and focused on similar goals that one could befriend; in such a community, one could devote oneself to political activity and philosophical reflection and thus have the best opportunity to flourish as a social and rational creature. One obvious question, then, is whether we have anything today equivalent to such a community, and thus whether Aristotle's analysis of justice even applies to us,[19] and, more specifically, whether New York City could possibly fit this model. Indeed, one characteristic of New York that is always cited as essential to its uniqueness and greatness is the remarkable diversity of its citizens and its immigrant enclaves. In what sense is New York even a *single* community, except insofar as its diverse population is (oh, so) crowded into one compact geographic area? In what sense can its citizens be thought of as engaging in like-minded projects or pursuing the same aims?

This leads to a second major issue: in today's Western, liberal society (and New York City specifically), is there anything like a common good, the pursuit of which could form the core of the Aristotelian notion of general justice? For the most part, don't individuals (like Frank) pursue their own narrow interests without giving much thought to the good of all? Indeed, given the diversity of our individual values and interests, could we even agree on what a "common good" would be?

A MacIntyrian Critique

One view is that Aristotle's political and moral theory does not apply to contemporary Western society because of our apparent lack of a coherent community and a common good. The contrary view is that there's nothing wrong with Aristotle's politics and ethics; they're still applicable. Rather, there's something wrong with Western, liberal society. This is the view of Alasdair MacIntyre.

For MacIntyre, contemporary Western society is pervaded by a radical individualism, a situation in which virtual strangers occupy a common physical space but possess and embody very different and in fact incommensurable values. In contemporary society there isn't, and couldn't be, anything like a common good. In his landmark *After Virtue,* MacIntyre says: "This notion of the political community as a common project is alien to the modern liberal individualist world. This is how we sometimes at least think of schools, hospitals or philanthropic organizations; but we have no conception of such a form of community concerned, as Aristotle says the polis is concerned, with the whole of life, not with this or that good, but with man's good as such."[20] Further, as I noted earlier, because of the lack of a conception of a common good, there is likewise no conception of what true human flourishing would be; subsequently, there is at best a drastically attenuated notion of the virtues and their role in human life.

In *25th Hour,* the diversity of New York and the lack of a cohesive community and common values are on dramatic display in the remarkable bathroom soliloquy. In that scene, Monty is having dinner with his father at the latter's tavern prior to meeting his friends. He goes to the restroom and finds "fuck you" scrawled on the mirror and then launches into a tirade against a number of different groups and types (indeed, stereotypes) of people in the city. He says his own "fuck you" to panhandlers, Pakistanis, Korean grocers, Orthodox Jews, Puerto Ricans, Bensonhurst Italian Americans, Upper East Side rich ladies, African Americans, priests, and al Qaeda terrorists, among others, and then to his own friends and family.

Monty articulates the most common stereotypes associated with these different groups, and by so doing, he expresses New Yorkers' great diversity. But of course, almost all these stereotypes are negative, so in running through this list, Monty puts on display the apparent vices of all these people and, by implication, brings into view their perhaps incommensurable outlooks and values. For example, Pakistanis are potential terrorists, Wall Street brokers are Gordon Gecko–style hucksters,[21] Jews sell "apartheid diamonds," Russians from Brighton Beach are mobsters, priests are child molesters, and so forth. Surely, a MacIntyrian would say, given these dramatic differences, it would be impossible for these people to agree on common values.

In case he missed anyone, Monty concludes: "Fuck this whole city and everyone in it. From the row houses of Astoria to the penthouses on Park

Avenue. From the projects in the Bronx to the lofts in Soho. From the tenements in Alphabet City to the brownstones in Park Slope to the split levels in Staten Island. Let an earthquake crumble it. Let the fires rage. Let it burn to fucking ash and then let the waters rise and submerge this whole, rat-infested place." A good MacIntyrian reading of this tirade is that precisely because of the radical incommensurability of the values and outlooks of the denizens of New York, there's no hope of cooperation, no hope of progress, and no hope of saving the place.

Monty concludes by adding himself to the list of the damned: "No. No, fuck you, Montgomery Brogan. You had it all and then you threw it away, you dumb fuck!" A MacIntyrian might approve of a certain amount of anger and frustration directed at the incompatible differences between people that make it difficult or impossible for them to cooperate effectively, but he or she would certainly disagree with Monty on one point—that he "had it all" before being arrested.[22] From a MacIntyrian neo-Aristotelian standpoint, in such a society it's impossible for any human being to fully flourish and thus have it all. So, to answer the question posed earlier, just because Monty isn't an unjust person doesn't mean that he is flourishing or that he even could flourish. It's just not possible in such a divided, pluralistic (indeed, often antagonistic) community.[23]

Internal and External Goods

MacIntyre makes a distinction between what he calls internal and external goods, both of which one might achieve by participating in certain cooperative activities with others (which he calls "practices"). Internal goods are achieved through a specific activity, and whenever anyone achieves them, all those who cooperate in the activity are benefited. For example, by playing chess, one develops analytic skills, problem-solving abilities, and strategic imagination; when any player develops these abilities and further contributes to the activity, all who play are benefited.[24] Or by playing basketball, one develops agility, discipline, strength, and the ability to function as part of a team. Cooperative activities such as architecture, farming, chemistry, baseball, and politics are the sorts of practices MacIntyre has in mind in which one can achieve internal goods.

External goods can be acquired through these activities, but they aren't integral to the activity itself—for example, money and fame. These goods are limited and thus entail competition.[25] Biologists compete for paid positions in research labs, for example, and not every baseball player earns the multimillion-dollar salaries or the World Series rings of the big leaguers.

It's crucial to note that in MacIntyre's account, exercise of the virtues is necessary for the achievement of internal goods.[26] That is, to become truly skilled and excellent, one must possess and utilize virtues such as justice, courage, and honesty in cooperating with others in these activities. If one fails to be fair and courageous, for example, one can't hope to excel at an activity. It's also crucial to note that practicing the virtues often prevents one from achieving external goods. That is, if one cheats at a practice (and doesn't get caught), one is more likely to win the competition and thus reap the rewards of winning (although this would deprive oneself of the internal goods that might be acquired through that practice). If one competes fairly, one is generally less likely to win competitions and gain fame and fortune.

Given this account of internal and external goods, MacIntyre tells us: "Without the virtues there could be a recognition only of what I have called external goods and not at all of internal goods in the context of practices. And in any society which recognized only external goods competitiveness would be the dominant and even exclusive feature."[27] MacIntyre is, of course, talking about Western, liberal society, where (he believes) the notion of the virtues has been all but lost and people typically concern themselves only with money, fame, and the like, not with what he calls internal goods.[28] And, given the intimate link between the virtues and eudaimonia, true human flourishing is impossible in such a society. A person concerned only with external goods is the stereotypical avaricious American so often depicted on reality TV shows, an individual with little conception of justice, courage, or temperance and who will do (virtually) anything to gain the wealth and material comforts that constitute the "good life."

We should note that MacIntyre's description of the disconnected, greedy individualist describes Frank very well. He displays much vice and few virtues, pursues solely external goods, and seems to have no interest in anything resembling a common good. It's interesting to note that in exemplifying MacIntyre's fears about Western society, Frank likewise embodies what some say was the reason for the terrorist attack against the United States (and particularly New York) in the first place: Americans are greedy, overreaching, soulless and godless capitalists.

So, on a MacIntyrian reading, our hopes for true happiness and flourishing, for the good life, are generally quite slim, given the inevitable conflict of our myriad perspectives on life, community, and what's important and valuable. Without a common vision and social cohesion, we in the United States live with the incompatibility between liberals and conservatives, believers and nonbelievers, city dwellers and country folk, old and young, and so forth. How can we possibly flourish as the rational, political animals we are, given that we're always in conflict with one another as individuals?

New York City and 9/11

As noted, *25th Hour* is set in the wake of the terrorist attacks of 9/11, and themes and issues of justice are at least hinted at in the film. An Aristotelian account of justice compels us to ask questions about community and the values shared by those living in that community. Indeed, these latter concerns lead us to a MacIntyrian critique of Western, liberal society, as well exemplified by New York City, with all its diversity, conflict, and competitive, materialist tendencies.

Although the values of New York City's remarkably diverse population might normally be incommensurable and thus make a common good unachievable, 9/11 gave us a brief glimpse of something different. That is, in the aftermath of 9/11 and the horrors of that mass murder, New York City became a closer-knit community with something very much like a common purpose, at least for a short time. That is, in the wake of the attacks and the collective grief that quickly ensued, in the midst of the rescue and recovery missions by the police and firefighters, one clearly witnessed people's genuine concern for others—not just family and friends but strangers, fellow citizens, visitors from around the country and around the world. For those days and weeks after the attacks, people were united in their grief in something like a common cause, and their virtues were on display. Out of an incredibly diverse plurality came unity: a common fellow feeling and fellow regard. The tragedy brought into relief what's normally missing but what's still possible. It gave us hope that despite our sometimes radical differences, we might look beyond our own narrow interests and selfish desires to the needs and interests of all, such that we might still coexist in a way that allows each to live the most fulfilling life possible.

And of course, the actions (so soon to follow) of those who would use this event and people's collective grief for their own political ends showed us quite clearly the fragility of those newly formed bonds and of the possibility of human flourishing that depends on them.

Notes

Many thanks to J. J. Abrams and David LaRocca for their helpful comments and suggestions on an earlier draft of this essay.

1. The plot is somewhat oddly driven by Monty's fear of prison rape. It's what he dreads and what everyone believes will break him.

2. Note that, for Aristotle, there's a difference between acting in a virtuous manner and possessing a virtue. For example, one might perform a courageous or just action without actually being courageous or just. Pleasure and pain are good indications of whether one has acquired the virtue. That is, if a person is still in the mode of practicing courage in the face of danger, and it grieves him to act this way, he hasn't yet acquired the virtue. If, in contrast, a person has had much practice and has developed a built-in propensity to act courageously in dangerous situations, and it doesn't pain her so much, then she has very likely acquired the virtue. See the *Nichomachean Ethics,* book II, for Aristotle's account of the virtues of character.

3. "The intemperate person acts on decision when he is led on, since he thinks it is right in every case to pursue the pleasant thing at hand; the incontinent person, however, thinks it is wrong to pursue this pleasant thing, yet still pursues it." Aristotle, *Nichomachean Ethics,* 1146b23–26, 102.

4. Further, the continent person is likewise different from the temperate person, who is virtuous. The former has strong desires, knows they're bad, and follows reason in denying them. The virtuous person isn't even tempted by such pleasures. He plainly recognizes their badness and they hold no appeal for him, so there is no struggle, no conflict for him.

5. Aristotle thinks that incontinence arising from weakness is worse than that based on impetuosity: "Among the incontinent people themselves, those who abandon themselves [to desire, i.e., the impetuous] are better than those [i.e., the weak] who have reason but do not abide by it. For the second type are overcome by a less strong feeling, and do not act without having deliberated, as the first type do." *Nichomachean Ethics,* 1151a1–4, 111. Presumably, he means that it's better to act impetuously and not think about what you're doing, rather than deliberating about it, realizing the action is wrong, and doing it anyway.

6. *Nichomachean Ethics,* 1129a34–b2, 68.

7. Built into this, of course, is the notion that there *is* an equitable distribution of goods in a community and that justice requires promoting and respecting that division of materials.

8. *Nichomachean Ethics,* 1129b, 68.

9. For a discussion of this view, see Plato's *Republic,* book I. The character Thrasymachus is the classic example of the relativist regarding justice.

10. *Nichomachean Ethics,* 1129b, 68.

11. Terence Irwin, *Aristotle's First Principles* (Oxford: Oxford University Press, 1988), 424.

12. Ibid., 426.

13. Admittedly, he's not *completely* vicious. Frank displays real concern for Monty's well-being, to the point of offering to "ugly him up" before he goes to prison so Monty won't be such an attractive prospective victim to the other cons. Let me point out what

a poor strategy this might turn out to be. It seems unlikely that hardened cons would care that a new inmate is bruised and cut up when they're searching for a new target. In fact, his wounds might give them the impression that he's easy prey for others.

14. http://rogerebert.suntimes.com/apps/pbcs.dll/article?AID=/20030110/REVIEWS/301100301/1023.

15. As the DEA agent tells him: "In New York we've got a wonderful thing called the Rockefeller laws. Let me educate you. You had a kilo in your sofa. That kind of weight makes it an A1 felony, fifteen years to life minimum for a first offense."

16. My thanks to J. J. Abrams for suggesting this idea to me.

17. One of the agents tells him: "When you're upstate taking it in the culo by a bunch of guys calling you 'Shirley,' you'll only have yourself and Governor Rockefeller to thank for the privilege."

18. "General justice turns out to be the same state of character as virtue as a whole; it refers to the concern of the virtuous person for the common good of the political community." Irwin, *Aristotle's First Principles,* 424.

19. The essential question here is whether Aristotle's political and ethical theory is tied to his historical time and to the political arrangements of his day, making it inapplicable to other historical periods and other political configurations.

20. Alasdair MacIntyre, *After Virtue* (Notre Dame, Ind.: University of Notre Dame Press, 1984), 156.

21. This is a reference to Michael Douglas's character in the Oliver Stone film *Wall Street* (1987).

22. It might be worth wondering in what sense Monty believes he had it all and how and in what way he believes he threw it all away. Did he have it all because he was a successful drug dealer and threw it away because he got caught? Or did he have it all because he had decent friends and family and threw it away by dealing drugs in the first place? A third alternative is that he was doing okay selling drugs when he was younger but threw it all away when he got involved with the Russian mobsters. This is unclear. Frank articulates the same sentiment later in the film, telling Naturelle that Monty "threw it all away," and he mentions the fact that Monty was kicked out of school for selling pot. However, Frank also blames Naturelle for not stopping Monty and letting him throw it all away, but since the two of them didn't meet until Monty was already a drug dealer, this doesn't clarify the issue.

23. Note that Lee provides a kind of alternative to perpetual conflict and injustice in the dream-fantasy sequence at the end of the film. In that segment, Monty's father proposes the possibility of not reporting to prison, of heading west and adopting a new identity and a new life. In the fantasy, Monty settles in a community, Naturelle eventually joins him, and they have children and grandchildren and end up sharing a long, happy life together. In this alternate reality, Monty attains a measure of flourishing and contentment. Is Lee suggesting that this is what justice would be for Monty? Given our Aristotelian, MacIntyrian reading, is he suggesting that flourishing is still possible in small, homogeneous communities that lack the inherent conflict in a metropolis like New York City? However we decide to answer these questions, we need to keep in mind that

this alternate reality is presented as a fantasy or dream, so in any event, it may remain unobtainable. (My thanks to both J. J. Abrams and David LaRocca for pointing out the importance of this scene for my essay.)

24. That is, when I become better at chess, the others in my chess club benefit, insofar as I can better challenge them and be a more skilled and more capable opponent in our games. In any activity, all benefit by the achievements of those individuals who are supremely and uniquely skilled and who expand what is possible in the practice—a Bobby Fischer in chess, for example. For MacIntyre's chess example, see *After Virtue*, 188.

25. "External goods are therefore characteristically objects of competition in which there must be losers as well as winners. Internal goods are indeed the outcome of competition to excel, but it is characteristic of them that their achievement is a good for the whole community who participate in the practice." Ibid., 190–91.

26. "*A virtue is an acquired human quality the possession and exercise of which tends to enable us to achieve those goods which are internal to practices and the lack of which effectively prevents us from achieving any such goods.*" Ibid., 191; emphasis in original.

27. Ibid., 196.

28. "We should therefore expect that, if in a particular society the pursuit of external goods were to become dominant, the concept of the virtues might suffer first attrition and then perhaps something near total effacement, though simulacra might abound." Ibid.

We Can't Get Off the Bus

A Commentary on Spike Lee and Moral Motivation

Gabriella Beckles-Raymond

On October 16, 1995, a million black men marched on Washington, D.C.,[1] answering Louis Farrakhan's call for reconciliation and atonement.[2] Not since the 1963 march for civil rights had so many Americans descended on Capitol Hill. Although the mainstream contemporary historical narrative suggests otherwise, Martin Luther King Jr., like Farrakhan, was a controversial figure in his time. Nevertheless, in spite of the varied perspectives within the African American community about Farrakhan's beliefs and methods,[3] his call to action was answered by thousands of African American men across the country.

The first anniversary of this historic occasion was marked by the much-anticipated release of Spike Lee's *Get on the Bus* (1996). This film remains the only feature-length depiction of the Million Man March, and despite being a fictional account, it provides us with a unique opportunity to explore the march as part of a social movement, a political event, and a commentary on the black community and race relations in America. Since both the march and the film, significant changes have taken place in the political landscape. Incredibly, just thirteen years after the march, America's first black president stood on the same steps where Farrakhan willed the nation's black men to take action. Is Barack Obama's unprecedented ascendance through the political elite a manifestation of the grassroots empowerment Farrakhan envisaged? Obama and Farrakhan share one thing: both managed to mobilize large numbers of people, particularly those deemed furthest removed from the political process.

Liberal theory suggests that such social political acts are disconnected from a person's identity. Based on this model, we would conclude that the reason thousands of people were moved to march on Capitol Hill or to vote was not a function of their personal values. This model of political interaction arises out of a certain understanding of members of the state and the relationship between justice and morality. In this unencumbered view of the self, a person's identity (particularly membership in or affiliation with groups, such as race, religion, or gender) is disengaged from his or her notion of justice. As such, individual members of the state are understood to have an abstract sense of fairness that is applied at the social political level regardless of their particular identity and moral commitments. However, if this is true, how can we explain the depressing reality of persistent injustices such as racism?

An alternative view proposes that our political ideals are a function of our conception of the good. In this case, one's political sense of justice is connected to one's identity and personal moral commitments. Based on this interpretation, those who marched for Farrakhan's cause or voted for Obama did so because those social and political initiatives resonated with their personal principles. This encumbered conception of the person arises out of the communitarian critique of the unencumbered self. In the unencumbered conception of self, a person's social identities (such as race) are disengaged or distinct from his or her moral values. Conversely, in the encumbered model, a person's identity is indelibly intertwined with his or her moral commitments, which in turn impact that person's beliefs about what is just. Our understanding of moral motivation as a driver of political activism differs, depending on which model of the self one ascribes to. This essay examines the film *Get on the Bus* to illustrate that the encumbered model is a more accurate account of moral motivation and, more specifically, to explain why people participate in events like the Million Man March.

First, I focus on the way Lee draws on the trope of individualism to show how life experience has shaped the character of each rider. Next I discuss the collective and representative nature of the characters in the context of America's racial consciousness. Finally, I explore individual characters' reasons for getting on the bus, highlighting the relationship between their personal sense of who it is good to be and the social and political good that attending the march represents. I argue that, as members of a racially conscious society, the characters in *Get on the Bus* cannot separate their conceptions of who it is good to be from their racial identity. Lee shows us how these men are encumbered. In other words, raced persons cannot get off the bus.

Individual Riders Board the Bus

Unencumbered individualism is a cornerstone of the American narrative of social, political, and economic relations. Without this notion it would be difficult to discuss American identity or the force that undergirds America's national spirit. This spirit of self-determination boldly proclaims that no matter who you are or where you come from, by the act of your own free will and hard work, you can be whoever you want to be. The rags-to-riches fable has been repeated, reworked, retranscribed, and redistributed generation after generation via every cultural medium, particularly in film. From *Rocky* to *The Pursuit of Happiness,* we are encouraged to believe that one's ethnic or racial identity has nothing to do with one's opportunity or willingness to embrace the values and commitments that are the American dream and to seize a piece of the oh so elusive pie.

Yet this rampant individualism is not simply the purview of mainstream America; philosophically, economically, and culturally, there is a long tradition of self-determination in the African American community. From Frederick Douglass and Booker T. Washington to Jay-Z and Spike Lee, the message is that as an individual in American society, you can transcend the boundaries of group identification and define your existence on your own terms. Indeed, it is interesting that even among those who advocate group-level agendas, as in the case of the great champions of African American freedom and liberation mentioned above, the methodology is, nevertheless, fundamentally individualistic.[4]

Thus, it is not surprising that as the characters of *Get on the Bus* board the Spotted Owl,[5] the audience is introduced to a collection of individuals, each with a discrete personality type. Indeed, Lee exploits this individualistic bent to carve out each rider's personal experiences, achievements, version of the good, political persuasion, and religion—each one unique, and each one distinct from the other. Heading up this intriguing ensemble is trip organizer, co–bus driver, and beacon of moral wisdom, George (Charles Dutton). The film's spiritual leader appears in the form of Jeremiah "Pop" (Ossie Davis), who dedicated his life to a large manufacturing company but suffered a breakdown, lost everything after being made redundant, and now suffers from heart disease. Initially, we get the sense that Jeremiah's soft-spoken, law-abiding, Christian demeanor speaks of a life worlds apart from that of the next characters who board the bus. Estranged father and son, Evan Sr. (Thomas Jefferson Byrd) and Evan Jr. "Smooth" (De'aundre Bonds), shackled together in state-issue handcuffs, have yet to achieve the quiet acceptance that comes with finally understanding life as Jeremiah does. Equally distant from the aforementioned characters are Kyle and Randall (Isaiah Washington and Harry J. Lennix), a middle-class gay couple whose relationship is about to end. Their tight-lipped restraint is similarly contrasted with the loud-mouthed, arrogant narcissism of Flip (Andre Braugher), an actor who is "in between jobs" and determined to be offensive every time he speaks. Flip's brashness is juxtaposed with the overly deliberate political correctness of Gary (Roger Guenveur Smith), a biracial, heterosexual (in contrast to Kyle and Randall) police officer. Wide-eyed film student Xavier "X" (Hill Harper) has yet to experience the turmoil of a long-term relationship. His documentary project serves as a narrative device for the film, and his quest to find the meaning of life distinguishes him from his fellow passengers with respect to the extent to which they have found those answers, particularly the group's griot, Jeremiah, whom he befriends. But unlike Xavier, not all young people enjoy the happy innocence of untarnished beginnings. Jamal (Gabriel Casseus) is a former member of the notorious Crips gang and a devout, recently converted Muslim, on the road to redemption from his troubled past. Rounding out this diverse group is the entrepreneur Jay (Bernie Mac), owner of a successful bubblegum company he built from the ground up. Self-made and hardworking, Jay is the embodiment of the American dream.

Thus, although the film's premise is a journey to the Million Man March, it becomes clear that any generalizations about a homogeneous black community would be overly simplistic and inaccurate and should be guarded against. Being black is seemingly the only thing the riders have in common, and as their differences illustrate, this identity is not sufficient to engender a collective or unified social perspective or political agenda. They are presented, and we are made to see them, as individuals with only loose connections to one another and to the larger black community. Consistent with the unencumbered conception of self, the characters' political affiliations and versions of the good, though obviously shaped by their life experiences, are apparently not governed by any particular "thick" identity commitments such as race, religion, sexual orientation, class, or occupation. Thick black identity includes "thin" black identity, with some additional elements (e.g., ethnicity, nationality, cultural kinship) that are understood as constitutive of a person's identity but not essential or permanent components of who a person is.[6] Rather, as Tommie Shelby's account of black solidarity predicts, the minimal "thin" black identity seems to be enough to bring this eclectic group together. Thin blackness is a socially imposed racial category that sweepingly includes all those persons who fit the phenotypical and genealogical criteria.[7] It does not, however, include personal commitments about the meaning or value of black identity. And yet, Shelby's liberal conception grounds the motive for solidarity in shared oppression—it is the struggle *against* antiblack racism that gives rise to black solidarity.[8] However, as Jessica Henry rightly notes, the Million Man March was "decidedly different" from other acts of solidarity. Whereas "most of the marches in Washington, D.C. have been part of a larger social protest movement against the government, this march was part of a movement for African American men to 'atone and reconcile' for the wrongs which they have committed."[9] It is clear that antiblack racism, insofar as it shapes society, had an impact on the behavior and life choices of the men attending the march. However, the notion of justice and its motivational force doing the work in Shelby's account (recognizing that one is a member of an oppressed group and standing against one's oppressors) does not provide a satisfactory explanation of one of the largest single examples of collective action and unabashed demonstration of African American solidarity in recent American history. So why did so many African American men, whether from Los Angeles or Baltimore, make this epic journey to the nation's capital? What was it that resonated with all those individuals such that they were willing—indeed, determined—to unite around the common cause of uplifting and transforming the African American community? *Get on the Bus* provides us with some insights into and explanations for these actual and metaphorical journeys. I argue that a better understanding of their motivation can be achieved by viewing these men as encumbered beings in the black experience.

Collective Consciousness in *Get on the Bus*

As the title of Joe Morgenstern's film review, "Spike Lee and a Cast of Millions," suggests, the characters in *Get on the Bus* represent "a microcosm of black male America."[10] Watching *Get on the Bus,* we realize that this collection of individuals is a very deliberate study of the people, attitudes, and issues that make up the larger African American community. In spite of their idiosyncrasies, our connection with and understanding of the characters is not merely a relationship with their individual sojourns toward atonement, reconciliation, or self-discovery. Rather, we can see past the individuals and understand that their stories are the stories of many other African American males like them. Yet they are not stereotypes, even though they are in some ways caricatures—an example of art imitating life. What are so often presented in the media as crass headlines or shock-tactic statistics are revealed as the stories of real human lives. This is precisely what gives *Get on the Bus* its power and exemplifies Lee's gift of bringing complex realism to the big screen. Through the characters' exchanges, the audience gets a glimpse of life as an African American man in its many different forms. We see what boils under the surface of angry, disenchanted young men like Smooth, who are closer to their "homies" than to the more savory influences society thinks they ought to associate with. Similarly, when Jamal describes his experiences as a young Crip, the audience hears the rationale of the seemingly unintelligible, too young gang-banger who willfully kills with no regard for human life. We are not asked to agree or condone, but we are invited to empathize. At the other end of the generational spectrum, Jeremiah reminds our often too short memories of the coping mechanisms African American men had to deploy, not so long ago, so that later generations could live as they do today. Endearing as this character is, his role is to tell not just his own story but that of all African American fathers and grandfathers and great-grandfathers—hence the nickname Pop. "The old ones remind us that slavery's chains / Have paid for our freedom again and again," Maya Angelou reminded the crowds at the march.[11] Kyle and Randall force the reluctant to acknowledge that the African American community has gay men too, and Republicans to boot! Gary extends the inclusive message to those of mixed parentage. Thus, through these eclectic characters, we recognize people we know, have seen, or have heard of. The crucial point is that none of the riders on the Spotted Owl strikes us as out of place or fanciful. This is why shooting the movie through Xavier's documentary lens works. One accepts the sometimes contrived elements of the plot as a function of filmmaking, squeezing three days' travel and more than 400 years of history into 120 minutes, yet the audience understands that the movie's messages are not fairy tales; they are social and political commentary.

Get on the Bus as social political commentary is necessarily a reflection on race and racisms in America. At first glance, we see a collection of individuals—Democrat and Republican, Christian and Muslim, homosexual and heterosexual—but all the riders get on the bus because they are African American. And Farrakhan was keen to impress this message on those attending the march:

> There's a new Black man in America today. A new Black woman in America today. Now Brothers, there's a social benefit of our gathering here today. That is, that from this day forward, we can never again see ourselves through the narrow eyes of the limitation of the boundaries of our own fraternal, civic, political, religious, street organization or professional organization. We are forced by the magnitude of what we see here today, that whenever you return to your cities and you see a Black man, a Black woman, don't ask him

> what is your social, political or religious affiliation, or what is your status? Know that he is your brother.[12]

The importance of African American solidarity is further emphasized by those who do not stay on the bus. When Craig (Albert Hall), George's original driving partner, is replaced by Rick (Richard Belzer), a white Jew, one instantly feels that Rick should have stayed with the broken-down bus and let Craig continue on the trip, or that the replacement driver should have been another African American. Despite initial reservations, Rick's presence is accepted by the passengers, but then Rick initiates his own exit when he refuses to go near anything associated with Farrakhan and promptly gets off the bus. Although Rick does this because of his own racial consciousness, the symbolic point is made: only African American men are on the bus going to the march. The encounter with Rick, and with the other white characters in the film, highlights the racial consciousness in America that colors our understanding of American society and is itself constitutive of that society, such that we can speak of different racial groups and the "African American community." According to Michael Banton:

> Racial consciousness is not easily defined because it is a distillation of personal experience. In one form it is an individual's interpretation of how his or her life is affected by the way others assign him or her to a racial category. In another form, it is an individual's tendency to assign others to racial categories. . . . If those who are assigned to a particular category are treated similarly they are likely to share this experience . . . men can experience a common bond with men in a different society; women with women, whites with whites, and blacks with blacks.[13]

In this sense, America is a racially conscious society. This becomes increasingly apparent as each rider's reasons for attending the march are revealed. In spite of, or maybe because of, their differences, the riders are aware of their racial identity and the significance of that identity in their society. To be black in America is to be perceived, treated, and responded to in particular ways. It means that one will inevitably encounter racial discrimination, albeit in different forms. Those inclined to forget are reminded by Gary's failed attempt to assert his status as a police officer, as he is promptly shown that this does not override his racial identity.

In one of the many examples of microcollective action, *Get on the Bus* lets the audience know that although the Million Man March is clearly for

African American men, simply being black in the thin sense is not enough, and "black on black" abuse will not be tolerated. So when Wendell (Wendell Pierce), Republican capitalist extraordinaire, joins the group for the sole purpose of financially exploiting the business opportunity, his offensive "Uncle Tom" attitudes and insistence on referring to his fellow riders as "niggers" promptly get him ejected. Wendell's presence in the film, however, is acknowledgment that despite his determination to distance himself from it, Wendell is indeed part of the African American community. Wendell symbolizes that element of the African American community that has internalized the racist, materialistic hegemony of the American narrative such that it has become self-hate, which in turn manifests as hate for one's own people. The riders, as metaphor and microcosm of the African American community, unanimously reject that element from their presence. Financial and moral success are not mutually exclusive, nor is the former more preferable. Indeed, there are no illusions that political action comes without collective fiscal action—the Million Man March is the first public march to provide an independent financial audit of its operations.[14]

Black Identity and Themes of Moral Motivation

This theme of marrying principles and actions brought out in the analysis of the Million Man March and *Get on the Bus* illustrates that it is not possible to separate the social and political from one's racial identity. Therefore, anyone hoping to mobilize others to political action must consider the target audience's identity commitments as integral to their moral and political motivation. However, it is the "thickness" of these identity commitments that is at stake here unless we accept Shelby's account, which would have us believe that recognition of membership in the group is all that's required. But as the history of any oppressed group attests, recognition of membership isn't enough to generate political or social action. Here, drawing on Charles Taylor's work, I explore in more detail the personal accounts of the riders' motivations in *Get on the Bus* to substantiate the claim that who one believes it is good to be necessarily provides the motivation for moral and social political actions.

According to Taylor, humans are beings with purpose. As such, humans engage in higher-order decision making; they evaluate which desires are more desirable. For Taylor, deliberations about how to behave when desires are incompatible are not merely a matter of contingencies; rather, they rest on and reflect the comparative worth of the action to the person doing the evaluating.[15] These "strong evaluations" appraise whether and to what extent motivations are noble, courageous, virtuous, and so forth, and they use terms such as *good* to indicate the worth of the desire or action. In this conception of human agency, some goods are of incomparable value to a person; they play a fundamental role in orienting that person's life. Taylor explains:

> For those with a strong commitment to such a good, what it means is that this above all others provides the landmarks for what they judge to be the direction of their lives. While they recognize a whole range of qualitative distinctions, while all of these involve strong evaluation, so that they judge themselves and others by the degree they attain the goods concerned and admire or look down on people in function of this, nevertheless the one highest good has a special place. It is orientation to this which comes closest to defining my identity, and therefore my direction to this good is of unique importance to me.[16]

It is my contention that, given America's racial consciousness, one's racial status invariably impacts the commitments that orient one's life, such that racial identity necessarily shapes a person's moral motivation. Indeed, all the riders on the Spotted Owl are going to the march because they are black. This is not to suggest that a particular racial identity status leads to a certain set of moral commitments, motivations, and actions. Rather, the point is to understand how racial identity intertwines with racial consciousness and the social and historical context that shapes it to produce unique yet related versions of who it is good to be. *Get on the Bus* allows us precisely such an insight because Xavier's narrative device requires the riders to answer one very explicit question: "So how come you're going to the march?"

As Taylor's encumbered model of self would predict, the riders' conceptions of who it is good to be are central to their reason for going to the march. Jeremiah's emotive and eloquent prayer that inaugurates the trip highlights this concretely. He proclaims, "And if there is anything dear Lord that we do need and pray for is that after this trip each and every one of us will be a better man than he was before." Indeed, it was precisely this theme, central to the march, that inspired such a phenomenal number of people to participate. As the Reverend Jesse Jackson rightly commented, "The pledge for personal atonement, so central to the gathering, was married to a commitment to political action. There is no contradiction here."[17]

Although making the trip was about the commitment to being better men, there were different perspectives about what that entailed. For Evan

Sr. and George, going to the march was about being better fathers and positive role models. These aims are not unique to African American fathers, even ones trying to forge better relationships with their sons. But why address a personal issue with a social political action? Why not take Evan Jr. to a baseball game or discuss their past difficulties over lunch? And what is the significance of this need to be a positive role model to George, who has a loving family and well-adjusted children? The answer is that for both men, being a better father and role model is inseparable from their racial status as African Americans. This racial identity is central to their sense of responsibility to their children. Both are explicitly aware of the need for young African Americans to have positive male role models, not simply because all young people benefit from such a thing but specifically because positive role models are an invaluable resource for combating the negative effects of racisms that African Americans inevitably experience. Hearing that Smooth would rather be with his homies, Evan Sr. retorts, "That's the very reason I'm takin' him to the march because the homies ain't doin' nothin' but killing each other. I wanna take my son to this historic event. I want him to see, uh, a million black men doin' something positive for the country." Thus, in taking his son to the march, Evan Sr. not only provides the much-needed role model but also moves closer to his ideal of being a more responsible father. Similarly, George appreciates, as do his wife and daughters, the importance of representing himself and their family on this historic occasion. Thus, George not only proves he is a good role model but also demonstrates his commitment as a father, husband, and member of the African American community.

This desire for internal moral consistency is also played out through Jay and Jeremiah. Jay already considers himself an independent, self-sufficient, financially responsible, hardworking African American man, and these values are important to his sense of self. As such, he wants to make a definite statement to that end. Jay also believes these values are necessary for African Americans to achieve the financial and personal success that enables them to triumph in spite of racism. Yet again, the motive is personal. Jay explains, "I'm going to the meeting for myself. I think it's time for brothers to stand up and be responsible and get out of the begging mentality we have, the hook me up syndrome; 'look out for a brother.' We need to start looking out for ourselves." Jay is rightly proud of his thriving business in a field in which no one would expect an African American to achieve success. Therefore, for him, going to the march is an affirmation of his principles and his endorsement of their applicability to all African Americans.

Unlike Jay, Jeremiah's professional journey is not one he is proud of. As we discover from the tragic story of Jeremiah's life, his regret is derived not from his financial misfortunes but from his loss of integrity. Jeremiah is going to the march to reclaim his self-respect. Having failed to attend the March on Washington in 1963 because of his desire to please and appease his new employers, he takes this march as an opportunity to express the sense of solidarity that he now understands is so important. For Jeremiah, being a better man is about being true to himself as an African American.

Also seeking atonement is Jamal, and his need for redemption is more obvious. His sins are not simply personal affairs. As Jamal himself recognizes, the violence of his former life as a gang member placed him at the heart of the tragic destruction of African American life. Having converted to the strictly principled Islamic faith, Jamal now has a very clear conception of righteousness. He is determined to follow these values for his own atonement and to share them in the hope of helping other young gang members who are still lost. Helping his community makes Jamal a better man.

Thus far, I have discussed those characters (Evan Sr., George, Jay, Jeremiah, and Jamal) whose motivation for attending the march is explicitly expressed as a function of their desire to be better people. Such motivation implicitly, yet no less significantly, involves their identity as African Americans. As I now demonstrate for the remaining characters (Xavier, Gary, Randall, and Kyle), who explicitly emphasize racial identity as their motives for attending the march, their interpretations of that identity, like those of the other characters, are rooted in their personal conceptions of who it is good to be.

Xavier, though characterized by his youthful exuberance, is educated and socially conscious and is going to the march to be part of history. He is media savvy and understands the significance of documenting that history for himself—hence his thesis project. But this is not just an opportunity to fulfill a class requirement; Xavier intends to show his documentary to his future children. If he doesn't, their image of African Americans will be based on Hollywood and the mainstream press and thus will invariably be negative. As he says, "summed up in the four R's—rap, rape, rob, riot." For Xavier, it is his moral responsibility as a filmmaker to present an alternative, more accurate picture. As the "Spike Lee junior" of the film, perhaps he is also articulating the sentiments of the man himself, whose filmography clearly speaks to this view.

Gary's desire to be part of history and to show solidarity with other African Americans is also motivated by his conception of what it means to be a good person. Being of mixed race and having suffered a tragic loss at the hands of a black gang member, he has an option and a reason to abandon the African American community.[18] Whether one takes the position that he is compensating for his lack of blackness or is driven by a desire to honor his father's death, being "one of the brothers" is important to Gary. By fighting crime and going to the march, Gary is showing the world and himself that he is not disloyal. In spite of his obvious discomfort and uncertainty, he believes it's the right thing to do. "I guess if the brothers are getting together, you know uh, talkin' about some things, tryin' to work things out, then I wanna be there, right?"

Randall and Kyle, rejected by certain sectors of the African American community because of their sexual orientation, also demonstrate the virtues of loyalty and commitment to their community. For Kyle, that connection seems to come from the unfortunate but apparently inevitable realization that no matter what he does for American society—even becoming a marine and risking his life in defense of the nation—he is still black. Randall's commitment, though also informed by his experiences as an African American man, is self-claimed. On the surface, others might think Randall fits the profile of the sellout (light skinned, middle class, and "well spoken"), but he does not comply with that stereotype at all. Indeed, defying it is precisely what Randall believes is the righteous thing to do; for him, doing so is a display of his masculinity. Thus, when the opportunity presents itself in the form of a discussion with Rick the bus driver, Randall shows that he is not intimidated and is definitely not afraid to directly challenge white Americans about their bigotry. Randall's stand lets the audience know that he may be gay, but he is still a man, and whether they want to admit it or not, he is unequivocally part of the African American community.

Drawing on Spike Lee's epic journey across America and into the hearts and minds of African American men, I maintain that, ultimately, people are motivated by their own desire to be good people, whatever form that might take. Simply fitting into a thinly conceived African American category isn't sufficient for a raced person to engage in acts of solidarity or collective action to fight against racisms. A stronger and, by extension, a qualitatively different kind of motivation is required to sacrifice the time and money and to risk all the other potential losses one is likely to experience by taking a stand against injustice. For the riders on the Spotted Owl, their racial identity is invariably included in conceptions of who it is good to be for African Americans in America. Wendell's failure is not an inability or an unwillingness to acknowledge his racial identity; rather, the reality of his racial identity has not been integrated into his conception of who it is good to be, which is precisely why he has no reservations when it comes to bandying about and assigning a derogatory term to his fellow African Americans. Being a "nigger," for Wendell, is clearly not a good thing.

Yet the treatment of Wendell juxtaposed to that of the other riders illustrates the wider moral point to be made here. Moral motivations born out of our sense of self are no less noble than moral motives stemming from an abstract, universal ideal of justice. Indeed, I don't think this moral ideal of purely selfless motivation is possible for humans to achieve. As the life journeys of the riders reveal, their attendance at the march is personal, not necessarily individual or singular, but definitely personal. Our longing for a pure altruism is not affirmed by the historical, social, psychological, or personal record, no matter how wonderful a vision it might be. Yet, if we are willing to question the legitimacy of the unencumbered moral ideal, the door is open for an improved conception of moral motivation to emerge. This, in turn, paves the way to developing more effective antiracism agendas. As *Get on the Bus* and the actual Million Man March emphatically demonstrate, an abstract, individualistic moral ideal is neither sufficient to explain nor, indeed, a necessary motivation for amazing acts of positivity, kindness, collective action, and genuine humanitarianism.

Notes

Thank you to Dr. Bill Lawson for suggesting the title of this essay and for our many discussions about black identity.

1. S. Craig Watkins, "Framing Protest: News Media Frames of the Million Man March," *Critical Studies in Mass Communication* 18, 1 (2001): 83–101. "The number of march participants emerged as a highly salient issue in the second and third phases of news coverage. Originally, park officials announced that 400,000 individuals participated. After substantial protest from march organisers, participants, and the circulation of video and still photos that suggested otherwise this number was recalculated to 800,000. That number would be revised later to roughly one million" (n. 2).

2. Louis Farrakhan's call originally appeared in *The Final Call,* December 14, 1994. It can also be found online at http://www.africawithin.com/mmm/mmmcall.htm.

3. Desda Moss, "Theme Timely, But Organizer Is Controversial," *USA Today,* February 16, 1996, http://www.usatoday.com/news/index/nman004.htm (accessed October 4, 2009).

4. "Frederick Douglass among the Romantics," in *The Cambridge Companion to Frederick Douglass,* ed. Maurice Lee (Cambridge: Cambridge University Press, 2009), 118–31. It is also worth noting that, as is the case with European Americans, such individualism is a largely male-endorsed ideal, and it is the inequality of gender power relations, in part, that led to the individualistic perspective being the dominant one.

5. The Spotted Owl is the name of the bus. Symbolically, as Wendell reminds us, it is an endangered species.

6. See Tommie Shelby, *We Who Are Dark* (Oxford: Oxford University Press, 2005), 207–16, for full descriptions of these forms of thick black identity.

7. Shelby defines thin blackness as "a vague and socially imposed category of 'racial' difference that serves to distinguish groups on the basis of their members having certain visible, inherited physical characteristics and a particular biological ancestry" (ibid., 7).

8. Ibid., 247.

9. Jessica M. Henry, "An Africological Analysis of the Million Man March: A Look at the Response to the March as a Measure of Its Effectiveness," *Harvard Journal of Communications* 9 (1998): 158.

10. Joe Morgenstern, "Spike Lee and a Cast of Millions," *Wall Street Journal*, October 16, 1996, http://online.wsj.com/article/SB845407708327868500.html (accessed October 8, 2009).

11. Maya Angelou's Million Man March poem, http://www.poemhunter.com/poem/million-man-march-poem/ (accessed October 12, 2009).

12. Excerpt from Farrakhan's speech at the march, transcript available at http://www.africawithin.com/mmm/transcript.htm (accessed October 12, 2009).

13. Michael Banton, *Racial Consciousness* (London: Longman 1988), 9.

14. The audit report is available at http://www.millionsmoremovement.com/mmm1995_audit.htm (accessed October 8, 2009).

15. Charles Taylor, *Human Agency and Language: Philosophical Papers 1* (Cambridge: Cambridge University Press, 1985), 18.

16. Ibid., 62.

17. Jesse L. Jackson, "After the Million Man March," http://www.hartford-hwp.com/archives/45a/042.html (accessed October 15, 2009).

18. The idea that persons with mixed-race identities can opt out of being raced is itself a fallacy of the unencumbered conception of self. On the encumbered model, the moral connectivity of all raced persons renders the severing of such ties untenable.

Monsters and Moralism in *Summer of Sam*

R. Barton Palmer

Controversial, Yet Unexpected

More than a decade after its release, *Summer of Sam* (1999) remains Spike Lee's most controversial film. In part, this is because *Sam* depicts in graphic detail the gruesome murders perpetrated in 1977 by a notorious serial killer who, in letters to the police and the media, referred to himself as "Son of Sam." Many of those involved in the case are still living, and families of some of the victims have objected to what they judge to be Lee's overly sensationalized exploitation of these horrific events. Somewhat strangely, perhaps, the killer himself, David Berkowitz, has complained from his prison cell that the film unfairly demonizes him. At the same time, *Sam* has been widely faulted for its frankly unromantic, starkly realistic (if hardly pornographic, in the usual sense) handling of sexual themes, as well as for its pervasive street language. According to those who take an interest in counting such things, *Sam* contains more than 400 uses of the F-word and its several derivatives, making it, according to that measure, one of the most profane films ever granted a general American release.[1]

It is hardly surprising, then, that *Sam* continues to be widely viewed as issuing a cynical appeal to trashy tastes, and this has prevented some critics from according it more than cursory consideration. What is ironic is that Lee, who throughout his career has made war on harmful stereotypes, was also pilloried for what some saw as his bitterly negative and even defamatory representations of white ethnic culture, even though cast members such as Ben Gazzara, who came from that background, have attested to the film's truthfulness, however unflattering some might think it.[2] Such objections to the film were perhaps to be expected. Any filmmaker who embarks on the re-presentation of actual events runs the risk of stepping on sensitive toes.

And Lee, from the beginning of his career, has demonstrated that he will not shy away from explicit sexual representation if the proper telling of a story requires it (as in *She's Gotta Have It* [1986]). His films have never been characterized by a hesitating political correctness but rather by the trenchant, if admittedly uncomfortable, probing of stereotyping and prejudicial thinking. To be sure, the director's critique of such destructive cultural attitudes has never spared blacks, but neither has he been moved to tread carefully around white sensibilities. Arguably, the "in-your-face" quality of Lee's social commentary is the most distinctive aspect of his wide-ranging engagement with a national culture of diverse racial and ethnic constituencies characterized by mutual antagonism and suspicion. Within the context of his filmic oeuvre, *Sam* is no exception.

But *Sam* did mark a significant departure from Lee's previous films in its focus on the cultural dynamics of an all-white community. The film is not about the Berkowitz killings per se but about how the young men and women of the East Bronx (one of the communities Sam preyed on) react to them. By the time he released *Sam,* Lee had firmly established himself both as a portraitist of contemporary African American experience, especially of the middle-class variety, which was familiar to him from his own upbringing (*She's Gotta Have It, School Daze* [1988], *Mo' Better Blues* [1990], and *Crooklyn* [1994]) and as a forceful analyst of American race and social class relations (*Do the Right Thing* [1989], *Jungle Fever* [1991], *Malcolm X* [1992], *Clockers* [1995], and *He Got Game* [1998]). Arguably, however, as the 1990s came to an end, Lee's interest in various aspects of black identity politics became stronger and more intense, leading him to become somewhat dissatisfied with the fictional format of mainstream commercial cinema, which limits and restricts the way social issues can be represented and treated. If he was to be a director who "uses the medium of film to foreground and contest race, class and gender politics," as one critic perceptively put it, then it made sense that Lee would find ways to use all the resources of the cinema, not just the ones provided by a commercial cinema interested more in emotional affect and entertainment value than in intellectual depth.[3]

This is perhaps the reason why there is such a strong nonfictional strain in the films he released in the closing years of the 1990s. *Get on the Bus* (1996) is a low-budget documentary-style account of the journey of a group of black men to the Million Man March, and *4 Little Girls* (1997) is a straightforward documentary essay on the notorious September 15, 1963, church bombing in Birmingham, Alabama, that killed four members of the girls' choir. Lee's 2000 release, *Bamboozled,* likewise delves deeply into racial politics, offering a savagely satirical send-up of white stereotypes of blacks and the collusion of some notable African American celebrities in their perpetuation. The show-within-a-show structure of *Bamboozled* renders it interestingly antifictional, calling attention to the director's somewhat strident critique. These films underscore Lee's increasingly passionate engagement with tragic milestones of African American history (an approach taken earlier in *Malcolm X*). In addition, they detail a range of contrasting political options open to blacks who seek to devise a workable modus vivendi (including both an anti-integrationist nationalism that emphasizes self-determination and an arguably servile cooperation with the white-dominated media).

Yet, as Paula Massood points out, it is undeniable that in this phase of his career (and even earlier) Lee also took up subjects that were "more broadly American," including the examination of "seminal moments in American history" (especially the civil rights era in *Malcolm X* and the post-9/11 years in *25th Hour* [2002], which, like *Sam*, is dominated by white characters).[4] A strong documentary impulse to explain key aspects of the national experience also makes itself felt in *Sam*, a film that offers, at least in part, a collective approach to historical memorialization and analysis. *Sam*'s communal scope is suggested by a title that evokes an entire period rather than its most notorious "public personality." A decade earlier, Lee first deployed this approach in *Do the Right Thing*, which deals (indirectly, if unmistakably) with another violent outbreak (the 1986 Howard Beach incident, described later) that similarly captured the attention of New Yorkers for some months. A number of that film's featured characters are white, and the narrative focuses with sympathy and insight on the struggles of an Italian American pizzeria owner and his grown sons to continue operating in a largely black neighborhood, with whose residents they have long enjoyed a mutually respectful if not conflict-free relationship.

In *Sam*, even more so than in *Do the Right Thing*, the broad political and cultural trends of the era are recalled with a potent mixture of horror, nostalgia, and disgust. But the particulars of New York City life in the summer of 1977 are not excepted from representation; *Sam* is, in this respect, more journalistic, although its main characters are purely fictional. It seems true enough, as critic Richard A. Blake observes, that as a filmmaker, Spike Lee remains fascinated by New York, where he spent most of his childhood. With its epic yet highly personal treatment of what many agree are key moments and cultural trends in the city's history, *Sam* demonstrates the depth of that fascination. Although the Lee family had deep roots in Atlanta, they moved to the Fort Greene section of Brooklyn when Spike was very young, and he spent his childhood and adolescence there before returning to Atlanta to attend Morehouse College. Like other directors with deep roots in New York (most prominently Martin Scorsese, Sidney Lumet, and Woody Allen), Lee finds himself telling over and over again the story of the city. New York (or, more precisely, some of the districts of the larger metropolitan area) is the place Lee cannot leave because it is, Blake suggests, "so much a part" of his "artistic and psychic sensibility" that it has become the basis for the "anthropological study of the dynamics of racial thinking" that characteristically dominates his films.[5]

Set in an Italian American neighborhood of the Throgs Neck area of the Bronx, *Sam* explores the insularity of a settlement closed in by geographic barriers (the East River and Long Island Sound) that exists literally in the shadow of bridges (the Whitestone and the Throgs Neck) that lead elsewhere, to the more prosperous and assimilated suburban towns of Long Island and Westchester. Lee's camera does not find a community with a vital center, such as the restaurant where neighborhood residents draw continuing nourishment in *Do the Right Thing.* In that earlier film, the violence is racial (a conflict between blacks and Italian Americans) rather than psychopathic, and it is meant to recall a 1986 incident in Howard Beach in which four black men, stranded after their car broke down on the highway, found themselves in an isolated white-only community. After eating a meal at a local pizzeria and using the pay phone to call for a tow truck, they were confronted and subsequently beaten by an angry mob of young white men. One of the victims, fleeing on foot, was accidentally run down and killed; another, found by the police wandering around, confused and wounded, was initially refused medical assistance and was treated as a perpetrator. A subsequent trial led to the imprisonment of a number of the attackers, and the police officers involved were severely censured by the city commissioner. In *Do the Right Thing,* Lee notably rewrites history by staging the violence in a multiethnic community where people who normally get along with one another, despite some mistrust and anger, are provoked by a heat wave into a confrontation that leads to a policeman unintentionally killing one of the black men involved.

Conditions in the East Bronx pictured in *Sam* are even more hopeless than in the notorious Bedford-Stuyvesant neighborhood of the earlier film (as many critics noticed, *Do the Right Thing* depicts Bed-Stuy more than a little idealistically, minus its pervasive litter and endemic drug addiction, and with brightly painted storefronts camouflaging the drabness of its brownstones). Community life, such as it is, in *Sam* revolves around a drug pusher and his buddies who work for the local Mafia and do business near an unwelcoming and barely accessible shoreline, seemingly a forbidden point of departure; a sign, featured prominently, marks the street as a "dead end," and this seems to be an appropriate prediction for the young lives dominated by indolence and petty criminality that are dramatized in the film. If politically incorrect, *Sam* conveys, often vividly, something of the claustrophobic homeliness of an inward-looking metropolitan urban enclave. Reviewers and audiences saw *Sam* as ethnographic reportage. Janet Maslin, writing about the film in the *New York Times,* pronounced a widely shared judgment: "Set in a xenophobic, embattled Bronx neighborhood where non-Italian-Americans are regarded with deep suspicion, 'Summer of Sam' shares the 'Do the Right Thing' affinity for local color."[6]

Despite its grim subject matter, however, *Sam* is more than a little nostalgic for the regrettable past it brings to life—the "bad old days," as journalist Jimmy Breslin ironically terms them. Lee has Breslin address the viewer in the film's prologue, which is stylized as a TV magazine piece. In the film's present, the New York City of 1999, Breslin says that "business is booming up, up, and up," while "crime is down, down, down." In confessing that New York is the city "I love and hate both equally," Breslin strikes a familiar stance (arguably, no other American journalist has so identified himself with his "beat"). He also seems to be a spokesman for Lee's own feelings about the events the film recalls and in part fictionalizes. The journalist's presence seems a down payment on the director's intentions to speak the era's truth (which, it turns out, is a complex mixture of good and bad).

Moreover, turning Breslin into the film's on-screen presenter recalls both his prominent public role in the Son of Sam case (the murder spree actually continued for more than a year during 1976–1977) and his best-selling novelization of the police investigation that eventually, after a series of embarrassing missteps, resulted in the arrest of Berkowitz. Breslin's *.44* is a finely crafted piece of noirish reportage, strongly evocative of Truman Capote's *In Cold Blood,* with its blending of the criminal and journalistic pursuit of answers to the various questions posed by the killings and the apparently mild-mannered and obviously deeply disturbed man eventually charged with them. The book shares with *Sam* a fascination with the more outré aspects of the case, including Berkowitz's bizarre psychopathology and the unusual brutality of murders committed with a large-caliber handgun. The names and details have been changed in the novel, but not the terror, which Breslin avers is "factual." The terror is factual in *Sam* as well, despite the dependence, except for Berkowitz himself, on strictly fictional characters. Both Breslin's novel and Lee's movie capture that summer's structure of feeling, and it is appropriate that the journalist was enlisted to present the film.

In contrast to *.44,* which confines itself to the crime and its unraveling, *Sam* offers a detailed portrait of the now strangely remote customs of an era very different from the more prosperous, law-abiding, post-Giuliani present inhabited by an older Breslin, who seems distinctly disappointed that his hometown has become a boring business center where few sensational crimes are committed. *Sam,* interestingly enough, treats the disco era's self-indulgence and rapidly evolving sexual politics through a fictional lens strikingly similar to that adopted in the period's own very successful attempt at self-promotion. John Badham's *Saturday Night Fever,* released in 1977, was playing in theaters when Berkowitz continued to be moved, as he put it himself, "to hunt and kill." Both films feature charismatic working-class Italian American "studs" who excel at doing the Hustle and find themselves drawn by their macho style and a seemingly unlimited supply of eager women toward sexual overindulgence. *Sam*'s Vinny (John Leguizamo) is a more tragic version of *Fever*'s Tony Manero (the glamorous role that propelled John Travolta to stardom); both are products of a moment characterized by equal amounts of ethical uncertainty and ostentatious public displays of style.

A notable sequence in *Sam,* in fact, seems like an homage to *Fever.* Vinny and his wife Dionna (Mira Sorvino) go to the local disco lounge, where they run through an elaborate dance routine that advertises itself as a calculated performance (not to mention an erotic display). Suddenly the club that is their stage inexplicably transforms into an abstract performance space, as the other dancers disappear and an elaborate visual style emerges to glamorize and idealize their carefully rehearsed gracefulness. There is something to love and as well as hate in the New York that Lee's characters inhabit. In contrast, *Do the Right Thing* has no such mixed tone; it delivers on the earnest moralizing promised in the title, delineating its gallery of characters with the calculated ordinariness of social realism, as each represents contrasting and political points of view.

In his somewhat sensationally titled narrative account, *The Bronx Is Burning,* journalist Jonathan Mahler sees the summer of 1977 as "a transformative moment for the city . . . [which was] straddling eras," reaching a nadir of "decay" that would soon give way to "rehabilitation."[7] He prefers to recall that moment through the bitter trials plaguing the hometown Yankees (particularly the ongoing quarrel between manager Billy Martin and star slugger Reggie Jackson, a conflict with distinct class and racial overtones). Those troubles, however, ended in the team's successful campaign for the American League championship and a stunning World Series triumph. Mahler's book was transformed into a celebratory ESPN miniseries (it debuted in 2007 after that year's Home Run Derby) dominated not by a catalog of ills, including the city's ongoing political crisis, but by Jackson's heroics (three consecutive home runs) in the game that gave the Yankees the series—

a shining moment for a professional sport now tarnished by the excesses of the steroid era. Lee's characters, to be sure, feel no such sense of communal victory. But, with the narrative at an end, Jimmy Breslin reappears to close his account with a brief evocation of Jackson's feats ("Mr. October!"), as well as, more glumly, a brief mention of Elvis Presley's death and a report on the conclusion of the Berkowitz trial (the killer was sentenced to twenty-five years to life) and the 3,700 arrests for various offenses committed during that summer's blackout (more about that later).

Allegory, not Ethnography?

Lee portrays Berkowitz's monstrosity in the etymological sense; that is, he emphasizes the killer's manifestation of otherwise hidden truths. And this kind of cultural archaeology says much about the director's approach to New York history. In *Sam,* characters struggle with a problem (the incredibly varied human capacity for violence and self-destruction) they can never fully grasp, much less resolve. And yet all is not lost. Life goes on, an unfathomable mixture of horror and accomplishment, leading to a present marked by a financial boom and a crime rate in rapid decline. That the director's on-screen spokesman is a white journalist correctly signals a shift away from identity politics. This surprised many who had become convinced that Lee's subject would always be the problems experienced by blacks in an America riven by racism and class inequality. Despite other obvious similarities, *Sam* radically differs in this respect from *Do the Right Thing,* which announces in the opening credits its engagement with the ongoing struggle against institutionalized racism with Rosie Perez's elaborate hip-hop routine choreographed to the strident strains of Public Enemy's "Fight the Power," arguably rap music's most celebrated number.

Certainly the politically infamous, tragedy-marked summer of 1977 offered Lee the opportunity to examine poorer urban blacks' dissatisfaction with their increasingly limited access to a prosperity that, even during a time of general economic retrenchment, New York's white communities seemed to be enjoying. Among several notable events that summer was the July 13–14 areawide blackout, which led to widespread looting and exacerbated tensions in mixed racial communities such as Bedford-Stuyvesant. Particularly because they were not ignited by some notable case of police brutality, real or supposed, these riots were a startling demonstration that the underlying economic and social problems that had led to widespread urban violence in the 1960s had by no means been solved. Instead, dissatisfaction and discontent were revealed to be simmering beneath the surface, ready to explode when the opportunity presented itself, as it did when the power failure made it difficult, if only temporarily, for the already frayed fabric of the social order to hold together. The blackout and its aftermath would have made an ideal subject for the kind of fictionalized analysis of the range of attitudes on both sides of the racial divide that Lee had perfected in earlier films. In fact, the project that became *Sam* would have made an ideal diptych with *Do the Right Thing* had Lee been eager to build the story around the July blackout.

Instead, working with a script penned by white screenwriters Victor Collichio and Michael Imperioli (the latter also partnered with him on the production), Lee chose to focus on the violent reactions of a group of young Italian American men from an all-white enclave in the East Bronx to the depredations of the era's notorious serial killer. In *Sam,* the blackout and its aftermath are evoked only briefly, just as black characters and their experiences are relegated to the film's margins. An uncharitable account of *Sam* might emphasize that, in this way, it replicates Hollywood films that have traditionally chosen to ignore African Americans' role in key events of American history. The blackout rioters—observed in on-scene television accounts narrated by black reporter John Jeffries (played by Lee himself), who assumes the role of an uninvolved emissary from downtown culture on the corner of 125th Street and Sixth Avenue in Harlem—constitute little more than local color. They serve as brief evocations of what else was happening that summer in New York City. These sequences were reportedly added by Lee to the original draft of the script, embellishing but in no way altering its focus. Thus the racial themes explored briefly in *Sam* constitute an afterthought of sorts. The film emphasizes, instead, how the blackout increases the self-isolating fears of the East Bronx community. Its residents are not interested in relieving shop owners of their goods but are desperate to prevent Son of Sam from exploiting the darkness, which affords him the perfect cover as police find themselves otherwise overwhelmed.

In an era of intense identity politics, Lee's move away from a focus on the African American experience has undoubtedly proved controversial. Ever the canny manager of his own public image, Lee anticipates such criticism in a scene that is wryly metafictional. On the eve of the anniversary of the first killing, John Jeffries, doing an on-scene report for his appropriately named segment "A Darker Perspective," interviews some of the residents of Bedford-Stuyvesant. One woman observes, "I thank God it is a white man who is killing all those people." A perpetrator of color, she plausibly opines, would mean an unimaginable vigilante vengeance visited on the city's black communities. Another passerby tells Jeffries, "I am surprised to see you in a black community. I didn't think you liked black people." In this ostentatious preemptive strike, Lee accuses his fictional alter ego of being something of a race traitor with no purported interest in "black people," sending up the filmmaker's chosen focus in *Sam,* whose villains and victims are uniformly white. By way of contrast, in *Do the Right Thing,* Lee plays a character from the Bed-Stuy community: Mookie works for the white-owned pizzeria and has a continuing relationship with the Nuyorican girl Tina (Rosie Perez), thus effectively connecting to the three ethnic communities portrayed in the film.

Critics, not surprisingly, have been eager to find some saving explanation for *Sam*'s exploration of events that do not involve the city's blacks. Most notably, Dan Flory insists that the film "offers a subtle and oblique form of racial analysis, for on the surface the narrative is not about race at all." Working by something like allegory, *Sam,* according to Flory, asks viewers to read its portrayal of vigilantism and mob hysteria within the all-white community as an extended allusion to "the histories of Black lynchings." Lee is said to guide viewers to such an interpretation through a number of significant details, including the hairstyle of the white character Richie (Adrian Brody), who comes close to being killed by his erstwhile friends and neighbors because they interpret his rejection of community grooming norms as dangerous deviance and mistakenly think he is the notorious Son of Sam. Richie, who has adopted a punk identity, including a Union Jack T-shirt and a Cockney accent, first sports a spiked 'do and then a spectacular blonde Mohawk. So the condemnation of his hairstyles as perverted "uncomfortably alludes to dominant white rejections of Black hair on alleged aesthetic grounds."[8] Although presumably interested in dealing with the theme of lynching, Lee decided against crafting a narrative that tackled this subject directly, apparently fearing that those filmgoers he was most intent on "reaching" might fail to engage sympathetically with the victims of such violence. Instead, the film is said to work indirectly to "convince whites to learn to listen to or observe sympathetically those who may be subordinate to them." As a result, *Sam* is supposedly dominated by a sermonizing rhetoric. The director's evident hope is that these filmgoers, witnessing the effects of irrational mob violence on one of their own, "might acquire a better sense of moral relevance . . . regarding racial injustice."[9]

Sam, in other words, is not about its ostensible subject—one of the most highly charged and socially significant moments in the history of Lee's native New York City. Instead, it is a gentle, carefully calculated attempt to change the hearts and minds of resistant whites through the drawing of a general truth—namely, that prejudice, fear, and mistrust can be an explosive mix, resulting in the victimization of the innocent. Such an allegorizing reading that rejects as forgettable the film's surface would make sense if one believes that Lee could not have otherwise devoted such time and energy to a dramatization of events from which black characters are almost entirely excluded. But the fact remains that, from the beginning, *Sam* was a personal project (Lee was enthusiastic about the script and devoted considerable time and energy to its modification and improvement).

Moreover, it is hard to imagine that if the never-reticent Lee were eager to make a film about lynching he would have chosen to approach it in such an oblique and indirect fashion that soft-pedals its horrific, shameful nature. It seems significant, moreover, that the vigilantes succeed in doing nothing more than roughing Richie up. We never learn whether they actually intended to kill him, and in any case, they are stopped when Richie's stepfather Eddie (Mike Starr) hears the commotion, grabs his pistol, goes out into the street, and fires a few shots, forcing Richie's tormentors to stop. The crowd quickly disbands once he tells them that the actual Son of Sam, now revealed to be Berkowitz, has been taken into police custody. And so no "lynching" takes place. As a comparison, note the direct, affecting fashion in which Lee presents murderous extralegal violence against blacks in the childhood sequences of *Malcolm X.* Within the context of Lee's career at this point, it certainly would have been understandable if he had taken on the lynching of blacks, which was then a prominent topic of discussion in American culture as a collection of "memorial" postcards and photographs of lynchings was making the rounds of American museums, eventually to be even more widely circulated in book form.[10] But this is clearly not the film he decided to make when he embarked on the project that became *Sam.*

Even more important for our purposes here, the kind of reading that Flory proposes offers a simplistic account of Lee's engagement with the film's social materials. But this engagement, as Jimmy Breslin makes clear, is a mixture of love and hate (which seems to be, among other things, a reference to *Do the Right Thing,* in which the Afrocentric character Radio Raheem wears matching rings engraved "love" and "hate"). For Flory, the director's intentions are reduced to the construction of a parable. To be sure, the moral of that parable—that the innocent are often victimized because of the irrational desires or fears of their fellows—clearly emerges from *Sam*'s closing sequences, and it has been seized on by those commentators sympathetic to Lee's overall political project. Richie is innocent, and his community is, albeit in extremis, exculpated as he is rescued and restored to his family. Good sense prevails, and damage to the social fabric is minimal (*Do the Right Thing* similarly ends with a moment of reconciliation after the violence has passed). In *Sam,* however, such an easy identification and condemnation of communal malfeasance emerge as an overly optimistic, liberal-minded interpretation. With some subtlety, the film actually shows that evil cannot be located only in the would-be perpetrators of extralegal violence and in the psychopath who is their unintentional inspiration.

To put this another way, these breakdowns in sanity, emotional restraint, humaneness, and respect for the social order are revealed not as deviations but as symptomatic, even exemplary. It is the decline of the social order itself in an era of rapidly changing values that is the film's main subject: the disordering that manifests itself in the lives of individual characters as well as in the widespread looting and unrest occasioned by the July blackout. Lee's customary concerns with community politics (and the way these conflicts are often susceptible to rational discussion and cooperative resolution) thus find themselves subsumed within a larger account of collective pathology, anomie, and rebellion. As Lee has maintained, "This film is not about David Berkowitz. It's not about Son of Sam. This film is about his evil energy that affected eight million New Yorkers."[11] And that energy is not dissipated by either the capture of Berkowitz or Richie's fortunate escape.

In *Sam,* the political filmmaker par excellence shows himself to be a moralist as well. It is important to note that Son of Sam, to whom this summer belongs, is never given an ethnic identity (interestingly enough, Berkowitz is actually something of a liminal figure—Italian American by birth but later adopted and renamed by a Jewish couple). He is never located precisely within the social space the film constructs; *Sam* does not treat the murders and their aftermath from a sociopolitical perspective. Thus the film does not follow *Do the Right Thing* in dramatizing the passions and fears of culturally divergent communities that share the same crowded urban space and find themselves economically, but not culturally, interdependent. In *Sam,* the vigilante violence that eventually results from Berkowitz's evil energy is not directed outward, toward some group that presents itself to be "othered" and scapegoated (as would be the case in a lynching, properly speaking), nor does it exacerbate already existing institutional problems (such as a police force long disposed toward the unjust treatment of "minorities," as in the earlier film).

"There Was Something in the Air That Night"

In the film's climactic sequence, Richie, innocent of violence or aggression toward anyone, is rescued from an undeserved and extralegal fate by the intervention of an ordinary citizen who "does the right thing." The injustice of this victimization is emphasized in this part of the film by Lee's use of affecting crosscutting between scenes depicting Berkowitz's capture and others devoted to the local vigilantes' decision to take Richie into custody. But this moralizing, with its intention to establish a clear, perhaps absolute distinction between good and evil, does not prevail throughout the film. In its anatomizing of the complex interplay of ethical values, *Sam* effectively dismantles any easily drawn contrast between the killer and the community of his innocent victims. The killer's evil (treated as inexplicable) leads to the similarly threatening evil of the misguided vigilantes, who, ironically enough, in their desire to extirpate the threat to their community, find themselves victimizing one of their own. The victimized become victimizers.

The film traces this pattern in Son of Sam himself. Like the vigilantes, he too finds himself moved to violence after it seems he can no longer endure what he understands, however insanely, as unmerited persecution. The police lieutenant in charge of the investigation reads one of the killer's letters to the incredulous Mafia capo of the East Bronx, whose assistance he seeks. In it, Son of Sam rants, with maniacal illogic, about his imprisonment and compulsive "hunting": "Papa Sam keeps me locked in the attic too. I can't get out. When I look out the attic window and watch the world go by. I feel like an outsider." The letter confirms Lee's representation of Berkowitz's madness, which opens the film. This terrifying spectacle is neither personalized nor psychologized. With no establishing shot or backstory provided, the camera simply finds Son of Sam as a barely human, howling presence seemingly trapped in a room filled with waste and garbage, where he suffers bitterly from the barking dog that later comes to play such a large role in his increasingly elaborate delusions. But in the next sequence he is suddenly empowered, shuffling from the shadows to which he has somehow been transported and moving toward his first intended victim to the eerily appropriate and frighteningly ironic sound of Abba's "Fernando" and its signature line "there was something in the air that night."

How this has come to pass does not receive even the briefest explanation. What that "something in the air" might be is never identified. Berkowitz is accorded no moment that reveals him in any meaningful sense as human rather than demonic. Lacking a history, a voice, or familial connections, he is simply "there." Seemingly out of nowhere, he appears before his victims to murder them, escaping afterward, apparently without any difficulty, into the anonymity of the city. Son of Sam, we might say, is the archetypically modern urban dweller, shut up alone in his room, cut off from meaningful relationships (the oppressive father, never depicted, is apparently a delusion), a grotesque flaneur roaming the streets in search of what will satisfy his desires and obsessions. In Lee's ostentatiously expressionistic depiction of his depredations, Son of Sam is represented either by the symptoms of his presence (the shattering blasts from his large-caliber handgun) or, like the monster in a horror film, by fleeting glimpses of his partially visible body. Eerily monstrous is the profound disgust for the city he expresses in the letter he sends to famed columnist Breslin (which is read in voice-over in the film). New York, he proclaims in the manner of a modern Elijah, is "filled with dog manure, vomit, stale wine, urine and blood." For him, the city is a sewer of unrelieved corruption that, as the tortured grammar of his ramblings reveals, somehow explains how he has come to be what he is.

Richie is not the terrifying psychopathic presence whose identity he is thought to occupy. The film reveals him to be gentle, tolerant, and open-minded. Richie has no obvious connection to the violent murders that seem to be motivated in some sense by the apparently sexual anger the real killer directs at attractive young women and dating couples. Richie is a focused character whose personality, history, and troubles are dramatized sympathetically, as Lee shifts to a blank, realist style to represent the inhabitants of one of the neighborhoods Son of Sam is terrorizing. He is not a loner but someone who is defined by his connections to others, including his mother and stepfather as well as his longtime friends (especially Vinny). When he unexpectedly appears just as the killings begin, his friends are appalled (he is initially unrecognizable), but they do not reject him. Despite his inability or refusal to find a respectable job, Richie emerges as the only young man who lives something like the examined life in a neighborhood filled with those who unquestioningly accept the ostensibly bankrupt ethnic culture that enfolds and entraps them, including its prejudices and narrow-mindedness.

Returning to the East Bronx from Manhattan, where he has been pursuing a not terribly successful career as a musician and has been caught up in the punk movement, Richie finds himself drawn to one of the girls he has known since childhood, Ruby (Jennifer Esposito). Ruby is likewise something of an outsider because of what the others regard as her promiscuity. A romance develops between the two. Richie at first rejects Ruby's sexual advances, unsure of his own interest and, perhaps more important, refusing to allow her to continue being the "whore" the others insist she is. Richie offers friendship instead, and Ruby accepts. Transporting themselves on weekends to the East Village, the two come to share an enthusiasm for the punk culture and music to which Richie finds himself drawn so intensely. At last comfortable with her affection for him, Richie and Ruby begin to make love in his garage apartment one night, and ironically, it is at the very moment when their "normality" as a couple emerges that the vigilantes show up to lure him outside, having convinced themselves that Richie is in fact Son of Sam and must be destroyed.

Such a plot summary is accurate enough, but it ignores aspects of Richie's alienation from community values that seem more troubling and undermine his sympathetic innocence. Richie's punk restyling is more than a fashion statement; it responds to the profound uncertainty he feels about his identity. His world is now one that offers substantial opportunities for self-fashioning. Perhaps such malleability is deceptive. Richie can make himself "British" by adopting a Cockney accent. He can indicate his rejection of bourgeois norms by his clothing (including a spiked dog collar) and hairstyle, but he cannot reject entirely the community of his birth. Gay liberation (the Stonewall revolt is eight years in the city's past) has made possible an open embrace of homosexuality, even in the traditionally minded ethnic enclave that is his home. The neighborhood gang includes a somewhat flamboyantly "out" young man who, like Richie, is accepted as one of the community, despite occasional razzing and mild mistreatment.

Richie, however, has a secret life. He makes money to support a marijuana habit by dancing in a male strip club that caters to a homosexual clientele; at the club he also engages in prostitution with some of the customers. Given his rejection of Ruby's advances and his willingness to participate in gay sex, Richie seems uncertain or ambiguous about his own sexuality. He even takes Ruby to the club so that she can see his act, in which the peace-loving Richie symbolically acts out his own disturbing connection between sexuality and violence. His dance involves two life-size canvas-covered dolls, one male and one female, with whom he mimes different sexual acts. Then he removes a jackknife from his pocket, opens the blade, holds it near his genitals, and, to enthusiastic applause and shouting, stabs and slices open the female doll, as feathers fly around the stage. The energy and self-abandon with which Richie dances suggest that he is in this for more than the money.

Son of Sam confesses that he is no woman hater, yet he targets only single young women and dating couples engaged in sex. In one of his letters he proclaims, "I love the world." Does he indeed, like Jimmy Breslin, love and hate equally? Does Richie? The sympathetic young man only mimes the homicidal anger that drives Son of Sam to a killing spree. His developing alienation from the identity offered by his culture never becomes pathological in any ordinary sense, even as his questioning sexuality seems to locate a "normal" object in Ruby, whom his affection rescues from self-destructive sexual overindulgence. Richie never exhibits the disgust that Berkowitz expresses at the abjectness of a city overflowing with waste. And yet his transformation of something resembling Son of Sam's eros-fueled anger into an act that receives enthusiastic acceptance from his audience suggests that there is little difference between perpetrator and performer. They are, to be sure, separated from each other by accidents of birth, upbringing, and psychology, but they give equal expression to that "something in the air."

Later in the film Lee makes a more specific connection between Richie and the monster for whom he is eventually mistaken. In fact, Richie becomes Son of Sam's stand-in, once again under the cover of artistic performance. His musical group, which now includes Ruby, is shown playing for a rave at an East Village punk club. The lyrics of the song he screams out in the requisite chanting style are the frightening words from the killer's letter to Breslin. The crowd goes wild at the mention of streets "filled with dog manure, vomit, stale wine, urine and blood," and the confession that initially aroused mass terror is now shown to be responding equally to the desires of a wider "clientele." It is deeply ironic, perhaps even poetically just, that Richie is nearly murdered as a consequence of the general loosening of moral and cultural restraints that allows him to become an "other" of sorts. In response to this freedom, he eagerly becomes Son of Sam's double, adopting an active role in aestheticizing and promoting the very social breakdown that nearly destroys him. He too finds himself split between hate and love. Richie even experiences, one might say, something of a lucky escape.

What If I'm Deviated?

Richie's friend Vinny is not so fortunate. Despite sincere attempts to reform, Vinny is unable to control his insatiable appetite for the zipless extramarital sex that is seemingly available everywhere in his world. In the process, his life is destroyed as he descends a slippery moral slope. If Richie is misidentified as Son of Sam, Vinny just narrowly escapes being one of his victims. Parked with his wife's cousin on a lonely byway, Vinny notices a figure in the shadows moving toward the car as they couple lustfully, even brutally; the man is frightened off by the arrival of another car. Sam moves on to other victims, while Vinny returns to the dance club where he has left his wife Dionna. Driving home, they pass by the latest crime scene. Vinny cannot resist looking inside at the mutilated and bloody corpses, a sight that sickens him. He confesses later to Richie, "It's an omen. He let me go. What does it mean? God is telling me that I'm going to burn in Hell unless I stop cheating."

Richie, who has no patience for metaphysical explanations, rejects the possibility of a larger moral purpose in his friend's escape: "God's got nothing to do with it." Vinny's problem, he confesses, is that although he finds Dionna beautiful, he cannot bring himself to make her the object of all his sexual desires, including "sixty-nine and doggie style"; these he can satisfy only with women he can treat purely and simply as objects. In a time of the dissolution of traditional gender categories, Vinny remains a prisoner of old-fashioned male attitudes: "You don't do that kind of shit with your wife." The more worldly and liberal-minded Richie advances the view that what seems morally wrong might actually be a source of vitality. "Evil," he reminds Vinny, "spelled backwards is live," a bit of philosophizing that Son of Sam himself, were he granted a moment of mental clarity, might find compellingly attractive as a motto. "What if I'm deviated?" Vinny whines, admitting the more frightening possibility of unconscious compulsions. If these prove too powerful to resist, as he predicts, his life will be "over."

And he is proved correct. Intending to hear Richie's group play at the punk rave, Vinny and Dionna make their way to the famous Studio 54 disco club, where they are picked up by a group organizing a trip to the notorious Plato's Retreat, a members-only club offering swingers an upscale venue for anonymous sexual abandon. The couple gets high on the cocaine provided by their hosts and, with Vinny taking the lead, spends the evening indulging in sex with strangers. Although Vinny is initially enthusiastic about the prospect of freedom from conventional moral restraints, in the aftermath of this indulgence, he cannot overcome his repulsion at what it means. Overcome with jealousy and fear of his own inadequacy, he accuses Dionna of being a lesbian and a whore, even though he encouraged another woman to approach her. When his wife throws the reproach back in his face, he responds, "I'm a man. I can't be a whore." But, sensing that the uncertainties of his culture are manifesting themselves in him, Vinny confesses, "The shit I'm doing right now isn't me." Perhaps with a bit of a heavy hand, Lee stages this monumental fight in a local cemetery, where the couple stops on the drive home, even though both Dionna and Vinny fear an attack from Son of Sam. But they prove perfectly capable of destroying their lives without his pistol passing judgment on them, and this is perhaps the director's point.

Richie, who has been to Manhattan, tells Ruby, "You can be whatever you want to be." And Ruby, who has spent her life in the East Bronx, responds, "You're born into a slot and that's it." *Sam* mediates between, but does not reconcile, these two positions on human freedom. Its ethnography, committed to the exploration of a transformational moment, surveys both the deep-rootedness of a traditional self-regarding ethnic enclave and the irrepressible urge for self-fashioning now proclaimed as a right by the wider culture. As in so much else, the psychopath is here exemplary. Son of Sam's self-understanding is hopelessly contradictory. Searching for a self-explanatory center in the letter to Breslin, he proclaims, "I don't hate women. I am a monster. . . . The women of Queens are prettiest of all. I live for the hunt . . . I love my work."

The film's finale offers no satisfactory account of these antinomies; nor can it explain his double nature as a prisoner and a perpetrator, as a creature who can be anything he wants to be, even as he finds himself occupying a slot of endless misery. In the end, all that seems to matter is that Berkowitz is apprehended, tried, convicted, and imprisoned, restoring the community's sense of safety. Likewise, the blackout episode concludes with the bringing to justice of the hundreds of New Yorkers apprehended for various criminal acts. Reggie Jackson's heroics proclaim the resurgence of a city thought to be on the ropes, and Lee can conclude with Frank Sinatra's musical paean to the city. And yet the "evil energy" that Son of Sam manifests and makes public (even though he is not its source) has not dissipated. After destroying Vinny, it finds a home in Richie, who experiences not only a bitter inner conflict but also the thought that his actions might not be his own.

Notes

1. This was most commented on, perhaps, by Janet Maslin in the *New York Times.* She observes, "What may surprise anyone following the publicity maelstrom around the director's latest effort is that its Son of Sam aspects, while fiendishly vivid, are only the backdrop for a film that is much more lurid in other regards. 'Summer of Sam' pushes sexual hot buttons even more emphatically, to the point where it also pushes the envelope for raw talk and raunchy eroticism on screen." "Red Hot Buttons in Lee's Steaming 'Sam,'" *New York Times,* July 2, 1999, http://www.observer.com/node/41715 (accessed January 20, 2010).

2. Critic Andrew Sarris, for example, whines, "I hate to use the reverse racist card on the self-righteous Mr. Lee, but if an Italian-American director caricatured and defamed African-American characters in Bed-Stuy as Mr. Lee demonizes Italian-Americans here, we'd never hear the end of it" (review of *Summer of Sam, New York Observer,* July 11, 1999).

3. Sean Redmond in *The Wallflower Critical Guide to Contemporary North American Film Directors,* ed. Yoram Allon et al. (London: Wallflower, 2000), 276.

4. Paula J. Massood, ed., *The Spike Lee Reader* (Philadelphia: Temple University Press, 2008), xvi.

5. Richard A. Blake, *Street Smart: The New York of Lumet, Allen, Scorsese, and Lee* (Lexington: University Press of Kentucky, 2005), 38, 218.

6. Maslin, "Red Hot Buttons."

7. Jonathan Mahler, *The Bronx Is Burning: 1977, Baseball, Politics, and the Battle for the Soul of a City* (New York: Farrar, Straus, and Giroux, 2005), xi.

8. Dan Flory, "Race and Black American Film Noir: *Summer of Sam* as Lynching Parable," in *The Spike Lee Reader,* 203, 205.

9. Ibid., 208.

10. See James Allen et al., eds., *Without Sanctuary: Lynching Photography in America* (New York: Twin Palms, 2000).

11. Prairie Miller, "*Summer of Sam:* An Interview with Spike Lee," in *Spike Lee: Interviews,* ed. Cynthia Fuchs (Jackson: University of Mississippi Press, 2002), 179.

Part II

Race, Sexuality, and Community

(Still) Fighting the Power

Public Space and the Unspeakable Privacy of the Other in *Do the Right Thing*

Elizabeth Hope Finnegan

Near the end of Spike Lee's *Do the Right Thing* (1989), the two Italian American brothers Pino (John Tuturro) and Vito (Richard Edson) are arguing in the back room of their father's pizzeria, where they work. Pino, the sullen, overtly racist older brother, is manhandling Vito, trying to impress on him the danger of getting too close to their multicultural—primarily African American—customers and, in particular, their delivery boy Mookie (Spike Lee). For Pino, the struggle is about maintaining a discrete and essential identity; earlier in the film he cautions his brother, "Remember who you are." What he means is both "Italian American" and "American" as white—a whiteness that is set in essential opposition to blackness and is possible only through the constitution of blackness as something fundamentally *Other.* As the brothers wrestle, the overhead light swings above them in a disorienting blur of cartoonishly orange light and shadow; the handheld camera jostles and edges around them, ratcheting up the tension. Vito finally finds a purchase on his brother and insists, "You don't *know.* You *think* you know, but you don't *know.*" What does Vito mean by this?

Before suggesting an answer, I would like to reflect on the fact that even twenty years after its release, *Do the Right Thing* continues to spark discussion and controversy. Although Lee's body of work is at times problematic, in particular with regard to its pervasive heteronormativity and its often troubling representation of women,[1] *Do the Right Thing* remains a film to be reckoned with. The film continues to engender acute discomfort among audiences (especially, but not exclusively, white audiences), raising a number of questions about why its confrontation of what Lee calls the single most pressing problem in America—race and racism—is so threatening to generally held assumptions about race in America.[2]

The film, set on the hottest day of the summer in a multicultural neighborhood in Brooklyn, created a stir with its uncompromising portrayal of racial inequities. The heat aggravates the already brewing conflicts among the central characters: Sal (Danny Aiello), the Italian American pizzeria owner; his sons Pino and Vito; his slacker, deadbeat-dad delivery boy Mookie; the implacable Radio Raheem (Bill Nunn), whose blaring boom box precedes him everywhere; and Buggin' Out (Giancarlo Esposito), a wannabe militant who decides to boycott Sal's for excluding African American celebrities from his all–Italian American "Wall of Fame." These conflicts—some petty and others more serious—escalate over the course of the day into a bitter confrontation between Sal and Radio Raheem, resulting in a riot, the murder of Radio Raheem at the hands of the police, and the destruction of Sal's Famous Pizzeria.

Vito's contention about the status of his brother's knowledge raises the question of claiming knowledge as the basis for dealing with others. *Do the Right Thing* mines this question and its consequences for how race-based injustices are framed and represented in American culture. In investigating how the film addresses race as an epistemological problem—that is, as a problem rooted in knowledge (or a lack of knowledge)— I begin with a brief synopsis of philosophical skepticism and suggest what is at stake in framing our relation to others as an epistemological question. In doing so, I use Ludwig Wittgenstein's private language argument and J. L. Austin's theory of speech acts to show that the film participates in a sustained engagement with the skeptical challenge and makes a crucial intervention in the discussion of race within the context of the kinds of knowledge claims we make, or say we cannot make, about others. Finally, I make a case that the cinematic grammar of the film directs us to reject the framing of racism as an epistemological problem at all, and I suggest what the film is ultimately asking of us.

The Skeptical Challenge to Our Knowledge Claims

Before returning to the fighting brothers in the back room of Sal's pizzeria, I'd like to take another leap backward in time, to the moment in 1641 when René Descartes decided that he could never be in a position to know anything outside of his own thoughts, effectively condemning us to an ineluctable state of doubt regarding the thoughts or feelings of others.[3] This means that our relation to others—for epistemologists, anyway—has been conscripted as an epistemological problem, that is, as a problem of *knowledge*, rather than as an ontological problem, or a problem of the *nature* of existence of the world or of others. The skeptical position with regard to what is called the "problem of other minds"—the problem of whether we can, with any degree of certainty, know (or be known to) another—is that since the Other cannot be known with certainty (because there is always the chance of being deceived or wrong about what we think we know), we cannot claim to know anything at all about others. Because I cannot verify that your cry of pain, for example, is genuine and not a pretense, I cannot be said to *know* that you are in pain. Descartes argued that knowledge has to begin with the mind, with what is private and interior to each person; that the barrier between ourselves and others is unnavigable; and that inference and observation cannot logically be trusted. Clearly, this is an unsatisfactory way of existing, and much of philosophy since Descartes has attempted to find empirical or commonsense data—enough evidence to say, "I *do* know"—to domesticate the skeptical threat.[4] This is likewise unsatisfactory, akin to using calculus to solve a crossword puzzle; it's an attempt to counter deduction with induction.[5] The problem with empirical or inferential data is that they are always subject to doubt; since we *could* be dreaming, hallucinating, or otherwise deceived, argues the skeptic, we cannot accept this kind of evidence either. In fact, the skeptic requires a standard of evidence that is simply impossible to satisfy.[6]

What precisely is so troubling about casting our relation to others as an epistemological problem—a problem of a certain kind of "privacy" of the Other (to, or from, me) that is logically unassailable yet might be accessible *if* we could amass a sufficient body of evidence? The answer, perhaps, is that doing so means, in the first instance, that we are given philosophical grounds to deny the humanity of the Other and, in the second instance, that we can simply ignore the logical force of skepticism, pretending it is not a genuine threat at all or in some cases arguing for a transcendent force such as the existence of God to reassure us (which is Descartes' end-run strategy). Rejecting both approaches, ordinary language philosophers Wittgenstein, Austin, and Stanley Cavell have taken up the skeptical challenge by examining the ways we use language in our everyday lives.[7] It turns out that our "ordinary" (as opposed to philosophical) language includes a large number of statements that are not empirically true or false but instead are *descriptive* of our experience and so are subject to neither empirical verification nor logical analysis; they are not, in other words, dependent on truth conditions (knowable as either true or false) to be meaningful. These uses of language, or what Wittgenstein calls our "forms of life,"[8] are part of what grounds our human community.

Nonetheless, for these philosophers, the threat of skepticism is real; it is urgent; to ignore it is to cut ourselves off from a community of Others as drastically as the skeptic fears we are already inevitably cut off. The skeptic is not so much the enemy as the messenger we would like to blame. The question of how to effectively respond to the message—the claim that we simply cannot know to any degree of certainty anything outside of our own inner states, emotions, or sensations—is inextricable from the question of how we are to engage with the Other at all in the face of the skeptical challenge. For the ordinary language philosopher, this engagement is freighted with an obligation to achieve an ethical intersubjectivity that is not contingent on knowledge claims at all.

Racism as Ignorance

What *Do the Right Thing* so strikingly illustrates, and situates as tragic, is the epistemological drama of what it would mean to say that we can or cannot know the (in this case racial) Other, and what is at stake in evicting that Other from the possibility of community as a consequence of our knowledge claims. To return to our two Italian American brothers, locked in a wrestler's hold: what Vito thinks he means in saying "You don't *know*" is that his friend Mookie is not really Other, or not *so* Other; he has gotten to know Mookie, and Mookie is all right (just as Mookie, earlier in the film, defends Vito from his black militant–wannabe friend Buggin' Out by saying, "Vito's alright. Vito's down."). This is the model of race relations that dominates our cultural myths about what racism is and how it can be overcome: without reference to the origins of racist assumptions, they are generally posited as being located in ignorance. Racism, in other words, is largely conceived as a class of epistemic failure; that is, it is a *failure to know.* We could say that racism is treated as a special class of the "problem of other minds."[9]

In the United States, the African American has been broadly constituted as an immitigable and unknowable Other in relation to the white Self, which is constituted as central and universal.[10] The mirror image of this claim, presented as its antidote, is that with the production of sufficient knowledge, racism (i.e., ignorance) could be overturned. Vito's assertion that Pino doesn't *know* (because he hasn't gotten to know Mookie the way Vito has) moves toward precisely the model of epistemic failure or success that the film dramatizes with regard to race.

The model of racism and its overturning endorsed by Vito has tremendous narrative power: it is clear; it is dramatic; it involves precisely the kind of transformative experience that, in classical theater, allows for audience catharsis; but above all, it is simple. What this model likewise supports is the overwhelmingly reinforced notion that racism can be defined, understood, and confronted solely on the level of personal bigotry. That is, such a model conveniently ignores the larger spectacle of a society grounded in white privilege and whose cultural, economic, social, and political institutions invisibly perpetuate "whiteness" as a normative state.[11] Furthermore, this model supports the equally popular notion of personal (rather than institutional) responsibility for success, and the corollary notion that the United States functions as a meritocracy, a system in which anyone who works hard enough (as Sal, who built his pizzeria with his "own two hands," does) will succeed according to their worth.

Do the Right Thing, however, demonstrates that claims to knowing the Other are insufficient to overcome racism precisely because racism is still built into our social, political, and economic institutions such as education, banking, housing, and even family systems—institutions that allow Sal, for example, "the time and strength—that Mookie has not—to forge ties of warmth and integrity with his sons. [Sal] has had the economic fortune—that Da Mayor [Ossie Davis] has not—to be able to be in the position to hand Da Mayor the broom to sweep his sidewalks with discretion and dignity, and to buy photos he does not want from the neighborhood crazy."[12] Sal recognizes neither his own privilege nor his customers' lack of it; he simply sees himself as a nurturer of the children who, he says proudly, "grew up on my pizza." Sal's framing of himself as the father figure of the neighborhood kids does not stop him from picking up a baseball bat—not because he has been physically threatened but because Buggin' Out questions his sovereign right to exclude photographs of African Americans from the pizzeria's "Wall of Fame." Sal's disproportionate and violent reaction to this insubordination signals his unquestioning investment in his own (institutionally sanctioned) authority.

I suspect that part of the media's negative—even hostile—reception of *Do the Right Thing* can be traced to its refusal to participate in the Hollywood version of the overcoming of differences through personal knowledge of a specific representative of the Other who "proves" that he or she is both knowable and, typically, committed to values consistent with white, middle-class notions of virtue. This suggests that white audiences, at least, are more comfortable with this epistemological model because it does not challenge them to address racism at a societal level but only at the level of the individual, who can always be recuperated through sufficient knowledge.[13] The burden of proof, either way, appears to be on the African American. *Do the Right Thing* was attacked by many critics in ways that suggest that Lee's film used complex strategies to unpack race problems from a perspective that made audiences and reviewers deeply uncomfortable.

Wittgenstein's Private Language Argument

Before turning to what the film itself does on a cinematic and narrative level to elicit this level of discomfort, I first want to sketch what is at stake in linking the idea of racism to epistemological claims regarding the knowledge of other minds. One way Wittgenstein has dramatized the skeptical challenge is through the private language argument.[14] Wittgenstein asks us to imagine a language that is intelligible to only one person, a language that no one else can know or learn and that refers only to things the single user of that language can know. He describes the language like this: "The individual words of this language are to refer to what can only be known to the person speaking; to his immediate private sensations. So another person cannot understand the language."[15] Both the language and the sensations it refers to, then, are necessarily private, unknowable to anyone else.

Wittgenstein uses the notion of a private language as a metaphor with which to engage the larger epistemological concerns about the privacy of sensations and thoughts and the implications these concerns have for human interaction. Rejecting the Cartesian move to begin with consciousness, Wittgenstein begins instead with human activity. He points out that using a language means following the rules of that language, and in order to know that one is following a rule, that rule (and therefore the language) must be public: "And hence 'obeying a rule' is a practice . . . it is not possible to obey a rule 'privately': otherwise thinking one was obeying a rule would be the same thing as obeying it."[16] Using the example of a language intelligible to only a single person, Wittgenstein argues (albeit indirectly) that this would logically mean that *all* inner sensations—pain, pleasure, emotions—would likewise be intelligible to only one person.

Thus he makes the point that Austin states more explicitly: if I cannot know that *others* have sensations (or language), then I cannot know that *I* have them either, because it is only due to our shared *linguistic* practices that I can know anything at all.[17] My "knowing" occurs *in* language. Our reaction when knowledge claims fail us is not the absence of knowledge but, more accurately, a condition of *speechlessness*.[18] Our relation to the world, and to others, is not a matter of knowing or not knowing but of knowing (or not knowing) *what to say*. What the skeptical threat registers is really our anxiety about our existential condition of separateness from and unintelligibility to one another; it is an anxiety about the legitimacy of our *own* experience, an expression of our own loneliness. As Cavell puts it:

> The fantasy of private language . . . can be understood as an attempt to account for, and protect, our separateness, our unknowingness, our unwillingness or incapacity either to know or to be known. Accordingly, the failure of this fantasy signifies: that there is no assignable end to the depth of us to which language reaches; that nevertheless there is no end to our separateness. We are endlessly separate, for *no* reason. But then we are answerable for everything that comes between us; if not for causing it then for continuing it; if not for denying it then for affirming it; if not for it then to it. The idea of privacy expressed in the fantasy of private language fails to express how private we are, metaphysically and practically.[19]

Ultimately, to deny the pain of others is to deny my own. And conversely, to say that I am in pain is to admit that anyone *can* be.[20] The private language argument dramatizes the problem of other minds because it provides an example of the consequences of declaring that someone is totally and inaccessibly Other. There is a reason that the private language argument, and much of the philosophical debate about epistemic privacy, focuses on the sensation of pain; pain is both the loneliest of sensations and the one that most urgently demands and foregrounds empathy. For Wittgenstein, Austin, and Cavell, the use of the word *pain* in our everyday language, our knowing what that word means, entails our ability to talk about others as well as about ourselves. Wittgenstein asserts, "You learned the *concept* of 'pain' when you learned the language."[21] If a person speaks a language (or has a pain, or has a history) that we *do not know,* we can conceivably learn it. If they speak a language (or have pains and histories) that we *necessarily cannot know and cannot ever learn,* any notion of human connection is vitiated. A private language entails extracting a person from the "form of life" that makes the very concept of language meaningful.

Saying "I am in pain" moves outside the privacy of one's pain into the publicness of language; it asks whether we understand what the words "I am in pain" *mean* within our shared practices. If we do, then we are "answerable" to one another, as though we have given our word, or our words, to one another. If we don't, then we are condemned to speechlessness, which is one way of describing solipsism. A language can be mine only if it can also be ours. And what is language for if not to express and to attend to the illimitable array of our human pains? To cast the acknowledgment of the Other as an epistemic problem rather than an ethical one is ultimately a strategy of abdicating, or repudiating, our human responsibility to one another.

The Public Space of Speech

We could say that what is dramatized in *Do the Right Thing* is the disaster of what it would mean to claim the essential privacy, the inexpressiveness, of the African American Other. If epistemic privacy means that we cannot, in some sense, *speak* to one another, because any speaking of oneself would be subject to doubt or certainty and thereby foreclosed, how can we construct an antidote to privacy? And what would it mean to make the private public?

Hannah Arendt's notion of public space elucidates the importance of publicness, of what she calls the "space of appearances," an arena where persons may congregate and speak and act in concert with one another. It is only, she elaborates, in a *public* space that we can use our words and actions to "insert ourselves into the human world."[22] Public space is not, in a strict sense, a physical space; it is less "the name of a realm than the voice we use in conversing with one another."[23] This understanding of public space demonstrates what is at stake in the notion of a private language—that it would incapacitate or invalidate our claims to being members of a community. If the (racial) Other is marked as private, that is to say, speechless,[24] this would mean that the public space, the space of appearances where speech and action come into being, is foreclosed to that Other. To demand knowledge of the Other as a condition for that Other to be allowed to speak his or her private self publicly is to evacuate that Other from the space of appearances. Public space and the conflict between public and private (where *public* means having a voice with which we can speak with and to others, and *private* designates a condition of speechlessness as a metaphor for inaccessibility) are central to the interwoven conflicts in *Do the Right Thing.*

The black characters in *Do the Right Thing* do not have access to the space of appearances in any meaningful sense. Power and powerlessness are played out in the film in terms of publicness; if the African American Other is constructed as essentially private, then entrance to the public sphere is logically impossible. The street is physically public, but as a political space, it is not animated by the power of its inhabitants to act; without this power, the space of appearances is "undermined."[25] The African Americans in the film are mostly un- or underemployed; they do not appear to own their homes or to have any access to political, economic, or social avenues of mobility or progress. The sole markers of "success" among the black teenagers are high-profile consumer goods, which are more accurately markers of an illusion of success; the film "shows what it is like to live in a community where personal identity is largely constituted by product fetishism—from Air Jordan sneakers to . . . elephantine boom boxes."[26]

In contrast, Sal's pizzeria is a kind of hybrid space: it is a public restaurant, but Sal's private ownership of it is highlighted in almost every scene. We could say that for Sal, it is *both* private and public; for the African Americans, it is effectively neither. Sal's Wall of Fame, a synecdoche of his private ownership of the major "public space" in the film, underscores the futility of Buggin' Out's attempt to enter the space of appearances through his misplaced "activism." The wall is so important to Buggin' Out precisely "because it signifies exclusion from the public sphere."[27] Ironically, Buggin' Out's deeply parodic portrayal of a militant in terms of his language stands in stark contrast to his not unreasonable request; he does not seek the removal of the Italian American photos but simply the addition of some "brothers" in recognition of the multicultural customer base that keeps Sal's business *in* business.

Picturing Public and Private: Visual Style as Polemic

On a purely cinematic level, *Do the Right Thing* addresses the problem of epistemic privacy and its consequences for action within a public arena that institutionalized racism has made inaccessible to people of color. The film's cinematic language specifically enacts the tension between public and private through the blending of two sharply differentiated visual styles.[28] In the scenes featuring the Italian Americans, Lee uses traditional Hollywood methods of character development, methods designed to create audience sympathy for and a sense of relation to the characters. Audiences are so familiar with these techniques that they are affected by them without realizing it; thus, these techniques are as effective—and as invisible—as white privilege itself. The Italians are given interiority—they talk about their feelings. We learn about Sal's history with the neighborhood and about Pino's struggle between loyalty to his father and the peer pressure of his friends, who ridicule him for working in a black neighborhood. Conversely, we don't learn much about Mookie, Radio Raheem, Buggin' Out, or the rest of the neighborhood residents. These characters are curiously flat, at times ironically caricatured. The film encountered a paradoxical attack for being too militantly in favor of black empowerment at the expense of whites (even endorsing, some claimed, black violence against white property),[29] on the one hand, and for representing black characters too negatively, one-dimensionally, or stereotypically, on the other,[30] as though the act of representation itself means that the artist is necessarily uncritical of what is being represented. The subtext that emerges here is that an African American filmmaker is apparently obliged to make films that can be used as public service announcements, an updated version of the 1960s social message films. Lee adamantly refuses the burden of speaking for his race, which is another source of the film's controversy.

For the most part, the scenes in the pizzeria, in contrast to the street scenes, are shot in a conventional shot–reverse shot technique that gives us each character's point of view and allows us to experience the illusion of spatial and temporal continuity. These scenes are thus more "realistic"; their naturalism folds us into the film world as though we were there with the characters, reaffirming the narrative interiority of their character development. The use of "normal" lenses that "see" in much the same way our eyes see—without distortion—combined with the naturalistic sense of space and depth created by the editing and the narrative depth awarded to the characters, puts us at ease with this space and these characters. We feel that we "know" them because their physical space and their emotional expressivity are much like our own, even if we do not agree with *what* they are expressing.

The style used to render the African American characters, in contrast, refuses us entry to the filmic world and to the interior world of the characters. The use of a nonnaturalistic color palette, the extreme low and high camera angles, the insistent use of a distorting wide-angle lens, the profusion of canted or "Dutch" angles, and the frequent disruption of the visual space of the diegesis (the film's fictional world) with nondiegetic sequences and shots that pull us out of the story world effectively create the sense of a world out of balance. This is more like a deliberately staged, theatrical tableau than a realistic illusion, a world where the image is expressive rather than depictive. The highly stylized cinematography makes us aware of itself *as* style, forcing us to come to terms with it.

The effect of this confrontational visual style is to effectively and overwhelmingly dissociate the viewer (of any race) from the African American characters in the film. We are both narratively and visually alienated by the jarring use of space and time and by the denial of interiority to these characters; we are prevented from relating to them in the way we have been conditioned to relate to characters in movies. This strategy forces us, in effect, to recognize them not as Other but as *othered*. Whereas bell hooks takes Lee to task for a cinematic style that promises an intimacy "the narrative does not allow,"[31] I argue instead that it is precisely the cinematography, not in opposition to but in tandem with the narrative, that keeps us at a distance from the African American characters, forcing us to recognize what the condition of Otherness *looks* like. As soon as Radio Raheem (or the sound of his boom box) enters the frame, the canted angles begin; he is always seen diagonally across the frame and from below, a move that produces a tension and dynamism that creates an unnerving dissonance with his otherwise impassive, brooding persona. The pervasive use of a wide-angle lens for his close-ups creates an unnatural and aggressive foreshortening. These techniques emphasize his profound isolation while marking him as threatening, looming over us in a way that makes it almost impossible to relate to him.

Similarly, when Buggin' Out confronts the white brownstone owner (John Savage) for smudging his pristine Nike Air Jordans, he is rendered both comic—through the extreme close-ups of his exaggerated reaction—and threatening—through the use of an extreme low angle to look up at him and his cohort. But here the standard use of low and high camera angles to signal power and powerlessness has been subverted: although physically, the white man's position on the stoop is higher than that of the African American teenagers on the street, Buggin' Out and his crew are seen from below, and the white man—who owns property in the neighborhood and insouciantly wears the jersey of a white basketball player (Larry Byrd)—is seen from above. This has the effect of underscoring the white fear of black violence, of representing not the *actual* power positions of these characters but the white *perception* of the menace of an angry young African American man whose (empty) status symbol—his Nikes—has been damaged. These kinds of inversions signal that the film is less interested in "telling it like it is" than in showing how it is *perceived* and *felt*.[32]

The camera here becomes an ethical instrument that reveals our own epistemological stance (that we can recuperate others through our knowledge of them) and empties it of meaning. Ultimately, the drama of privacy as explored by Wittgenstein in terms of the failure of epistemological claims to know or fail to know the inner state of another is literalized in the cinematography and narrative structure of *Do the Right Thing*. Because the film addresses that which is hidden, it hides from us what we feel we ought to see. The visual, aural, and montage system of the film (with regard to the black characters) does not represent to us the inner states, motivations, and intentions of its characters; instead, it visually (and so on) represents to us (1) what it looks like, or maybe what it feels like, not to be represented at all; and (2) that the failure to "get to know" these characters is, or should be, irrelevant to how we engage with the events that unfold in the film, irrelevant to the obligation entailed in the "form of life" of the film itself. What is being expressed is what the "necessary inexpressiveness"[33] of epistemic privacy would *look like* from the outside.

Who Throws the Trash Can—Mookie or Spike Lee?

Much of the criticism of the film has been couched as an attempt to interpret the characters' intentions, as though this would change how we see their actions. The major action critics have focused on is Mookie's hurling a garbage can through the window of the pizzeria. Lee and some of his critics have argued that the white media's response to the film largely read Mookie's vandalism as the central act of violence in the film (rather than the choking of a black teenager by the white police).[34] Some reviewers, taking the act out of the context of the crowd's horror and anger at witnessing Radio Raheem's brutal death, even claimed that the film encouraged black viewers to destroy white-owned property. Other critics (by far the minority) have argued that by diverting the crowd, Mookie is trying to save Sal's life.[35] The first reading, to be sure, is patently absurd, and the latter is simply not there on the screen; in fact, *any* reading of Mookie's intentions is purporting to do precisely what the grammar of the film tells us it does not want us to do. Mookie's action may (and likely does) save Sal's life, but we have no access to Mookie's interior life—because the film has made sure that we don't—so we cannot address his intentions. All we have to go on is his *action*. Like the statement "I am in pain," at stake here is whether empirical observations can satisfy epistemological concerns. And what is at stake in *that* question is whether our existential relation to one another is something that can be satisfied *by* those epistemological concerns.

The anxiety over whether this single event in a two-hour film is meant to constitute "doing the right thing," and whether the director's casting himself in this role means that Spike Lee as well as Mookie is somehow symbolically committing or endorsing this action, reflects the white anxiety over what "power" would mean for an African American and the assumption that this power will be—indeed, must be—enacted through violence. Mookie's act is not an act of power; it does not change the structure of power in the community. To suggest that Lee thinks it does strikes me as bizarre. Mookie's action is precisely the act of the powerless; it has psychological but not political force. The destruction of property does not, in itself, effect entry into the space of appearances.

When Spike Lee (director) has Mookie (character) smash the plate glass window, he is perhaps rendering visible his own transgressive breaching of the (allegedly) transparent boundary that exiles African American speech—and art—from the public realm. Hollywood is a public space from which African American voices are largely excluded; in a way, the pizzeria is the only space in the film that offers (through the ownership of private property, which provides the credentials for access to public space) a platform from which a person can "legitimately" speak from and in and to the public sphere. Although Lee's status, even in 1989, was hardly that of a marginalized Hollywood outsider—the film was distributed by Universal Studios, after all—he nonetheless was (and still is) one of the few African American directors whose films have garnered mainstream attention. In spite of Lee's subsequent success and cultural power, African American film artists in general—directors, writers, actors, cinematographers—remain a tiny minority in Hollywood, often restricted by stereotypes of what is appropriate for an African American story or character. Paradoxically, if Lee's gesture—making this film—succeeds in breaking into a white-dominated space, this only highlights the failure of Mookie's gesture—throwing the trash can—to do so. If anything demonstrates that the character is not the on-screen stand-in for the director, it is the sharp deviation between the act and the representation of the act: Mookie is, for all purposes, mute within the public space, but Lee certainly is not. Mookie, after all, is not the one whose film is under discussion here.

The Racial Slur Montage: Speech as Action

The publicness of speech and its power to move beyond the intention of its speaker is most clearly enacted in the sequence Lee calls the "Racial Slur Montage." In this sequence, we are ejected from the world of the narrative and forced into a disorienting series of vignettes during which the camera rapidly tracks in to each speaker, each in his own separate space. Each delivers, directly to the camera, a sustained litany of ethnic slurs, quickly and without particular emphasis, as if reading from cue cards.[36] By removing this sequence from the diegesis (the story world), we are not given an opportunity to become involved narratively with any potential motivations, intentions, or justifications for the words. The words are simply there—inescapable, commanding our attention, simultaneously making us the object of these words and condemning us as potential speakers of them. Just as we are denied the interior life of the African American characters, here we are denied any context for the words being projected at us. Later in the film, in the scene that drives us toward the final tragedy, Sal for the first time calls Radio Raheem and the rest of the black teenagers "niggers." Because of the power of the Racial Slur Montage, the context of Sal's (not unprovoked) anger—that is, his frustration, the heat—is ultimately destabilized as a mitigating factor. The word leaps out at us as though jettisoned from its ostensible context, freezing any possibility of justification.

Critical race theorists,[37] who argue that race is part of a socially constructed system of discrimination rather than a biological set of attributes, often invoke Austin's theory of speech acts to categorize racial slurs as what Austin calls "perlocutionary acts," a class of "performative utterances."[38] The articulation of language as performative is meant to underscore that the power of speech has the same substantive force as action; some kinds of speech do not merely report on the world but are bound up in our ability to act in the world. A perlocutionary utterance is one in which, by speaking, I am performing an action that intervenes in the physical world in some way: I ask a question or make a statement that elicits a response from you. In doing so, I am not making a claim about the world that can be determined to be true or false through recourse to evidence or logical analysis; I am making a claim on *you.* And not only this: I am giving, in some sense, my word *to* you. Language is a public practice, not a representation of inner states. When I call you a name, I am doing more than describing you; I am publicly constituting you (and my relation to you) in language. A speech act, then, is very much a public act.

In making *us* the object of these performative words, Lee makes us feel their force, and he does so without giving us any narrative context with which we can try to organize or explain—or excuse—them. The intentions or internal states of the speakers are literally irrelevant to us and to the story; in this sequence, they are not even part of the story. By restricting this kind of language (for the most part) to a single, concentrated sequence, its power to wound is brought into sharp focus.

Mister Señor Love Daddy's Antiracist Speech Act

In another (quasi-)nondiegetic sequence, Mister Señor Love Daddy (Samuel L. Jackson), the DJ of the local radio station, recites a list of names of prominent African American musicians. This litany is offered as though it were a kind of antidote to the Racial Slur Montage; they are parallel in structure, in the sense that they are both recitations of names outside of a narrative context. The (linguistic) difference, though, is that Mister Señor Love Daddy's list is merely ostensive; the names themselves are not *doing* anything in the world, they are only pointing to something (to the performers themselves). I submit, however, that in this special case, Mister Señor Love Daddy's list of names *is* in fact invested with perlocutionary force. The recitation takes on a kind of hypnotic power by virtue of its very length and breadth, as though speaking the names to this particular community *does* command a response similar to the asking of a question or the issuing of a challenge. The DJ watches from his glass booth like an oracle, invoking these names like a kind of mystical incantation. In hearing the names, we hear, in a sense, more than the names. We are responsible for understanding the power of those names; we are called on to recognize them as present and accounted for. A claim has been made on us; likewise, a promise has been made *to* us.

Beyond Knowledge to Acknowledgment

Both these sequences demonstrate that we can learn something about our world by learning about our words and about how we use our words to deny or acknowledge our world, to deny or acknowledge the claims made on us. Cavell argues that the commonly cited argument that American slave owners did not consider their slaves human beings is a misreading, a claim to a kind of ignorance that cannot be truly meant. It cannot be sincerely argued, says Cavell, that the slave owners did not *know* their slaves were human, which is not far off from saying "they didn't know any better." The claim that racism is based on ignorance—that is, that it is an epistemic problem—strikes me as similarly suspect. How *can* such a claim be meant? It cannot be the case that a racist does not *know* that blacks are people with pains, thoughts, histories. We might call it willful ignorance, but it is more a kind of hiding, a wishing not to know, a wishing not to *be* known; as Cavell says, it can be understood as a wish to be private *from* the slave.[39] Where does such a wish come from, if not from a fear of our own unintelligibility to others, of our irrevocable *outsideness* to others? It is not a failure of knowledge but a failure to acknowledge, or more like a refusal to acknowledge. The desire or "fantasy" of a private language is rooted, we could say, in shame, in the twin longing for and terror not just of knowing the Other—with all the responsibility that would entail—but also of being known *to* the Other.[40] If we insist that the Other is private—that is, unknowable—then *our* privacy is safe: we are private, unavailable for knowledge—or love or hatred or blame or forgiveness. In this way, we draw a veil over our loneliness and disguise it as solipsism, for it is the publicness of our language that reveals how separate we really are.

Do the Right Thing forces on us the truth of skepticism: that we *cannot* claim to know the internal state or intention or motivation of others; that we can choose to give or to withhold our acknowledgment of them, but our assertion of knowledge claims—that we either can or cannot know another person's pain—does not reach the depths of the other's pain; nor does it fail to. Empirical evidence cannot fight the power of skepticism any more than it can fight the power of racism; knowledge is not what will overcome these afflictions. Our responsibility to others does not begin with our knowledge of them nor end with its repudiation. The visual grammar and narrative structure of *Do the Right Thing* emphasize that the problem of other minds is not ultimately an epistemological problem at all but an ethical one. The film does not offer a solution to how or whether we *can* know; far more radically, it reminds us that whether we know or not, our existential human commitment to one another remains unconditional.

The commitment to others, to unconditional acknowledgment, is open to our consent or withdrawal; making that choice is part of what being human means. What *Do the Right Thing* shows us is the price of that withdrawal, and the film's insistence on putting us in the position where we might choose to believe that withdrawal is justified because we have not been given sufficient knowledge to make that commitment to these characters is its most contrary, most frustrating, and most devastating victory. The film does not illustrate what "doing the right thing" would be; it offers us no role models and at every turn denies us catharsis, resolution, and relief. Turning its camera eye upon us, this film challenges us to step into our words and into the world, a world in which speech becomes the condition for fighting the power.

Notes

1. *Heteronormativity* is the assumption that heterosexuality and traditional gender identities are universal and natural, thus marginalizing those who, because of their sexuality or gender identity, do not adhere to social norms. For further reading, see especially Robert K. Lightening, "The Homophobia of Spike Lee," *CineAction* 29 (1992): 35–39; bell hooks, "Whose Pussy Is This? A Feminist Comment," in *Reel to Real: Race, Sex, and Class at the Movies* (London: Routledge, 1996), 227–35; and Michelle Wallace, "Spike Lee and Black Women," in *The Spike Lee Reader*, ed. Paula J. Massood (Philadelphia: Temple University Press, 2008), 23–29.

2. Michael T. Kaufman, "In a New Film, Spike Lee Tries to Do the Right Thing," *New York Times*, June 25, 1989, H1.

3. René Descartes, *Discourse on the Method and the Meditations*, trans. John Veitch (Buffalo, N.Y.: Prometheus Books, 1989).

4. In particular, see A. J. Ayers, *The Foundations of Empirical Knowledge* (London: Macmillan, 1940); Bertrand Russell, *The Analysis of Mind* (1921; reprint, New York: Humanities Press, 1971).

5. *Induction* and *deduction* are the two major types of logic. Inductive reasoning is based on observation and experience and develops a claim to a universal principle

based on specific examples. Deduction works from the other direction; deductive logic assumes the truth of a general premise and then applies that premise to particular instances to demonstrate its validity.

6. Though giving rise to what is called Cartesian skepticism, Descartes himself is not a skeptic. Descartes' purpose in the First Meditation is to examine our knowledge claims by subjecting them to the most radical doubts possible to show that all our beliefs about the external world are subject to *possible* doubt. In the Second Meditation, however, he argues that he can know that he himself exists because, although inductive knowledge of the external world is always prey to doubt, deductive knowledge, reached entirely by his own internal logical processes, proves that his mind exists. Because his awareness of the working of his own mind is not dependent on sensory information, he argues, his existence likewise does not depend on the existence of the external world. This would be true even if he were being deceived, hallucinating, or dreaming (because even in these cases, *someone* is having the dream or hallucination). The problem with Descartes' challenge to skepticism is that its logical consequence is solipsism.

7. Specifically, see Ludwig Wittgenstein, *Philosophical Investigations,* 3rd ed., trans. G. E. M. Anscombe (Upper Saddle River, N.J.: Prentice-Hall, 1958), and *The Blue and Brown Books* (London: Basil Blackwell, 1958); J. L. Austin, "Other Minds," in *Philosophical Papers,* 2nd ed. (London: Oxford University Press, 1970), 76–116, and *How to Do Things with Words: The William James Lectures Delivered at Harvard University in 1955,* 2nd ed. (Cambridge, Mass.: Harvard University Press, 1962); Stanley Cavell, *The Claim of Reason: Wittgenstein, Skepticism, Morality, and Tragedy* (1979; reprint, Oxford: Oxford University Press, 1982).

8. Wittgenstein repeatedly uses the phrase "form of life" to refer to language as the context in which we form a community; for example, he says, "the *speaking* of language is part of an activity, or of a form of life" (*Philosophical Investigations,* §23).

9. Charles Mills uses the term "epistemology of ignorance" in his discussion of the cognitive dimensions of ignorance that allow the domination of "white" knowledge as universal when it is in fact profoundly exclusionary; see especially *The Racial Contract* (Ithaca, N.Y.: Cornell University Press, 1997).

10. For more on the epistemology of race in philosophy, see Shannon Sullivan and Nancy Tuana, eds., *Race and Epistemologies of Ignorance* (Albany, N.Y.: SUNY Press, 2007).

11. Some helpful investigations of white privilege are Noel Ignatiev, "The Point Is Not to Interpret Whiteness But to Abolish It" (speech given at the conference "The Making and Unmaking of Whiteness," University of California, Berkeley, April 11–13, 1997); Howard Winant, "Racism Today: Continuity and Change in the Post–Civil Rights Era," *Ethnic and Racial Studies* 21, 4 (1998); David T. Wellman, *Portraits of White Racism* (New York: Cambridge University Press, 1993); Paula S. Rothenberg, ed., *White Privilege: Essential Readings on the Other Side of Racism* (New York: Worth, 2004).

12. Jennifer Radtke, "*Do the Right Thing* in Black and White: Spike Lee's Bi-Cultural Method," *Midwest Quarterly* 41, 2 (winter 2000): 223.

13. Textbook examples of Hollywood films that cast racism as a function of an

epistemic claim include virtually all the "social issue" films of the 1960s such as *In the Heat of the Night* and *Guess Who's Coming to Dinner?* Both these films from 1967 feature white characters overcoming their racist assumptions because they "get to know" a (spectacularly) nonthreatening, unimpeachably admirable, and in all ways "worthy" black character, thus carefully suppressing the historical context of the very prejudice the films ostensibly condemn. For further reading, see Susan Courtney, "Guess Who's Coming to Dinner with Eldridge Cleaver and the Supreme Court, or Reforming Popular Racial Memory with Hepburn and Tracy," in *Hollywood Fantasies of Miscegenation; Spectacular Narratives of Gender and Race* (Princeton, N.J.: Princeton University Press, 2004). Post *Do the Right Thing,* the trend to read racism as a matter of isolated events and individual prejudices that hinge on ignorance continues, with a far bleaker twist, in *Crash* (2004). *Crash* insists that racism is both universal and unavoidable, it renders bigotry as random and individual, and it ignores the history of institutional racism altogether. See Susan Searls Giroux and Henry A. Giroux, "Don't Worry, We Are All Racists! *Crash* and the Politics of Privatisation," *Third Text* 21, 6 (November 2007): 745–59, and David G. Holmes, "Symposium: Paul Haggis's *Crash:* The Civil Rights Movement According to *Crash:* Complicating the Pedagogy of Integration," *College English* 69, 4 (March 2007): 314–20.

14. Wittgenstein did not invent the idea of the private language, but because of his use of and attack on it in *Philosophical Investigations* (§§243–315), it has been associated with him. He was likely responding to remarks about a "perfect" language that could logically only be private in Bertrand Russell, "The Philosophy of Logical Atomism," in *Logic and Knowledge: Essays 1901–1918,* ed. Robert Charles Marsh (New York: Capricorn Books, 1918), 178–269.

15. Wittgenstein, *Philosophical Investigations,* §243.

16. Ibid., §202.

17. Austin's argument in "Other Minds" is that the skeptical argument that I could be wrong about another's feelings (because I can know only what I directly feel myself), and therefore cannot say I know another has those feelings at all, does not follow the way we really use language. If I turned out to be wrong, I wouldn't say I *didn't know* the person was, say, in pain; I would say I was *wrong,* which is not, in ordinary language, the same thing. Further, he argues that such knowledge claims operate more like promises than logical propositions; that is, if I make a promise I cannot or do not intend to keep, I would not deny the promise had been *made,* only that it had not been *kept.* The promise would be what Austin calls "infelicitous" (it failed), but it would still be a promise. If I fail to keep a promise, I have broken a covenant.

18. Austin repeatedly recasts or translates the epistemological propositional form "I don't know that a proposition (P) is true" as " I don't know *what to say.*" Specifically, see "Other Minds," 88.

19. Cavell, *Claim of Reason,* 369.

20. Moreland Perkins, "Two Arguments against a Private Language," *Journal of Philosophy* 62, 17 (September 9, 1965): 445–46.

21. Wittgenstein, *Philosophical Investigations,* §384.

22. Hannah Arendt, *The Human Condition* (Chicago: University of Chicago Press, 1958), 176.

23. Andrew Norris, "Political Revisions: Stanley Cavell and Political Philosophy," *Political Theory* 30, 6 (December 2002): 830.

24. I am not relying on her methodology or referring to her work here, but Gayatri Spivak's scholarship on and theory of the condition of the racial, ethnic, or otherwise colonized or subordinate Other as necessarily speechless is related to my concerns, and although my own theoretical commitments are rooted elsewhere, I want to acknowledge her profound contribution to the understanding of this issue. In particular, see "Can the Subaltern Speak?" in *Marxism and Interpretation of Culture,* ed. Cary Nelson and Lawrence Grossberg (Urbana: University of Illinois Press, 1988), 271–313.

25. Arendt, *Human Condition,* 200.

26. W. J. T. Mitchell, "Seeing *Do the Right Thing,*" *Critical Inquiry* 17, 3 (spring 1991): 607. Mitchell provides a persuasive analysis of the role of commodity fetishism in the film as an illusory kind of access to the public sphere, one critiqued by the film as ineffective and deeply compromised. Mitchell's essay is a response to Jerome Christensen's argument that the film aggressively promotes corporate capitalism and racial essentialism; see "Spike Lee, Corporate Populist," *Critical Inquiry* 16, 2 (spring 1991): 582–95.

27. W. J. T. Mitchell, "Violence and Public Art: *Do the Right Thing,*" *Critical Inquiry* 16, 4 (summer 1990): 894.

28. For detailed discussions of the film's cinematography and especially the key differences in style between the street scenes featuring the black characters and the interior scenes featuring the Italian American characters, see Ted Kulczycky, "By Any Means Necessary: Conflict and Its Resolution in *Do the Right Thing,*" *CineAction* 40 (May 1996): 48–56; Ed Guerrero, *BFI Modern Classics: Do the Right Thing* (London: British Film Institute, 2008). Radtke, "*Do the Right Thing* in Black and White," provides a sustained discussion of the treatment of the white and black characters, particularly in terms of narrative and character development.

29. See especially Joe Klein, "Spiked," *New York,* June 26, 1989, 14–15; Stanley Crouch, "Do the Race Thing," *Village Voice,* June 20, 1989, 73–74, 76; Terrence Rafferty, "Open and Shut," review of *Do the Right Thing, New Yorker,* July 24, 1989, 78–81; Murray Kempson, "The Pizza Is Burning!" *New York Review of Books,* September 28, 1989, 37–38.

30. See, for example, Brent Staples, "Spike Lee's Blacks: Are They Real People?" *New York Times,* July 2, 1989, sec. 2, 9; bell hooks, "Counter-Hegemonic Art," in *Yearning: Race, Gender, and Cultural Politics* (New York: South End Press, 1999), 173–84; Wahneema Lubiano, "But Compared to What? Reading Realism, Representation, and Essentialism in *School Daze, Do the Right Thing,* and the Spike Lee Discourse," in *The Spike Lee Reader,* 30–57.

31. hooks, "Counter-Hegemonic Art," 174.

32. Lubiano, "But Compared to What?" 41. Lubiano gives a sustained and not unpersuasive critique of what many of Lee's supporters praise as his naturalism or "authenticity" in terms of "telling it like it is" and argues that, far from "telling it like it is," the film is plagued by a "conventional Calvinist realism."

33. Cavell, *Claim of Reason,* 351.

34. See, for example, Peggy Orenstein, "Spike's Riot," *Mother Jones,* September 1989, 32–35, 43–46; Spike Lee and Henry Louis Gates Jr., "Final Cut," *Transition* 52 (1991): 177–204.

35. See especially Mitchell, "Violence and Public Art," 897, and Radtke, "*Do the Right Thing* in Black and White," 224–25. Both are trying to "recoup" Mookie's action from critics such as Joe Klein and Stanley Crouch, who claimed the film would incite black violence.

36. This sequence contains the bulk of the explicitly racist language in the film; other than Pino, the characters rarely use racial epithets. Unlike *Crash,* in which the characters feel compelled to get as many racist and sexist slurs into each sentence as possible, *Do the Right Thing* does not give us a chance to become inured to these words.

37. See especially Mari J. Matsuda, *Words that Wound: Critical Race Theory, Assaultive Speech, and the First Amendment* (Boulder, Colo.: Westview Press, 1993), and Janet Hill, *The Everyday Language of White Racism* (Chichester, U.K., and Malden, Mass.: Wiley-Blackwell, 2008).

38. See Austin, *How to Do Things with Words,* and "A Plea for Excuses," in *Philosophical Papers,* 175–205. Austin argues that whereas some kinds of utterances, which he calls "illocutionary," are obviously performing actions (such as "I marry you," "I christen this ship," or "I promise"), perlocutionary acts of language are not less forceful but simply less obvious.

39. Cavell, *Claim of Reason,* 272–78.

40. I am indebted for this thought to Cavell's essay on shame in *King Lear* and its roots in skepticism; see "The Avoidance of Love: A Reading of 'King Lear,'" in *Must We Mean What We Say?* (Cambridge: Cambridge University Press, 1969), 267–356.

Coworking in the Kingdom of Culture

Identity and Community in the Films of Spike Lee

Charles F. Peterson

> He [the Negro] simply wishes to make it possible for a man to be both a Negro and an American, without being cursed and spit upon by his fellows, without having the doors of Opportunity closed roughly in his face. This, then, is the end of his striving: to be a co-worker in the kingdom of culture, to escape both death and isolation, to husband and use his best powers and his latent genius.
>
> —W. E. B. DuBois, "Of Our Spiritual Strivings"

W. E. B. DuBois's essay "Of Our Spiritual Strivings" provides one of the most revered articulations of Afri-US[1] psychoracial identity; even more, it stands, as I believe DuBois intended, as a statement on the very nature of U.S. citizenship. DuBois's focus on the manner in which Afri-US (Negro) identity, citizenship, and social life were experienced as divided, antagonized, and marginal serves as a model for a new American urban sensibility. By the time "Of Our Spiritual Strivings" was published, the swelling ranks of the "tired . . . poor and huddled masses" that filled the cities of the United States had begun a churning process of ethnically redefining themselves over and against their peer groups in the context of a transforming/transformed adopted society. Nowhere was this process more extensive than in New York City. The streets and neighborhoods of New York City, with their ethnic tensions, contrasts, and inflections, became a vast cauldron of social and cultural combustion. As Robin D. G. Kelley writes in his biography of Thelonious Monk:

> With a diversity of peoples came a diversity of cultures. On West 63rd Street alone, the aroma of Southern styled collard greens cooked with ham hocks mixed with the distinct smell of Jamaican rice and peas and fried plantain. English was the main language of the community, but it came in a Carolina twang and a West Indian singsong lilt, in addition to a distinctive New York accent. Spanish and French were spoken on those streets, with German and Yiddish along the white dominated avenues.[2]

This atmosphere, energy, and *process of societal creation*—and the extent to which they would affect the American sensibility—would be apparent nearly 100 years later in the films of Spike Lee. Working beyond the archetypal class, spatial, and ethnic locales of his noted New York director peers (Woody Allen, Martin Scorsese, and Francis Ford Coppola), Lee consistently analyzes the multicultural realities of race, class, and ethnicity—in short, identity—in New York City. Unlike his cinematic models and peers, Lee has trained his lens on the complexities of racialized (marginalized) life for those whose lives are *in* but ambivalently recognized as *of* America. This essay focuses on Lee's artistic vision as one concerned with the hyphenated nature of life and community in contemporary America as represented by New York City.

Race, Identity, and Images of Old New York

The 1989 film *New York Stories* features short films celebrating the then reigning directors of New York film life. Allen, Coppola, and Scorsese were and are hailed as cinematic masters in depicting life in New York City, and each director's vignette focuses on characters and situations deemed representative of life in the city. However, in light of the turbulent nature of race, class, and civic relations in 1980s New York City, one voice is missing from the film. Lee's contribution to 1989's cinematic output was a small-budgeted film titled *Do the Right Thing.* Set over the course of a day in the Bedford-Stuyvesant neighborhood of Brooklyn, the uneasiness of U.S. racial relations was put on display. A snapshot of late-twentieth-century urban America, Lee's film is populated by the waves of peoples that flowed into New York in that century. Afri-US, Afri-Caribbean, Latinos, and Asians are gathered into the arteries of New York City's civic body. In an earlier filmic age, depictions of New York street life would have focused on western European ethnics (e.g., the Irish street toughs of the Bowery Boys serials of the 1930s and 1940s); later, the struggles of eastern and southern European immigrant populations would be explored (e.g., 1961's *The Young Savages*).

But Lee's New York is one where race and class have joined hands, as those who desired white privilege[3] or those willing to commit to Anglo-Saxon hegemony were granted "whiteness"[4] and, for their efforts, were allowed to step outside the quarrelsome reality of "race" in the United States and live in a fictional and ordered "white" America.

The Euro-ethnic obsession with and embrace of whiteness displayed by Lee's characters exists as a negative definition and is apparent in relation to people of color. Yet the insecurity around the credibility of their whiteness becomes apparent out of sight of the gaze of both WASPs (white Anglo-Saxon Protestants) and peoples of color. The intragroup expression of insecurity around their whiteness is definitively displayed, for example, in Lee's film *Jungle Fever* (1991). In that film, as a group of Italian American men sits around a local newsstand, one of the customers, Sonny (Steven Randazzo), derides another, Frankie (Michael Badalucco), who is drinking (chocolate egg creams) to get over a lost girlfriend:

> Sonny: That's five egg creams you're eatin'. What has Donna got you in a state? I bet she's banging that big blonde guy. Y'know the one there with big blue eyes.
>
> Frankie: What's that supposed to mean? Just cause I don't look like that. Tall, blonde, blue eyes. That don't mean I don't feel like that. What am I, some kind of Neanderthal? These fucking Italian girls, they're all the same. You'd think they'd want their own kind. Naw, naw, what do they want? Fuckin' Robert Redford, Harrison Ford. Who's that other WASP . . . white Anglo-Saxon pricks . . . William Hurt!

Frankie's miseries are a result of his own uncertain racial position and aesthetic value. He articulates a larger critique of Italian American racial consciousness, its insecurities, and the desire to be, as newsstand manager Paulie (John Turturro) states, "regular white guys." The criteria for and absolute nature of white racial identity (that of WASPs) destabilize the psychological, social, and cultural positions of non-WASP Euro-American communities and lead them to gain racial and social self-certainty only in direct relationship to black people.

How the Italians Became White

Lee's most direct example of the dialectic of presence and identity or ethnicity is *Do the Right Thing*. Sal (Danny Aiello) and his two sons, Pino (John

Turturro) and Vito (Richard Edson), the owners of Sal's Pizzeria, believing themselves to be apart from the chaos of contemporary (*working in it but not of it*) urban life, cross over from Bensonhurst to ply their trade in the heart of a seemingly chaotic mishmash of multiethnic urban U.S. life. Sal believes himself to be a contributor and benefactor to the Bedford-Stuyvesant neighborhood, while his son Pino, dogged by his disdain for the neighborhood residents and the ridicule of his Bensonhurst companions, attempts to draw hard lines of racial separation between himself and his customers.

> PINO: I'm sick of niggers. It's like I come to work and it's the Planet of the Apes. I don't like being around them. They're animals.
> SAL: Why you got so much anger in you?
> PINO: My friends they laugh at me, they laugh right in my face. They tell me, aahh, go to Bed-Stuy, go feed the moolies.

Both characters think of themselves in relation to a white identity, one that creates a sense of separation and highlights the differences between the lives and experiences of Sal and Pino and those of the residents of the Bedford-Stuyvesant neighborhood. Sal's difference manifests itself as paternal concern, whether through his long employment of Mookie (Spike Lee) as a pizza delivery man or through his pride in providing pizza to the community for twenty-five years ("For Christ sake Pino, they grew up on my food, *my* food"). Pino's whiteness is a binary negation (them-us, animals-humans, moolies-whites) whose certainty is suspect due to proximity (being among *them*) and subject to assault by the derision of his friends. Pino's whiteness is constructed in a negation of blacks, but it is maintained by the affirmation of the community of white friends and neighbors ("What can I say? I don't want to be here, they don't want us here. We should stay in our own neighborhood, stay in Bensonhurst and the niggers should stay in Bed-Stuy."). Geographically and racially, Sal and his sons can assert a difference that allows them to be white, with all its attendant characteristics. However, this position is illusory, as their claims to racial identity are dubiously based on geography. Bensonhurst, though an aggressive white neighborhood, is in the midst of growing enclaves of color. It is urban and dense, and it is not Long Island, a Zion of whiteness for Euro-ethnics in New York City.

In a series of scenes that break the fourth wall, Lee films monologues spoken by denizens of the neighborhood, revealing the city's unconscious thinking about issues of race and ethnicity. Starting from within Sal's Famous Pizzeria, ground zero of race and identity in the film, Mookie gazes into the camera and says, "Dago, wop, garlic-breath, guinea, pizza-slinging, spaghetti-bending, Vic Damone, Perry Como, Luciano Pavarotti, Sole Mio, non-singing motherfucker." Mookie's confession does not note or speak to Pino's "whiteness" but marks him as an ethnic minority by utilizing slurs that set Italian Americans apart from WASP culture and by attacking popular icons most strongly associated or identified with Italian national and Italian American culture.[5] The diatribes continue as Pino unfurls the Afri-US racial slurs de jour: "You gold-teeth, gold-chain-wearing, fried-chicken-and-biscuit-eatin', monkey, ape, baboon, big thigh, fast-running, three-hundred-sixty-degree-basketball-dunking spade Moulan Yan." A cross section of New York City's communities is included, as Koreans are subject to distortion by Latino resident Stevie (Luis Ramos): "You slant-eyed, me-no-speak-American, own every fruit and vegetable stand in New York, Reverend Moon, Summer Olympics '88, Korean kick-boxing bastard." Officer Long (Rick Aiello), who is white and in a position of power, democratizes the proceedings by including every worn-out stereotype of Latinos: "Goya bean-eating, fifteen in a car, thirty in an apartment, pointed shoes, red-wearing, Menudo, meda-meda Puerto Rican cocksucker." Not to be left out—and counter to the established stereotype of the reserved and sagacious Asian personality—Sonny (Steve Park), the Korean grocer, unloads on his stereotypical ethnic competition: "It's cheap, I got a good price for you, Mayor Koch, 'How I'm doing,' chocolate-egg-cream-drinking, bagel and lox, B'nai B'rith, asshole." The climax of the series of speeches is local DJ Mister Señor Love Daddy's (Samuel L. Jackson) exhortation to "Take a chill. . . . Y'all need to cool that shit out!" Lee's goal is to throw up a mirror to the seething underbelly of racial tensions in New York. Having been dedicated to Yusuf Hawkins, victim of white terrorism in the Bensonhurst section of Brooklyn, Lee's film is an attempt to draw attention to the dynamics of race in the late-twentieth-century United States.

Home to the Bronx

Lee's 1999 offering, *Summer of Sam,* is ostensibly his take on the social and cultural effects of the series of murders committed by David Berkowitz in the summer of 1977. Informed by the cultural energies of disco, the tensions generated by a record-breaking heat wave, and the paranoia engendered by the "Son of Sam" killings, *Summer of Sam* is a study of the effect of the fear of difference in a small Italian community in the Bronx. A secondary character, local boy Richie (Adrian Brody), eschews the cultural and music scene created by disco and lives a punk rock life in the midst of the working-class Bronx. Richie's dress (bondage light), hairstyle (spiked), music, and lifestyle choices make him an object of concern and derision and—as the tension created by the killings grows—an object of fear. Richie's dress and interests mark him as outside the normal appearance of "manhood" in his neighborhood, and he is judged by the standard effected by Joey (Michael Rispoli), Brian (Ken Garito), and Anthony (Al Palagonia). This Italian chorus's view of masculinity is exemplified by their encounter with Bobby Del Fiori (Brian Tarantina)—or, as he is called, "Bobby the Fairy." Bobby is hit with run-of-the-mill homophobic jibes laced with fear of the .44 Killer (Son of Sam):

> Anthony: It said in the *Post* the killer's a woman hater. That's you Bobby, you could be the killer . . .
> Joey: The .44 caliber queer . . .
> Anthony: Yeah a real HOMO-cidal maniac . . .
> Brian: He's guilty, put him through the penal system . . .

Because of his sexuality, Bobby is not one of the guys, and he extends that mark of difference when he greets Richie after an apparently long absence with an admiring appraisal: "Long time no see. Very Lower East Side—I like it." Later, when Richie is revealed to be a bisexual hustler on the side, Bobby's remarks add not just a musical, cultural, and sartorial difference to Richie but a sexual one as well. Whether Richie's sexuality is known to the neighborhood guys or not, he is out of sync with the parochial hypermasculinity of the community, and this becomes a source of tension between him and the street-corner regulars. The sense of threat, though linked to sexuality and cultural interests, is seen in Brian and Anthony's questions about Richie's relationship to Ruby (Jennifer Esposito), a neighborhood girl. Anthony asks, "Richie, why buy the cow when everyone else is getting their milk and steaks for free." Richie responds, "I like the cow." Ruby, designated as "loose," is seen as someone not to be respected as a sexual partner, and seemingly any man willing to take her seriously has questionable values and lacks good sense.

As Joey, Brian, and Anthony are established as communal voices, their rejection of Richie is a larger social rejection. States Brian, "Hey Rich, not for nothing' but are you startin' to get the feelin' you're not welcome around here? Do I gotta spell it out for you?" The three characters exemplify the growing communal dis-ease over the murders. The perceived threat from the outside makes visible preexisting internal tensions. In the midst of their escalating theories on who the killer is and their manic search for him (provoked by a Mafia bounty), the trio represents the community's increasing paranoia. The fear of the Other increases as the once familiar becomes unfamiliar and the known, unknown. These three become suspicious of all those seen as living outside of acceptable community norms; the divorced, lonely, unemployed, gay, stranger, and even friend are refused the most human offerings: food (Richie, sitting with the main character Vincent [John Leguizamo], is refused dinner in a neighborhood diner) and shelter (Richie's mother and stepfather force him to live in their garage). The trio uses violence to express concern, as even longtime residents are subject to harassment and beatings. The everyday parochialism of the neighborhood transforms into a siege mentality.

Gradually, Richie's reaction to his ostracism becomes the ground for the belief that Richie is the .44 Caliber Killer. Again, Bobby marks Ritchie's difference or Otherness and reports Richie's "strangeness" after seeing him dance in a gay club. Interestingly, although Bobby is marked as gay, his homosexuality, though derided, is "acceptable" because it manifests itself in the cultural and social familiarity of the Italian American neighborhood. His dress, language, references, and (nonsexual) habits are those of his neighbors. In contrast, Richie's dress, language, beliefs, and affectations accentuate the questions about his sexuality and identify him as absolutely alien. The neighborhood's avenging spirits proceed to hunt Richie down and, in a climactic scene, beat him in his literal and figurative bosom of safety, outside his mother's house. In *Summer of Sam,* Lee's examination of a community reliant on its sameness and confident in its durability reveals how, when external pressures are applied, fissures appear at points of difference, change, and growth. Those fissures appear at the intersections of sexuality, masculinity, parochialism, and cosmopolitanism when Richie attempts to bring bits and pieces of the outside world home to the Bronx.

Fear and Trembling in New York City

In *25th Hour* (2002), Lee examines the idea of New York City as a whole community surviving in the shadow of its most self-conscious moment—the terrorist attacks of September 11, 2001. Nominally, it is the story of Monty Brogan (Edward Norton), a midlevel drug dealer who is spending his last day of freedom before serving seven years in prison for drug possession and distribution. However, the film is also a view into a city still struggling to come to grips with itself in the wake of incredible tragedy. An ode to the city, a love letter written in the 1s and 0s of digital code, *25th Hour* simultaneously unifies and disaggregates the city. On the main menu of the *25th Hour* DVD, there is a continuously running fast-motion shot of Times Square with an inset portrait slide show of various communities within New York

City. The anonymity of the people racing through the heart of Manhattan is counterbalanced by the slow still shots of smiling faces, as if to give specific identity and humanity to Times Square's faceless throngs. Embracing New York City as unified in its vulnerability, Lee follows Monty through the streets of Manhattan. Intimately stepping past schools, churches, houses, and offices, Monty lingers in alleys, chats with children; in his brooding steps, he seems to be memorizing every detail of the urban landscape. It is the spatial eye of the camera that lets the physicality of the city speak for itself. Whereas Daniel Kasman cites the "intimate character conversations that make up the simple, but rich urban texture of *25th Hour,* a picture of city life that is created and exists solely through these people's off topic dialogue and the context in which the dialogues take place (apartment over Ground Zero, trendy club, Irish bar, bathroom mirror etc.),"[6] I argue that Lee's sets and cinematography represent the intimacies of collective life in New York City. Akin to Woody Allen's Gershwin-backed opening credit sequence in *Manhattan* (1979), Lee sets his opening credits amid the Manhattan skyline and lets Terrence Blanchard's somber arrangements sing the city's cri de coeur.

Yet despite the sensitive rendering of the city and its life, Lee avoids treacly romanticism and reminds the viewer of Monty's profession through his memories and the discussions of those around him: girlfriend Naturelle (Rosario Dawson), friends Frank (Barry Pepper) and Jacob (Philip Seymour Hoffman), and father James (Brian Cox). As well, Lee reminds us of the city's bruised spirit. In the opening credits, the New York City skyline is split by the spotlights that stand where the Twin Towers once stood. Lee includes montage shots of the street memorials for the missing and the dead, and Frank's apartment overlooks the World Trade Center cleanup operation. As Frank and Jacob meet in Frank's apartment before a final night out with Monty, the grim will to survive 9/11 comes through in their conversation:

> JACOB: Jesus Christ! [overlooking the cleanup]
> FRANK: Yeah.
> JACOB: Yeah, the *New York Times* says the air is bad down here.
> FRANK: Well, fuck the *Times*... I read the *Post*... EPA says it's fine.
> JACOB: Well, somebody's lying.

In the wake of 9/11, Lee suggests that along with its panoramic skyline and its universally recognizable landmarks, there is something else that brings its citizens together, one more thing they have in common and have a common investment in: the need to heal the city's civic and psychological wounds. In this commonality a type of community is achieved, but Lee has not strayed from the path of the urban cauldron that is New York City.

Hearkening back to the dissonances and tensions of some of his earlier work, Lee, in the midst of the unity of memory, disaggregates New York along its many economic, social, ethnic, and racial fault lines. In a stunning montage-backed monologue, Monty eviscerates New York City's social and racial order from top to bottom while taking a bathroom break in his father's Irish pub on Staten Island. Reenacting the fourth wall–breaking confessionals of *Do the Right Thing,* Monty's reflection in the mirror gives vent to his angriest thoughts. Though covering the traditional laundry list of ethnic slurs—"Fuck the Korean grocers with their pyramids of overpriced fruit and their tulips and roses wrapped in plastic. Ten years in the country, still no speaky English?"—Monty's id updates the city's narrative of the disruptive migrant to include more recent communities, in light of current events: "Fuck the Sikhs and the Pakistanis *bombing* down the avenues in decrepit cabs, curry steaming out their pores, stinking up my day. Terrorists in fucking training." Unlike in the monologues of *Do the Right Thing,* socioeconomic class is held up for scrutiny. Monty belches equal bile for the wretched of the earth and the captains of finance: "Fuck the panhandlers, grubbing for money, and smiling at me behind my back. Fuck the squeegee men dirtying up the clean windshield of my car. Get a fucking job. . . . Fuck the Wall Street brokers. Self-styled masters of the universe. Michael Douglas, Gordon Gekko wannabe motherfuckers, figuring out new ways to rob hardworking people blind. Send those Enron assholes to jail for FUCKING LIFE!"

Thundering a profane jeremiad, Monty preaches against the sins of New York City's people. Vanity: "Fuck the Upper East Side wives with their Hermes scarves and their fifty-dollar Balducci artichokes. Overfed faces getting pulled and lifted and stretched, all taut and shiny. You're not fooling anybody, sweetheart!" Corruption: "Fuck the black-hatted Chassidim, strolling up and down 47th Street in their dirty gabardine with their dandruff. Selling South African apartheid diamonds!" Violence and betrayal: "Fuck the corrupt cops with their anus violating plungers and their 41 shots, standing behind a blue wall of silence. You betray our trust! Fuck the priests who put their hands down some innocent child's pants. Fuck the church that protects them, delivering us into evil."

In Monty's purifying anger, those nearest and dearest to him come up for judgment, too: "Fuck Jacob Elinsky, whining malcontent. Fuck Francis Xavier Slaughtery my best friend, judging me while he stares at my girlfriend's ass. Fuck Naturelle Riviera, I gave her my trust and she stabbed me in the back, sold me up the river, fucking bitch. Fuck my father with his endless grief, standing behind that bar sipping on club sodas, selling whisky to firemen, cheering the Bronx Bombers."

For Monty, the tensions, corruptions, and failings of the city are absolute, all-embracing, and should be universally damned: "Fuck this whole city and everyone in it. From the row houses of Astoria to the penthouses on Park Avenue. From the projects in the Bronx to the lofts in Soho. From the tenements in Alphabet City to the brownstones in Park Slope to the split levels in Staten Island. Let an earthquake crumble it. Let the fires rage, let it burn to fucking ash and then let the waters rise and submerge this whole rat-infested place." Having delivered his final judgment on New York City, Monty confesses a final judgment on himself and the source of his personal damnation: "No. No, fuck you, Montgomery Brogan. You had it all, and then you threw it away, you dumb fuck!"

In the context of this reading of Spike Lee's work, the point of the monologue is not Monty's self-realization (he is finally honest with himself, if with no one else in the movie) but the rhetorical dissection of New York City piece by piece. Monty's monologue, though jagged and critical, presents a panoptic view of the city. His analysis is one from the inside, revealing the frailties and weaknesses of the city. But in the almost absolute nature of his reflection's recollection (no group is left untouched), Monty (Lee) recognizes each piece as a real and necessary part of the city, each contributing to its totality. Each, despite its flaws, weaknesses, and failings, contributes to the community, making New York City what it is. In *25th Hour*'s social and cultural vision, Lee, echoing New York City journalist Jimmy Breslin in the opening scene of *Summer of Sam,* seems to state, "I love New York City and I hate New York City, equally." The testimony to that love and hate is the recognition and embrace of New York City as a singular, convoluted, and complicated space in the imagination of Spike Lee.

At present, Spike Lee is seen as a hyphenated (Afri-US) director, and that has narrowed how his work is perceived and discussed. Indeed, his work has largely focused on historical and contemporary issues related to Afri-US life and culture. However, Lee's work reveals that he ascribes to the tradition of Afri-US social thought that utilizes the experiences of Afri-US people as only the tip of the spear to discuss larger issues in American life. Lee, in his depictions of identity, difference, and community in New York City, evokes DuBois's schoolboy self-awareness of being "like mayhap, in heart and life and longing" like his white peers.[7] Cognizant and forthright in his articulation of the problems of cultural and racial difference, Lee's work also understands that the "life and longing" (the basic desires and goals) of Afri-US people are in line with those of other racial, ethnic, and cultural groups. Lee depicts the complicated nature of multiethnic and multicultural communal life in New York City as representative of the dynamics of race and culture in the United States. He examines in all their gory glory the churning, rough-and-tumble, inter- and intracommunal interactions of the various bodies that seek to find purchase in U.S. society. Lee's films show that the formation of a truly inclusive U.S. character is not a smooth linear path or the "melting pot" of high school civics courses; rather, it is one fueled by contradictions, conflicts, misunderstandings, and the birth pangs of a new society. In the search for identity and community, Lee does not assume assimilation or acculturation but demands that the viewer understand the tragedy and the majesty of community within the United States in its heteroglot character. Inclusive in its possibility, differences in race, class, ethnicity, and sexuality are the fundamental characteristics of Lee's view of the U.S. character. A roiling, ongoing debate on the ways the many can become one, Lee's vision is one in which there are many gates to the Kingdom of Culture.

Notes

1. I use the term *Afri-US* in place of the more common *African American.* In this essay, Afri-US denotes peoples of African descent in the United States. African American denotes the larger grouping of peoples of African descent within the Americas of the Western Hemisphere (North, South, and Central America).

2. Robin D. G. Kelley, *Thelonious Monk: The Life and Times of an American Original* (New York: Free Press, 2009), 18.

3. James Baldwin, "On Being White and Other Lies," in *Black on White,* ed. David Roediger (New York: Schocken, 1999).

4. Noel Ignatiev, *How the Irish Became White* (New York: Routledge, 2008).

5. Mookie does not use any of the traditional slurs against whites employed by Afri-US people (e.g., ofay, redneck, honkie, cracker, white devil). Mookie's slurs tap into Pino's fear. In his insults, Mookie does not recognize Pino, Sal, and Vito as *white.* Akin to their fears, he recognizes them as *not white.*

6. Daniel Kasman, *25th Hour* review, http://www.d-kaz.com/reviews/review.php?id=110.

7. W. E. B. DuBois, "Of Our Spiritual Strivings," in *W. E. B. DuBois: A Reader,* ed. David Levering Lewis (New York: Henry Holt, 1995), 28.

Feminists and "Freaks"

She's Gotta Have it and *Girl 6*

Karen D. Hoffman

Shortly after the release of *She's Gotta Have It* (1986), Spike Lee's first full-length feature film, feminists began discussing the lead character, Nola Darling (Tracy Camilla Johns), and questioning the extent to which she embodies a liberatory ideal of African American female sexuality.[1] Involved with three different men without being committed to any of them, Nola initially appears to be a woman who knows what she wants and how to get it. But, upon deeper inspection, she is also revealed to be a rather superficial woman who embodies problematic gender stereotypes, has very few female friends, and is ultimately punished for her sexual appetites. As a result, feminists like bell hooks are led to conclude that Nola objectifies her own sexuality, and "in so doing, her character becomes the projection of a stereotypical sexist notion of a sexually assertive woman—she is not in fact liberated."[2]

Given these concerns about Nola Darling, who appears to be a model of sexual empowerment, viewers might have had little hope of finding an emancipatory image of female sexuality in *Girl 6* (1996), particularly considering that the title character is a failed actress working as a phone-sex operator who caters to the fantasies of male callers. If the female lead of *She's Gotta Have It* objectified herself in her sexual relationships with men, surely a female lead paid for sexual labor would be engaged in an even deeper and more problematic self-objectification. Thus *Girl 6* would be of even greater concern to feminists than Lee's earlier film. Yet hooks suggests that this is not the case. Instead, she contends that *Girl 6* "critically examines sexism and misogyny" and displays a "complex awareness of sexual politics."[3] Her commentary on Lee's ninth film suggests that she might support the director's contention that *Girl 6* is "very experimental and, unfairly, the most underrated" of all his films.[4] Indeed, hooks goes so far as to claim that the film is Lee's "gesture of resistance. Combining strategies of experimental filmmaking, refusing to give us race as we conventionally see it at the movies, or sex, or class, he risks that audiences will be unable to appreciate the significance of this work, . . . [which] offers viewers the most diverse images of black female identity ever to be seen in a Hollywood film."[5]

In this essay I discuss some of the concerns feminists have raised about the portrayal of female characters in Spike Lee's films. Although these concerns extend to much of Lee's oeuvre,[6] I focus on *She's Gotta Have It* and *Girl 6*, since questions about female sexuality, empowerment, and liberation are central to both these films. Separated by ten years, both films feature young African American women who explore their sexuality and do so in at least partial defiance of many social conventions concerning acceptable behavior for women. Although issues of race and its connections to gender are also central to both films, I concentrate on the films' treatment of female sexual expression and empowerment.

In discussing the extent to which *She's Gotta Have It* and *Girl 6* can be considered feminist, it is important to keep in mind that there are multiple approaches to feminism and myriad definitions of the term. One way to approach the different types of feminism is to distinguish its three waves, representing different historical periods and ideological commitments.[7] In what follows, I focus on the second- and third-wave feminism of recent history. I suggest that there is good reason to suspect that neither "freak" Nola Darling nor Girl 6 (Theresa Randle) presents a model of female sexuality and empowerment that is likely to fully satisfy many second- or third-wave feminists. However, I also suggest that, besides presenting a strong, liberated female lead, there is at least one other way for a film to be feminist: it can identify some of the forces of oppression that keep the characters from becoming liberated. Although *She's Gotta Have It* fails to be feminist in this second sense, there is reason to think that *Girl 6* succeeds in revealing some of the social and institutional forces that perpetuate the oppression of women.

Feminist Perspectives

The first wave of feminism is generally considered to include the suffrage and women's rights movements of the early twentieth century, with an emphasis on ensuring that women were granted equal rights and opportunities. First-wave feminists work to open more options for women, particularly in the public domains of workplace and politics, primarily by identifying and removing impediments to women's participation and by acknowledging the positive contributions of which women are capable. Sometimes called "liberal" feminists or "equity" feminists, such thinkers typically do not call for a radical restructuring of society or for a radical rethinking of sex and gender. They typically do not believe the social game needs to be radically changed. Instead, women just need to be allowed to play on equal terms, and the rules need only be adjusted to remove inequalities.

Many second-wave feminists wonder whether removing inequalities and impediments is enough. Typically associated with much of the feminist literature from the 1960s and 1970s, second-wave feminists typically encourage the introduction of more radical social change to improve the lives of women. Many second-wave feminists worry that treating women equally is not analogous to treating them the same as men, particularly in patriarchal societies, where women have been disadvantaged and oppressed. Instead, they argue that to treat women equally and fairly, women might have to be treated differently.

Many second-wave feminists also suggest that we should rethink what it means to be a woman and explore how definitions of womanhood and femininity are conditioned and constructed by culture and society. These thinkers express concern about gender stereotypes and the extent to which femininity and female sexuality are defined by that which is pleasing to an oppressive male gaze—a gaze that sexualizes, binds, infantilizes, objectifies, and subordinates women. Pointing to things like high heels, which make a woman's walk less stable, or corsets, which physically restrict a woman and make her take up less space, or the practice of shaving, which makes a woman's body more closely resemble that of a child, some feminists of the second wave called on women to burn their bras and protest beauty pageants. Often associated with the slogan "the personal is political," second-wave feminists also began to think about how social and cultural images of femininity are constructed and reinforced by personal choices. They note that even though a woman's decision to do something like wear makeup might appear to be purely a matter of personal preference, she is thereby helping to create an image of what it means to be a woman. Her "personal" choices have "political" implications. Feminists worry that the objectification of women is perpetuated when women turn themselves into stereotypically beautiful feminine objects.

Frustrated with the social and cultural position of women, and concerned about the ability to change the status of women within patriarchal institutions, some second-wave feminists suggested the need for separate spaces where women could develop their own communities. Some began to articulate some of the important differences between men and women, particularly in terms of their different processes of socialization and economic, political, and social power. Thinking about the differences between men and women led to reflection about the differences in women's backgrounds and experiences, and it raised questions about the extent to which race, class, sex, and gender also play a crucial role in understanding oppression. It also led to increasing divides among the different schools of second-wave feminism.[8]

Despite the disparate schools of thought, many second-wave thinkers agree that sex (being biologically female) differs from gender (being identified as feminine) and that a number of current gender stereotypes are problematic, particularly for women. Second-wave feminists who eschew stereotypical images of femininity are not likely to view lead characters who embrace these images as models of feminist liberation.

By contrast, some contemporary third-wave feminists are more sympathetic to feminine gender performances. In part, this is because they are likely to view the adoption of a particular gender as just that: a performance, as something one does rather than something one is. Just as a transvestite plays a woman by adopting stereotypically feminine characteristics, so too, they argue, does a biological female play at being a women when she displays stereotypically feminine gender characteristics. The awareness that one is "performing" gender opens the possibility for the playful adoption of characteristics and even the exaggeration of stereotypically gendered traits, sometimes in the hope of calling further attention to the fact that gender is, in fact, a performance. The desire to playfully perform gender has given rise to what has been called "lipstick" or "girlie" feminism,[9] which often exaggerates rather than condemns gender stereotypes. Because these stereotypes are mere performances, they are constructed; thus they can be deconstructed. Most third-wave feminists think there is no essence of femininity, no true or genuine way of being female or being a woman.[10] And they are concerned that many attempts to identify the essence of what it means to be a woman have been oppressive to women, particularly when these attempts promote heterosexism (the view that "real" men and women are "naturally" heterosexual).

There is much more that could be said about third-wave feminism, including the diversity of positions it contains and some of the contemporary responses it has received. However, it is most important here to note that although these feminists are aware of the problematic history of femininity and its potential role in oppressing women, a number of third-wave feminists revel in the performance of femininity. Thus, such thinkers are likely to be more sympathetic to female characters who embody feminine traits.

Feminism and the Character Nola Darling

At first glance, the character of Nola Darling, the "freak" who has "gotta have it," appears to be a model of liberated female sexuality. Shot in black-and-white in a confessional, documentary style that brings to mind Akira Kurosawa's *Rashomon, She's Gotta Have It* tells the story of an attractive young woman who has three lovers competing for her attention.[11] There's serious, stable Jamie Overstreet (Tommy Redmond Hicks), who plays a kind of yuppie father figure; pretty boy Greer Childs (John Canada Terrell), an attractive but arrogant male model; and young Mars Blackmon (Spike Lee), a sneaker-clad, hip-hop street hood. Given Nola's interest in playing the field on her own terms and her apparent disinclination to eliminate any of the players, she initially appears to be what some critics have called her: "a direct challenge to a society that expects women to be submissive and ready to settle down, while men are encouraged to be sexually aggressive."[12] Reinforcing the idea that he intends Nola to be a strong woman who reverses stereotypical gender roles, the director said he decided to "make a film about a woman who is actually living her life as a man," at least with respect to the frequency and casualness of her sexual activities with multiple partners.[13]

Lee thus seems to intend Nola to be a model of a modern, liberated woman. There are numerous scenes in which she appears to support this characterization by being the one who initiates sexual encounters and controls the sexual situation. However, there is a rape scene late in the film that calls for Nola to relinquish her seeming control, to submit to one man (Jamie) and acknowledge the depth of her submission by answering his demeaning question "Whose pussy is this?" with the docile reply, "Yours."

About this pivotal scene in the film, hooks says, "It is difficult for anyone who has fallen for the image of [Nola] as sexually liberated not to feel let down, disappointed in her character and in the film. Suddenly we are not witnessing a radical questioning of female sexual passivity or a celebration of female sexual self-assertion but a reconstruction of the same old sexist content in a new and more interesting form. . . . [T]he uppity black woman [has] been put in her place. . . . [W]e have witnessed a woman being disempowered and not a woman coming to power."[14] She rightly notes that Jamie's forcing himself on Nola suggests he is claiming ownership of her and her sexuality, and Nola's submission to him suggests that her seeming strength and independence were rather ephemeral, that she is willing to lose herself as an autonomous subject and become the conquered object of male desire.[15] The message seems to be that women who attempt to be sexually assertive will end up becoming sexually submissive—forcibly, if necessary.

Once she is no longer in immediate physical danger, and even after she has had time to reflect on what has happened, Nola continues her submissive response to Jamie by furthering her relationship with him. As a result, it is not only Nola's sexual autonomy but also her critical faculties, good judgment, and capacity for honest self-reflection that are called into question. Her response to the assault requires viewers to reassess Nola's character and bolsters the charge that she represents an attractive object that is ultimately vapid and vacuous, lacking any substantive appeal. The film ends with Nola's explanation that her relationship with Jamie is over and she has realized, "It's about control. My body. My mind." Yet viewers are given no indication of what character development has prompted this decision. Moreover, her final question, "Who's gonna own it, them or me?" is less defiant and self-assertive than a declarative sentence would have been. Viewers can be forgiven for thinking that Nola's question is one she has not thought very deeply about and whose answer is not entirely clear.[16]

Nola's rape is deeply problematic for the film, and Lee has admitted as much. In an interview with George Khoury in 1999, Lee indicated that the one thing he would like to do over, out of all his films, is the "rape scene in *She's Gotta Have It*."[17] In 2005 he elaborated: "The rape scene, that is the one scene in all my films that I would redo. I think the rape and especially its aftermath were too flippant. I didn't really show the violation that it is."[18]

But even leaving aside the rape and Nola's response to it, there are other reasons for feminists to be concerned about Lee's first full-length feature film. Apart from Nola's submission when assaulted by Jamie is the fact that all the men in the film seem to want to domesticate Nola and turn her into someone she is not, to transform her "from a 'jezebel' . . . to a nice girl; an unrefined to refined woman; or a whore to what Mars referred to as a 'righteous' woman."[19] None of the male characters really accepts and appreciates Nola for who she is.

Complicating matters is the fact that the character of Nola seems to be undefined. It might be true that she's gotta have it, but it's never really clear who Nola is, exactly what she wants, or how she wants to have it. Unlike the male characters in the film, who are much more developed and who are, arguably, the real subjects of the film, Nola lacks a well-developed personality.[20] She takes pleasure primarily in her ability to please. Her desire is to be desired by the men in her life. But this makes her desire derivative: she wants to be what the male characters want her to be, and they want her to be a beautiful body.[21]

Interestingly, Nola shows no desire to be desired by the female characters in the film, whether as a lover or as an intimate friend.[22] Nola's connections with other women seem tenuous, and her lesbian friend Opal Gilstrap (Raye Dowell) comes across as a shallow sexual predator rather than a true confidante.[23] Dismissing out of hand Opal's suggestion that there is a certain plasticity to sexuality and sexual desires that might extend beyond heterosexuality, Nola does not want to even consider the possibility Opal raises. As a result, some feminists express concern about the film's heterosexist gender stereotypes—stereotypes that claim there are two sexes and two genders, with men typically defined as desiring subjects and women as desired objects (who desire to be desired by men).

Although the film seems to want to defy such stereotypes by suggesting that Nola has strong sexual desires and actively pursues her would-be sexual partners, the film ultimately reinforces the fact that Nola wants to be an object of male desire. She indicates this not only by her response to the rape but also by her undeveloped character. If she is an individual who is supposed to have autonomous sexual desires, it is essential that she give viewers some indication of what these are if she is to be seen as a strong, desiring subject.

But the concern about heterosexist gender stereotypes runs deeper: even if Nola presented herself as a desiring subject and consistently adopted a stereotypically masculine role in the film, merely switching the roles of masculine and feminine does little to call these roles into question. When third-wave feminists talk about performing gender, they typically do so as part of a project to undermine any essentialist notions of gender stereotypes and to call attention to the extent to which such stereotypes are socially constructed rather than part of some kind of biological determinism. If Nola merely plays a man's role, as Lee describes her as doing,[24] and if the role itself has not been reimagined, then the seeming revolutionary or emancipatory potential of *She's Gotta Have It* in overturning problematic gender stereotypes and in fostering new reflections about human sexuality and sexual relations is actually quite limited.[25] And Heather E. Harris and Kimberly R. Moffitt are right to worry that "the outcome, though probably not intended, is mostly recycled stereotypical images and fantasies of black women, through the gaze of black men—a sexist bamboozling of sorts."[26]

Feminism and the Character Girl 6

Having explored some feminist perspectives on *She's Gotta Have It,* I now turn to an examination of *Girl 6* and a discussion of the lead character, who is known throughout the film either by her position as the number-six girl of a phone-sex business or by the telephone moniker she adopts: "Lovely."

It is only toward the end of the film that viewers learn her real name is Judy. And given the prominence of fantasy and the film's emphasis on the lead character's performance of her roles, it seems appropriate to refer to her here as Girl 6.

Lee clearly intends for there to be a connection between the two films. In a 1996 interview with Charlie Rose, Lee explains that the story idea for *Girl 6* came from thinking about *She's Gotta Have It* and Nola Darling's sexual encounters with her lovers. Lee notes that the earlier film was made before the full impact of the AIDS epidemic and before the phone-sex business was a multibillion-dollar industry. Taking these things into account, Lee claims that *Girl 6* is "really a look at how things have changed in the past ten years."[27] Lee also calls attention to the fact that the monologue Girl 6 reads in her auditions for Quentin Tarantino (with which the film begins) and for Ron Silver (with which the film ends) was actually spoken by Nola Darling in *She's Gotta Have It*—signaling an intentional and explicit connection between the two films.[28] It's even possible that Girl 6 is auditioning for the role of Nola Darling.

Like Lee's first full-length feature film, *Girl 6* follows a young African American woman as she struggles to define herself, to explore her sexuality, and to find her place in the world. Unlike *She's Gotta Have It,* which focuses on the private life and the real sexual escapades of its female lead, *Girl 6* focuses on the professional life and the sexual fantasies delineated by the title character.

The story of *Girl 6* is relatively straightforward: unwilling to subject herself to the kind of exploitation required to work as an actress in New York, Girl 6 takes a position as a phone-sex operator, where she devotes her time to satisfying the fantasies of her male callers. Pretending to be an attractive, young, heterosexual white woman (unless a customer requests a different character), Girl 6 eventually begins to lose herself in the fantasies she constructs. She becomes superficially attached to one of her repeat customers, Bob (Peter Berg), and is disappointed when he fails to show up at an arranged meeting. Retreating into an increasingly private realm, Girl 6 leaves her office cubicle and coworkers and begins to work from home. Eventually threatened by a customer (Michael Imperioli) who is into snuff fantasies and claims to be coming to her apartment to kill her, she awakens to the dangers of her current profession. Emerging from her life of fantasy, she quits her job, says good-bye to her ex-husband (Isaiah Washington) and to her only close friend, Jimmy (Spike Lee), and moves to Hollywood.

Because it begins with its lead character speaking lines delivered by Nola Darling, *Girl 6* invites viewers to compare the female protagonists. Both women struggle to come to terms with their sexuality and find the proper avenues for expressing it. Both are stereotypically feminine heterosexual women who cater to male fantasies and who work to make themselves desirable to men. Like Nola, Girl 6 does not seem to possess sexual fantasies of her own, other than in a derivative sense: she wants to be wanted. However, Girl 6 has other strong desires—namely, to succeed as an actress (and retain her dignity in the process). She also seems to desire meaningful personal connections with men that transcend purely physical encounters.

It is not clear that she desires meaningful personal relationships with other women, however. Her best friend in the film is her neighbor Jimmy. Like Nola, Girl 6 seems to be somewhat alienated from other women and lacks close female friends. Despite the fact that she leads a life in which female characters play an important role, they do so as her bosses and coworkers, not as her personal friends and confidantes.[29] Like Nola, Girl 6 gives no indication that she is actively cultivating deeper relationships with women or that she puts a premium on doing so.

Despite these similarities, there are some noteworthy differences between the two female leads—differences generated primarily as a consequence of Girl 6's profession. Because she is paid to pretend to be the various female characters her callers want her to be, Girl 6 is aware of the extent to which she is performing her gender. Told what kind of character her customer desires, she constructs feminine personas of varying ages and ethnicities with differing sexual predilections.[30] The film makes it clear that Girl 6 is an actor playing a part, not someone who is turned on by the fantasies she constructs.[31] As she takes on various personas during her calls, she begins to experiment with different images of femininity in her life outside the office. She seems to become increasingly aware that gender is socially constructed and performed—issues that are of particular importance to many feminists.

Her gendered performance extends beyond physical appearances. As Charlotte Kroløkke and Anne Scott Sørensen note in their discussion of Kira Hall's 1995 study of phone-sex workers, employees in that industry "must mimic the inequality between the sexes, perform submissiveness, and give 'lip service' to the male customers. In this way, they draw on the stereotypes of women's language that are part of (White, heterosexual) conventional wisdom and expectations . . . [and] cater to hegemonic male perceptions of the ideal woman."[32] In other words, phone-sex workers like Girl 6 are putting on an erotic performance that extends beyond physical descriptions of themselves and includes the way they relate to their customers as deferential, dominating, or submissive. Girl 6 repeatedly performs as a woman who is erotically engaged by her male callers, who desires to be desired, and who enjoys participating in the acts they want her to describe. She performs to fulfill conventional masculine expectations about the ideal woman and thereby helps unmask the socially constructed content of these expectations.

For these reasons, feminists might be much more sympathetic to viewing Girl 6 (as opposed to Nola Darling) as an emancipated woman. However, I suspect that many feminists would have other concerns about the title character that undercut her ability to serve as a model for liberated sexuality. First, there is the problem of her name. The fact that for almost the entire film she is known only as Girl 6 or by her adopted moniker "Lovely" suggests that she is primarily defined by the role she plays; she has no independent identity apart from it. Although viewers eventually learn her real name, it is not clear, even by the film's end, that Judy is a fully developed character. At best, she appears to be on her way to self-definition. And although this is important, it is not sufficient to constitute a model for liberation.

As mentioned earlier, there is the problem of her failure to cultivate any strong relationships with other women. And with the exception of Jimmy and her somewhat estranged ex-husband, she does not have close personal relationships with men either. Although she seems to desire meaningful relationships, it is not clear that she has them. She remains somewhat isolated and aloof. Perhaps as a result of loneliness, she also has some difficulty maintaining an appropriate professional relationship with her male callers and goes so far as to agree to meet a client in person, although he ultimately disappoints her by failing to appear for their rendezvous. Girl 6, however, shows up at the agreed time and thereby makes her professional life inappropriately personal.

Late in the film, she also finds herself increasingly preoccupied with images of falling and with reflections about a young girl who falls down an elevator shaft. Eventually, her loss of control and escalating fear culminate in threats by one of her male clients that he will come to her home (from which she is now working), put a bag over her head, and kill her. As in *She's Gotta Have It, Girl 6* seems to suggest that women who are too sexually active or attractive will be punished by at least the threat of physical violence. The film thus implies that Girl 6 is mistaken when she thinks she is safe and in total control of the fantasies she constructs; even in the privacy of her own home, far from the physical presence of her customers, she may be subjected to violence from men. It is her recognition of this that prompts her to leave New York and the phone-sex industry and move to Hollywood to try her luck as an actress.

It might seem that she thereby escapes the institutions that are the source of her oppression and succeeds in becoming a liberated woman. But once she arrives on the West Coast, it becomes clear that she is still plagued by fantasies of old Hollywood gender stereotypes in the tradition of Dorothy Dandridge. Imagining herself in the black-and-white images of old Hollywood, she continues to audition and perform, retaining the moniker "Lovely" rather than reverting to her own name. Although there is, as hooks rightly notes, a sense of resistance and "a spirit of hopefulness" at the end of the film,[33] when Girl 6 refuses to remove her top for director Ron Silver and remains fully clothed as she repeats the lines from *She's Gotta Have It* that she was prevented from delivering in the film's initial scene, these are only early steps toward the title character's emancipation. She is beginning, but she has not yet arrived.

In the end, then, many feminists will find the character of Girl 6 not much more of a model of personal and sexual liberation than Nola Darling is. Both lead characters express their sexuality in ways that defy social conventions about how "good girls" are supposed to behave, and both at least appear to be initially empowered by doing so. But both women are eventually punished for their excessive sexuality or sexual expression by physical or verbal assaults. A closer examination of *Girl 6* and *She's Gotta Have It* shows that female leads who might initially appear to be models of liberated sexuality are not, in fact, fully developed characters and are not fully emancipated women.

Feminist Critique of Oppressive Industries and Institutions

Despite doubts about whether the lead characters of *Girl 6* and *She's Gotta Have It* embody feminist ideals of liberated women, it is important to keep in mind that feminism aims to identify and eventually eradicate the social, cultural, political, and economic sources of women's oppression. So a film that helps identify such sources of oppression can be considered feminist to the extent that it does so. With that in mind, we should explore whether *She's Gotta Have It* or *Girl 6* can be considered feminist in the sense of providing a critique of oppressive industries and institutions.

As we reconsider *She's Gotta Have It,* it appears that not much is accomplished toward this end. The sequence in which viewers are presented with a series of terrible pickup lines spoken by male "dogs" points to some of the ways men stereotypically objectify women. But this sequence takes only a few minutes of the film and is not substantial enough to constitute an exposé of how such stereotypically masculine discourse perpetuates the oppression of women.

Girl 6, in contrast, does contain an exposé of the sources of the oppression of women. From its opening scene, in which the lead character auditions for a part in a Quentin Tarantino film, *Girl 6* seems designed to explore how the entertainment industry functions to oppress women. Tarantino, who plays himself, repeatedly interrupts Girl 6 and instructs her to "listen," explaining that he wants to cast a woman who represents the "total package" of the ideal woman, and he will know her when he sees her. It is clear from the beginning that his gaze is what counts; it does not matter what Girl 6 says or does. What matters is how she looks, whether she "oozes sexuality," and whether she fits the ideal image that exists in his mind. He does not need to hear her perform the monologue she has prepared; he only needs to see what she looks like without her clothes.[34]

Despite being a white male, Tarantino maintains that he is going to direct a picture that reflects the perspective of an African American woman. He seems to undermine his own claim that the lead character's perspective is the locus of the film by noting that all the principal male "supporting roles" have been filled by important actors who (he seems to imply) are likely to carry the film.

By calling attention to the way Girl 6 is treated by male directors, by her agent (John Turturro), and by her acting coach (Susan Batson), Lee's film functions to expose some of the ways the film industry itself oppresses women and renders it impossible for them to escape being problematically objectified. Perhaps Lee means to call attention to his awareness of the fact that, as a director and author working in the industry, his films might be complicit in such objectification. Prior to writing the screenplay for *She's Gotta Have It,* Lee interviewed several female friends in an attempt to accurately represent women's voices, particularly about their sexuality and sexual experiences; however, by the time of *Girl 6,* he may be more aware of the difficulties involved in taking those experiences out of their particular contexts. Moreover, he may be more aware that those experiences can reinforce rather than revolutionize problematic sex and gender stereotypes. It is not enough to reverse the stereotypical roles and introduce a promiscuous female character in a relationship with a man who desires to be monogamous. Instead, the stereotypes themselves need to be called into question.

As Girl 6 turns to images from popular culture and mass media, she encounters nothing but problematic stereotypes of beauty, sexuality, and femininity. She is unable to find a satisfactory image to emulate. As hooks rightly notes, "By relying on mass-media images to structure her sense of self and identity, Girl 6 can find no representations of liberatory sexuality. She must be either victim, vamp, or castrator. All of these roles still require that she shape her sexuality in response to the eroticism of the patriarchal phallic imaginary."[35] Inasmuch as *Girl 6* shows this, it provides a critique of oppressive institutions that is consistent with the goals of feminism. Thus, even though the film's title character ultimately does not represent a model of liberated female sexuality, the film helps reveal some of the social and cultural forces that inhibit Girl 6's emancipation, and feminists might, on closer examination, find much to admire in this film, which is one of Spike Lee's most underrated.

Notes

I am grateful to Mark Conard for his helpful suggestions and thoughtful editorial remarks that improved this essay.

1. bell hooks maintains that the film "generated more discussions of the politics of race and gender, of rape and violence against black women, than any feminist article or book on the subject at the time." bell hooks, *Reel to Real: Race, Sex and Class at the Movies* (New York: Routledge, 1996), 4.

2. bell hooks, " 'Whose Pussy Is This': A Feminist Comment," in *The Spike Lee Reader*, ed. Paula J. Massood (Philadelphia: Temple University Press, 2008), 1–9.

3. hooks, *Reel to Real,* 5.

4. Spike Lee, *Spike Lee: That's My Story and I'm Sticking to It,* as told to Kaleem Aftab (New York: W. W. Norton, 2005), 211.

5. hooks, *Reel to Real,* 18.

6. See, for example, Michele Wallace, "Spike Lee and Black Women," in *The Spike Lee Reader,* 23–29; Wahneema Lubiano, "But Compared to What? Reading Realism, Representation, and Essentialism in *School Daze, Do the Right Thing,* and the Spike Lee Discourse," in *The Spike Lee Reader,* 30–57; Anna Everett, "Spike, Don't Mess Malcolm Up," in *The Spike Lee Reader,* 91–114; Beretta E. Smith-Shomade, " 'I Be Smackin' My Hoes': Paradox and Authenticity in *Bamboozled,*" in *The Spike Lee Reader,* 228–42; Mark Lawrence McPhail, "Race and Sex in Black and White: Essence and Ideology in the Spike Lee Discourse," in *Fight the Power! The Spike Lee Reader,* ed. Janice D. Hamlet and Robin R. Means Coleman (New York: Peter Lang, 2009), 274–86; Sharon Elise and Adewole Umoja, "Spike Lee Constructs the New Black Man: Mo' Better," in *Fight the Power!* 287–301; Heather E. Harris and Kimberly R. Moffitt, "A Critical Exploration of African American Women through the 'Spiked Lens,' " in *Fight the Power!* 303–20; Maurice E. Stevens, "Subject to Countermemory: Disavowal and Black Manhood in Spike Lee's *Malcolm X,*" in *Fight the Power!* 321–41.

In their introduction to *Fight the Power!* Hamlet and Coleman raise the question of whether Lee has "embedded in his work heterosexism and homophobia, sexism and misogyny, a masculinist aesthetic and a middle-class sensibility" (xx). They note that a number of the essays in their volume are devoted to discussing how Lee's films might be guilty of perpetuating problematic racial, class, sex, and gender stereotypes. The concern is that many of Lee's films evince a commitment to essentialist ideas about what it means to be a woman or, even more problematically, what it means to be a "real" woman, without an awareness of the extent to which what it means to be a woman is socially constructed in a particular cultural context. Many of Lee's male characters are depicted as subjects who desire women as objects, while many of his female characters are depicted as objects to be desired. Implicit in these stereotypes is a view of women as what Simone de Beauvoir calls the "second sex"; they are derivatively defined as not being men and are considered primarily in terms of their relationships to men and their desirability to men. Heterosexuality is assumed, and "characters located outside of the racialized gender normativity that [Lee] represents" are "uniformly marginalize[d], pathologize[d], or [made] suspicious" (Stevens, "Subject to Countermemory," 338).

In addition to the feminist concerns related to *She's Gotta Have It* and *Girl 6* explored here, Wallace notes that the female characters in *School Daze* (1988) are portrayed as passive consumers who are unconcerned about larger cultural and political issues. As a result, she argues that the film perpetuates problematic images of women: the Gamma Rays are shown in their "falseness, which reflects both their 'wanna be whiteness' and their femininity—as though they were black women in white women's drag. Jigaboo women, on the other hand, are natural women with natural hair; the film focuses on them primarily as objects of ridicule, humor and negation" (Wallace, "Spike Lee and Black Women," 26). Lubiano adds that *School Daze* "unfortunately and myopically, presents aesthetics as formal matters of physical appearance in which women only participate. Men *do*. . . . Women, on the other hand, *show*. . . . [T]he film is incapable of showing that women do anything other than look like components of male aesthetics" (Lubiano, "But Compared to What?" 50). Building on the concern that women in Lee's films show, while men do, Everett notes that women's agency in Lee's films "often bifurcates in terms of that familiar Madonna/whore construct so characteristic of mainstream Hollywood" ("Spike, Don't Mess Malcolm Up," 108). Raising concerns about the female roles in *Malcolm X* (1992), she notes that the film gives "short shrift" to Malcolm's widow Betty Shabazz and is guilty of "complete narrative erasure of Malcolm X's sister Ella" (ibid., 106).

7. For a more detailed discussion of the waves of feminism, see Charlotte Kroløkke and Anne Scott Sørensen, *Gender Communication Theories and Analyses: From Silence to Performance* (Thousand Oaks, Calif.: Sage Publications, 2006), particularly chapter 1, "Three Waves of Feminism: From Suffragettes to Grrls."

8. For a discussion of the different schools of feminist thought, see Rosemarie Tong, *Feminine and Feminist Ethics* (New York: Wadsworth, 1993). There she notes that feminists hold radically different attitudes toward femininity based on differing beliefs about its role in perpetuating the oppression of women.

9. Kroløkke and Sørensen, *Gender Communication Theories and Analyses,* 15.

10. Some question whether the biological category of *woman* can be consistently maintained. For some of the reasons to think that sex as well as gender might be socially constructed, and for some of the problems feminists face in defining what it means to be a woman while rejecting problematic essentialism, see Mari Mikkola's "Feminist Perspectives on Sex and Gender" in *Stanford Encyclopedia of Philosophy,* http://plato.stanford.edu/entries/feminism-gender/.

11. Released in 1986 and distributed by Island Pictures, the eighty-four-minute *She's Gotta Have It* was reportedly shot in only twelve days on the paltry budget of $175,000. The film, which lists Lee as director, author, producer, and editor, grossed more than $8.5 million. Lee notes that the similarity to *Rashomon* was intentional and that he used black-and-white film not to cut costs but because that was the way the images came to him. He used color for the birthday scene as "a little homage to *The Wizard of Oz.*" Marlaine Glicksman, "Lee Way," in *Spike Lee: Interviews,* ed. Cynthia Fuchs (Jackson: University Press of Mississippi, 2002), 7.

12. Dennis Abrams, *Spike Lee: Director* (New York: Chelsea House, 2008), 28. He adds, "What makes the three men so uncomfortable . . . [is that] Nola is in control—not only of herself, but of them as well. The traditional roles have been reversed, and none of the men in Nola's life are in the least bit happy about it" (ibid.).

13. Glicksman, "Lee Way," 8.

14. hooks, "'Whose Pussy Is This,'" 7–8.

15. George Khoury notes that "the great betrayal occurs when Nola announces that her body belongs to Jamie, who used violence to control her. At this moment, she announces the defeat of her individuality and beliefs. Had Nola said that her body belonged to her and her alone, she would have demonstrated strength and shown Jamie what power really is." George Khoury, "Big Words: An Interview with Spike Lee," in *Spike Lee: Interviews,* 153.

16. Though her final statement that she is not a "one-man woman" is probably supposed to reveal Nola's independence, it is spoken without the conviction needed to be convincing. More important, the film fails to make clear why being promiscuous and refusing to limit one's self to a single partner should serve as the model of a sexually liberated woman. The danger of equating sexual freedom and promiscuity seems particularly great for African American women, who have sometimes been stereotyped as promiscuous and sexually available. For a discussion of some of the problematic stereotypes and sources of oppression suffered by women of particular racial and ethnic groups, see Elizabeth Spelman, *Inessential Woman* (Boston: Beacon Press, 1988).

17. Khoury, "Big Words," 152.

18. Lee, *Spike Lee,* 47.

19. Harris and Moffitt, "Critical Exploration of African American Women," 306.

20. Wallace adds that Nola's language is "inane and self-canceling, as if she were selling something in a TV commercial" ("Spike Lee and Black Women," 26). It is worth noting that this may be the result of bad acting. Lee says of *She's Gotta Have It,* "Of the five films I've done to date, this is the one I don't, can't and refuse to watch . . . because

of the filmmaking and the performances." Spike Lee, "Introduction" to *Five for Five: The Films of Spike Lee*, by Terry McMillan and David Lee (New York: Stewart, Tabori and Chang, 1991), 13.

21. Lee admits that in his early films, his male characters are "more fully developed" than his female characters. Erich Leon Harris, "The Demystification of Spike Lee," in *Spike Lee: Interviews*, 134.

22. In one scene of the film, Nola dreams that three women (each jealous of Nola's relationship with one of the men she is seeing) are trying to set her on fire. It is interesting that Lee has Nola's fears take the form of other women, when it is Jamie, the seeming gentleman of the group, who goes on to assault her.

23. Stevens notes that "Lee's films uniformly marginalize, pathologize, or make suspicious characters located outside of the racialized gender normativity that he represents" ("Subject to Countermemory," 338).

24. Lee says of *She's Gotta Have It:* "The film is still told from a male perspective, and it's about these men's perspectives on this woman who is leading her life as a man as far as her sexuality is concerned" (Lee, *Spike Lee*, 29). Yet hooks believes the film's focus on the men's perspectives is problematic and turns it into a "male-centered, male-biased patriarchal tale" in which Nola is the "object that stimulates the discourse" but in which the men "are its subjects" ("'Whose Pussy Is This,'" 4).

25. Perhaps the image of Nola's bed as it appears in the film serves as a partial reflection of the difficulties here. Unconnected to any of the walls in the room, Nola's bed is a free-floating object that can be considered to exemplify freedom and detachment. But, as she explains to viewers, it is the only place she has sex. Perhaps, then, the bed represents not ultimate freedom and independence but imprisonment within a narrowly defined private space and dependence on those who visit there. What initially appears to be emblematic of liberation ultimately introduces another level of dependence.

26. Harris and Moffitt, "Critical Exploration of African American Women," 309.

27. Charlie Rose, "Interview with Spike Lee," in *Spike Lee: Interviews*, 117.

28. Lee, *Spike Lee*, 206.

29. Harris and Moffitt discuss Girl 6's alienation from other women in the film and argue that she "is given the opportunity to interact with other women, but it remains superficial . . . their connection seems to be one-sided and limited, focusing primarily on 'Judy's' life problems as well as their work-related adventures on the telephone" ("Critical Exploration of African American Women," 312).

30. *Girl 6* also raises some interesting questions about race and ethnicity as part of gender performance, particularly since the phone-sex operators are told to perform as white females unless a customer explicitly requests otherwise.

31. Although the film suggests that Girl 6 eventually finds it difficult to fully differentiate fantasy and reality, for much of the film she is able to separate herself from the fantasies she performs, at least while she is performing them, and does not appear to be erotically engaged in her calls. Her difficulties separating fantasy and reality begin when her callers engage her in real conversations about their lives. Thus it is not fantasy that bleeds into reality, but reality that bleeds into fantasy. As some of her callers reveal

details about their lives, the line between customers and friends begins to blur. Later in the film, as fantasy indeed begins to invade the lead character's life, it is not primarily sexual fantasies that preoccupy her but fantasies about what it means to live as a woman: fantasies about the vulnerability of the young woman falling down the elevator shaft and the receptivity to violence and loss of self such a fall represents, as well as fantasies about the strength of established and powerful adult women who, like Foxy Brown, are able to fully defend themselves against external threats.

32. Kroløkke and Sørensen, *Gender Communication Theories and Analyses,* 132.

33. hooks, *Reel to Real,* 18.

34. After briefly exposing her breasts, Girl 6 decides she is not comfortable continuing the audition topless and leaves. She receives no support from her agent or her acting coach, who both insist that nudity is a requirement for working in the film industry and who both indicate they can no longer work with her.

35. hooks, *Reel to Real,* 13–14.

The Dialectic of King and X in *Do the Right Thing*

Michael Silberstein

It is a hot summer Saturday in Bedford-Stuyvesant. The streets are trashed from violent confrontations between residents and police over the latter's killing of an African American. The scene of the crime, Sal's Famous Pizzeria, is pillaged and burned to the ground in response to the young man's death, while Sal (Danny Aiello) and his sons (John Turturro as Pino and Richard Edson as Vito)—the only whites on the block—look on in horror. Although there are no easy explanations for either the death or the violence that follows, *Do the Right Thing* (1989) illuminates key issues and themes central to the racism that can be the catalyst for such violence. Although the film by no means offers a solution, it does explore those features of racial injustice that are insidious and difficult to grasp. One of the film's strengths is not only its portrayal of the perplexing issues confronting minorities but also its evocative representation of those who seek to counteract racism, albeit by different means. Understood as a political objective, the question of how best to achieve racial harmony is, of course, highly controversial, and no simple resolution is offered. Rather, the film is responsive and sensitive to the nuances and subtleties of the family of problems surrounding racism.

The story functions as a microcosm of the problem of racism, as well as a challenge to the correctness of liberalism. Indeed, can we all get along with one another? And if so, what becomes of "tribal" loyalties, such as those found among the different ethnic groups in the mythic "melting pot" of American culture? The good liberal honors the concept of tolerance of differences and at the same time declares those differences to be unimportant, as a means of unification. The oppressed struggle to find their own voice, with the knowledge that it is only through that voice that their differences will be heard and, perhaps, honored and respected.

Thomas Jefferson's pluralism, which champions religious and political tolerance and is designed to ensure peace and harmony, is immediately challenged by the history of Africans in America. About black men and women in America, Jefferson famously said that "nothing is more certainly written in the book of fate than that these people are to be free." However, he also said: "Nor is it less certain that the two races, equally free, cannot live in the same government."[1] Jefferson knew slavery was wrong, but he also worried that emancipation was insufficient to solve the problem of slavery and save pluralism. Even Jefferson considered the possibility that expulsion might be necessary, given the slaves' differences from white Europeans. So although our democracy is founded in part on Jeffersonian pluralism, even he worried that too much racial and ethnic heterogeneity might defeat it.

Do the Right Thing is, in microcosm, a representation of this deep-seated problem and a reminder that the problem has not gone away but only changed shape. This is a challenge not only for the Jeffersonian pluralism derived from white European thinkers but also to the unity of the African American community, as represented by competing internal ideologies regarding how to respond to racism in America. Therefore, determining the right thing to do is an urgent issue for white and black peoples alike.

Martin Luther King Jr. versus Malcolm X

Here, *Do the Right Thing* is examined in light of two ideologies rooted in the African American community as they relate to the question of what it means to act rightly when confronted by social wrongs such as racism, prejudice, and discrimination. The ideological perspectives expressed through the characters in the film are those of Martin Luther King Jr. and Malcolm X. The film invites this analysis repeatedly throughout and ends with the following quotations:

> Violence as a way of achieving racial justice is both impractical and immoral. It is impractical because it is a descending spiral ending in destruction for all. The old law of an eye for an eye leaves everybody blind. It is immoral because it seeks to humiliate the opponent rather than win his understanding; it seeks to annihilate rather than to convert. Violence is immoral because it thrives on hatred rather than love. It destroys a community and makes brotherhood impossible. It leaves society in monologue rather than dialogue. Violence ends

> by defeating itself. It creates bitterness in the survivors and brutality in the destroyers. (Dr. Martin Luther King Jr.)

> I think there are plenty of good people in America, but there are also plenty of bad people in America and the bad ones are the ones who seem to have all the power and be in these positions to block things that you and I need. Because this is the situation, you and I have to preserve the right to do what is necessary to bring an end to that situation, and it doesn't mean that I advocate violence, but at the same time I am not against using violence in self-defense. I don't even call it violence when it's self-defense, I call it intelligence. (Malcolm X)

The film is, in part, an exploration of these opposing themes. Thus, this discussion initially focuses on the most formulaic points of contention between the two men at a certain point in their lives as Lee presents them in this snapshot.

Bear in mind that these were real men, not billboards for ideologies, who were trying to think their way through troubled and morally complex times. Although they have become icons—pictures on the wall—that does not reflect their reality. For example, there is no presupposition here that King was always persuaded of the rightness of nonviolent methods or that Malcolm X advocated Black Nationalism and separatism throughout his life. Also, keep in mind the limited scope in which these philosophies are explored herein. For instance, it is not clear whether Malcolm X would have applauded the tactics employed by characters such as Radio Raheem (Bill Nunn) and Buggin' Out (Giancarlo Esposito), who obviously embrace the concept of Black Power, in their dealings with Sal. One of the problems here is that both X's and King's thinking evolved over a relatively short period (X's in the last year of his life, in fact) and was shaped by quickly moving events and a mercurial history. Here, the two men are treated as two interlocutors in an ethical dialogue about racism and prejudice, but be wary about letting this device obscure how complex the men and their ideas really were.

What will become clear is that the differences between King and X are much deeper than simply the question of which tactic works best. Doing the right thing for these men is not merely a question of tactics but also a question of how one understands human nature, what one believes constitutes a good person and the good life, one's conception of justice, where one believes the present is heading, and which moral authorities one accepts as more credible than others. It will also become clear that although X and King start out in very different places on all these questions, they eventually converge on some of these points.

We also get some insight into the problem of unification among members of the African American community, exemplified in the preceding quotations from King and X. Indeed, from the film's first few images, the viewer is introduced to the conflict between the ideologies of King and X. We see the autistic Smiley (Roger Guenveur Smith) peddling the photograph of the two men shaking hands as he stammers out their names in a barely intelligible or audible fashion. The image is disarming and symbolic, as the viewer must likewise struggle to understand Smiley.

What, then, are the main differences between King and X that foster this internal struggle within the black community? As the preceding quotations suggest, King disavows the use of force and violence to end racial oppression, while Malcolm X defends the use of such strategies and believes they are sometimes the only means available to fight injustice. The former defers the issue of race as such for a (perceived) higher moral imperative of nonviolent resistance in the belief that, given time and incentive, white society will eventually recognize the common humanity shared by all races. One might say that King is using white Americans' Christian and democratic values against them, helping them to see that if they are serious about being good Christians and good Americans, they must accept racial equality and all it implies. This is not to deny that King's nonviolence movement is sometimes militant and proactive. However, it is fair to say that King believes that racism is more likely to be defeated by the New Testament emphasis on love as opposed to the Old Testament emphasis on retributive justice.

By contrast, Malcolm X pushes the whole issue of race to the foreground, where the Black Muslim movement and later the Black Power movement serve as self-protection from a fundamentally flawed and inhumane social order. X explicitly invokes the Old Testament eye-for-an-eye style of justice that is more prevalent in the Muslim tradition. King refuses to exploit the race issue and adopts a kind of "color-blind" morality. Recall his "I have a dream" speech: "I have a dream that my four little children will one day live in a nation where they will not be judged by the color of their skin, but by the content of their character." Malcolm X, however, uses the very issue of race to gain leverage on the uneven playing field of society at large. X says that society must first promote racial justice and reconciliation before it is possible to create a racially color-blind society. This is because color consciousness has been used to create and maintain white privilege for centuries. Thus, advocating for color blindness before racial reconciliation has been achieved is playing right into the hands of the status quo of white privilege in general and racists in particular. Indeed, at various times, X called King a "traitor to his race," "an agent of the white man," and a "religious Uncle Tom." It is worth noting here that white opponents of affirmative action and the like often quote King on color blindness as part of their justification.

King proposes that certain moral truths be preserved no matter what the particular situation. One such moral truth is that violence is always wrong; here, King appears to be defending an *absolute* (as opposed to a *situational*) moral ethic,[2] one he claims to have obtained from the authority of Jesus. In fact, both King and X operate with a theologically informed natural law–rights background.[3] In King's case, his rights stem from his sense of *imago dei* in the Christian tradition; in X's case, from the Islamic tradition. X views the Nation of Islam as the counter to the antiblack, white-centric ideology of Christianity; the Muslim faith provides a divinely justified defense of African American human rights. X often characterizes Christianity as a slave religion of white origins used to pacify blacks, claiming that Jesus was in fact a black radical willfully misinterpreted and misappropriated by white Christians.

Even if violent means are more expedient to the interests of the black community, King believes they are inherently wrong. In short, the ends do not justify the means. However, King is also sure that blacks would be slaughtered by whites if they attempted violent revolution, given the superior firepower and greater number of whites. This is perhaps King's best argument against X's rhetoric. In contrast, X asserts that it is a "crime in the face of all the violence that's been perpetuated on the Negro to expect them to be nonviolent." Accordingly, violence is sometimes both "appropriate" and "intelligent," as implied in the title of one of his most infamous books, *By Whatever Means Necessary.* Extreme measures may be the only way to bring about change. For this reason, the ends may very well justify the means if the end one seeks is a just society for all. X alleges it is better to die fighting for justice than to acquiesce to the white tyrants.

Thus, once again, X would say that King's nonviolence plays right into the hands of white supremacy. One should be wary of simplistic comparisons, however. King is clear that he is not merely defending an absolute deontological Christian ethic of nonviolence.[4] Following Gandhi, he believes that, in the long run, violent means only beget more violence (a cycle of violence) and thus thwart social justice in the end. This is, of course, a teleological or consequentialist justification.[5] Note, however, that although King mixes deontology and teleology when making the case for nonviolence, the "violence begets violence" argument is secondary to his claim that violence is always and everywhere wrong. King also repeatedly emphasizes that the ends and the means of moral action are inseparable. Likewise, it is clear that X is not merely providing a consequentialist defense of the use of violence; he is saying that blacks have been forcefully oppressed for centuries and therefore have the *right* to "self-defense" and retaliation. In short, X is claiming that a war on whites would be a *just war*—indeed, a just holy war from the Islamic perspective.[6] Again, keep in mind that his views became more nuanced toward the end of his life. King and X both changed their views over time and minimized their differences, as we shall see.

The Right Way to Realize Social Justice

Historically, change comes about through impassioned struggle and commitment. But how does one struggle with love or hate? The character of Radio Raheem literally wears this puzzle on brass knuckles—four-fingered rings that state LOVE on one hand, HATE on the other (an homage to Charles Laughton's 1955 film *The Night of the Hunter*)—as he parades the street to the prophetic beat of Public Enemy's "Fight the Power." Is one approach more pragmatically useful or morally superior than the other? Or does the photograph of King and Malcolm X shaking hands perhaps signify the hope of reconciliation both ideologically and within the black community? The photograph becomes an object of intrinsic interest because we entertain its very presence as posing this question. This is the same photograph that eventually finds its way on to Sal's "Wall of Fame" following the riot. The photograph is also the last image we see in the film. Malcolm X considers violence in response to oppression and injustice to be a form of self-defense, whereas King believes that through negotiation and dialogue, and by putting universal humanity and principles such as nonviolence before color, we will ultimately achieve racial harmony in America. However, within the context of the film, no conclusion is ever reached regarding the question of which ideology is more *right*. This is hardly surprising, since one of the characteristics of a rich and thought-provoking film is that it raises important questions without imposing definitive answers. Viewers are left to fend for themselves and consider the merit of each position.

King's conviction that people are basically good and fair-minded and that, in the end, they will prove themselves as such contrasts sharply with that of Malcolm X, who holds the issue of race up to the oppressors' faces like a mirror, forcing them to gaze in. He places the burden of proof directly on the shoulders of white society to reflect a sense of justice and decency. As X says:

> First of all, the white man must finally realize that he's the one who has committed the crimes that have produced the miserable condition that our people are in. He can't hide this guilt by reviling us today because we answer his criminal acts—past and present—with extreme and uncompromising resentment. He cannot hide his guilt by accusing us, his victims, of being racists, extremists and black supremacists. The white man must realize that the sins of the fathers are about to be visited upon the heads of the children who have continued those sins, only in more sophisticated ways.[7]

The views of both men presented here can be found in *Do the Right Thing*. For example, when Buggin' Out tries to recruit Mookie's (Spike Lee) sister Jade (Joie Lee) to boycott Sal's because of the pizzeria owner's refusal to hang pictures of famous African Americans on his "Wall of Fame," she responds, "Yeah, I'm down, but I'm down for doing something positive in the community, are you down for that?" Buggin' Out argues that Sal is obliged to meet his request on the grounds that it is primarily "black folk" who patronize his restaurant and therefore support his financial survival in a predominantly black community. Furthermore, by refusing, Sal exposes himself to be a racist, from Buggin' Out's point of view. Since African Americans constitute the majority of Sal's business, they are entitled to certain *rights*. Therefore, Sal has an obligation to honor and respect those rights, and by refusing, he shows his true colors, so to speak. But does Sal have such an obligation? Should Sal include his black patrons' heroes as part of the restaurant's decor because their money supports the business? Sal argues that it is, after all, *his* restaurant, so *he* decides what goes on the walls. And he tells Buggin' Out that when he owns his *own* restaurant he can hang whatever pictures he chooses. Of course, there is a ring of irony in Sal's statement, since the prospects of Buggin' Out ever owning such a business are not favorable. The question of whether a white man *ought* to own a business in a black neighborhood arises again when Sal's son Pino begs his father to consider relocating the pizzeria to their "own neighborhood." But Sal defends the respectability not only of the business but also of those who patronize it. He stands firm in his conviction that he does belong there, and he is proud to have watched the neighborhood children grow up on his food. Even when the white police officers inquire "how long" he plans to stay, Sal concludes that he has been there for twenty years and is not going anyplace.

The question of *rights* and *obligations* is presented in other scenes as well. One such scene is when Clifton (John Savage) accidentally rides his bicycle over Buggin' Out's "bran-new Jord-ens," leaving a small but detectable smudge on the toe. Buggin' Out hurries after the culprit, demanding retribution, as Clifton attempts to enter his house. Although the dialogue that follows between Clifton and Buggin' Out seems comical and lighthearted enough (with a group of black teens chanting "beat 'em up" and "take his bike" in the background), the argument becomes not about shoes but about the right of a white man to live in a black neighborhood. Clifton says, "I own this brownstone," to which Buggin' Out retorts, "Who said you could live on my side of the street? Mother fuck gentrification! Why do you want to live in a black neighborhood anyway?" Clifton responds, "As I understand it this is a free country and a man can live wherever he wants." But *should* he? Clifton may have a *legal* right to live wherever he desires, but Buggin' Out questions his *moral* right to do so.

According to King's scheme of things, Buggin' Out's objection runs counter to the goal of unification—living together in integrated, color-blind harmony. But in the Malcolm X worldview, Buggin' Out's words are a declaration of independence. They are a challenge to a white man's presumption of innocence, to his assumption that, having committed no wrongs, he can live where he wants. Clifton chooses to live in the neighborhood, and King might appreciate his residency decision as a kind of declaration of color-blind morality. The difference between the two views is King's concept of "integration" versus X's view of "segregation." As X puts it:

> But if he [the white man] doesn't want a mass movement of our people away from this house of bondage, then he should separate this country. He should give us several states here on American soil, where those of us who wish to can go and set up our own government, our own economic system, our own civilization. Since we have given over 300 years of our slave labor to the white man's America, helped to build it up for him, it's only right that white America should give us everything we need in finance and materials for the next 25 years, until our own nation is able to stand on its feet. . . . Wasn't it impractical that the Supreme Court could issue a desegregation order nine years ago and there's still only eight percent compliance? Is it practical that a hundred years after the Civil War there's not freedom for black men yet? On the record for integration you've got the President, the Congress, the Supreme Court—but show me your integration, where is it? That's practical? Mr. Muhammad teaches us to be for what's really practical—that's separation. It's more natural than integration.[8]

Thus X might question the legitimacy of a white home owner in a black neighborhood, given his doctrine of "separate but superior." Indeed, Buggin' Out views Clifton's presence as both bizarre and disrespectful to the African Americans who own so little of this "free country" of which Clifton speaks so patriotically. After all, one major reason the whites own so much and the blacks so little is slavery and its after-effects, such as legal segregation, lynching, housing covenants, unequal educational opportunities, and the like. The game of capitalism has been and continues to be fixed in white people's favor.

Racism, Prejudice, and Discrimination Are More than Skin Deep

Common to the views of both X and King is the fundamental issue of respect. We observe in the film various racial and ethnic power groups, such as black teens, Latino teens, white police officers, Korean grocery store owners, and so on. At one point each raps a barrage of racial epithets in a serial monologue targeting another group, exposing the racism and prejudice in every ethnic subculture. Lee calls this the "Racial Slur Montage" in the script, and it consists of "a quick-cutting montage of racial slurs, with different ethnic groups pointing the finger at one another. Each person looks directly into the camera." For example:

> MOOKIE: Dago, wop, garlic-breath, guinea, pizza-slinging, spaghetti-bending, Vic Damone, Perry Como, Luciano Pavarotti, Sole Mio, non-singing motherfucker.
>
> PINO: You gold-teeth, gold-chain-wearing, fried-chicken-and-biscuit-eatin', monkey, ape, baboon, big thigh, fast-running, three-hundred-sixty-degree-basketball-dunking spade Moulan Yan.
>
> STEVIE (Luis Ramos): You slant-eyed, me-no-speak-American, own every fruit and vegetable stand in New York, Reverend Moon, Summer Olympics '88, Korean kick-boxing bastard.
>
> OFFICER LONG (Rick Aiello): Goya bean-eating, fifteen in a car, thirty in an apartment, pointed shoes, red-wearing, Menudo, meda-meda Puerto Rican cocksucker.
>
> KOREAN CLERK SUNNY (Steve Park): It's cheap, I got a good price for you, Mayor Koch, "How I'm doing," chocolate-egg-cream-drinking, bagel and lox, B'nai B'rith asshole.

This scene is absolutely essential because it suggests that racism, stereotyping, and prejudice are deeply rooted in human beings of all races, cultures, and ethnicities, including those that are minorities themselves.[9] It suggests that the treatment of blacks by whites is a subset of a much bigger problem—the problem of a common lack of *respect* and cooperation driven by some deep-seated "tribalism."

Needless to say, this recognition is not intended to let whites off the hook but to illustrate the scope of the problem. The universality of prejudice and discrimination is also meant to make us reflect on the exclusivist Black Nationalism of X versus the more inclusive liberal approach of King, whose goal is to unify the oppressed of all races, ethnicities, and religions against all the oppressors, whoever they might be. From King's perspective, X is playing into the hands of powerful oppressors of all stripes. Social justice and true equality require a universal Christ-like value of tolerance and respect applied to everyone equally. King realizes early on that we either stand together or hang alone, and that divide and conquer is the most potent and insidious strategy in the arsenal of the power brokers. It is worth mentioning here that at the end of the film, after setting Sal's place on fire, the mob led by M.L. (Paul Benjamin) heads for the Korean market, with M.L. exclaiming, "It's your turn now, sucka!" The owner Sunny tries to fight them off with a broom while screaming, "I no white! I black! You . . . me . . . same! We same!" trying to convince the mob that he is one of them. Coconut Sid (Frankie Faison) says to M.L., "Leave the Korean alone! He's alright!" and the mob eventually begins to disperse, sparing his store.

This perceived lack of respect eventually leads to violence at the end of the film when Radio Raheem incites a confrontation with Sal by refusing to lower the volume on his radio in the restaurant, and Sal in turn refuses to serve him until he complies. An offended Radio Raheem later joins forces with an offended Buggin' Out to challenge Sal on general principles. All three feel disrespected, ultimately precipitating the hostile and deadly sequence of events when Radio Raheem and Buggin' Out return to the pizzeria to confront Sal. It is hot, it is late, the radio is loud, and Sal's patience has worn thin. He becomes enraged, wielding racial epithets: "You Nigger son of a bitch!" With bat in hand, he proceeds to smash the radio to smithereens. Sal, who had never used such dehumanizing phrases before, crosses the line into racism in the eyes of his patrons, who are observing events from the sidelines. Radio Raheem attacks Sal, choking him, in retaliation for Sal's attack on his black identity and dignity and for destroying his prized material possession. Soon Sal and his sons, Radio Raheem, and Buggin' Out are a ball of flailing limbs. As the fight spills out onto the sidewalk, a crowd gathers, the police eventually arrive, and Radio Raheem is choked to death by an officer.

As James Cone points out, one thing unifying X and King is that "'respect as human beings' was the central theme of both . . . in the black freedom struggle."[10] In the beginning, X thought the best route to respect was Black Nationalism, and King thought it was being a good American and a good Christian first and an African American second. Interestingly, on this matter, they both moved toward each other in the end. Again, the essential and counterintuitive irony here is that every ethnic group and all individuals within those groups crave respect, yet they all frequently withhold it from other groups they have labeled as the Other.

Who Is Responsible for the Death of Radio Raheem?

Is Sal responsible, and does he prove himself to be a racist after all by yelling epithets at Radio Raheem and Buggin' Out? Does it matter that Buggin' Out calls Sal a "guinea" first? In considering the question of whether Sal is a racist, it is critical to consider what kind of evidence counts toward labeling one a racist and how to define the term. Of course, being a racist is not an all-or-nothing situation, so Sal may be a racist to some degree and in certain respects but not in others. Sal is certainly not a card-carrying white supremacist, but he does subscribe to many stereotypes and is often insensitive to the plight of blacks, let alone the history of their persecution. Some of Sal's attitudes about African Americans are likely due to his own enculturation in the Italian American subculture, which is not meant to excuse but rather to explain his behavior; consider, for example, Pino's preceding rant. However, Sal sometimes appears to express real affection and concern for many of the African Americans in the neighborhood, even over the racist objections of Pino. Sal even says of Mookie, "He's like a son to me," and he is forgiving of Mookie's laissez-faire attitude toward deliveries and his inconsistent work ethic. Sal's pizzeria would have been closed on that fateful night when Buggin' Out and Radio Raheem arrived if he had not unlocked it after hours to feed a few neighborhood kids.

Furthermore, Sal's racial slurs are uttered after he is pushed to his emotional limit. They are arguably more reflective of his building anger and frustration toward Radio Raheem than his considered views about black people. No doubt there are racist dispositions latent in all of us that might manifest under the right circumstances. So we might say that if Sal had controlled himself and reacted better, the chain of events leading to Radio Raheem's death may not have been set in motion. However, it is clear that Sal did not intend any such harm and was horrified by Radio Raheem's death and the subsequent riot.

Are Radio Raheem and Buggin' Out themselves to blame? It is hard to ignore the fact that Radio Raheem was choking Sal and was eventually choked to death himself. Although Radio Raheem's violent reaction and Buggin' Out's persistence certainly contributed to developments that eventually resulted in the former's death, it is a mistake to conclude that either brought it on themselves. Clearly, Radio Raheem did not deserve such a fate. These two had also been driven beyond their emotional limits and were reacting not to a single event but to an ongoing pattern of disrespect and systematic abuse by the culture at large.

Are the police responsible for Radio Raheem's death? Recall that the officers involved in the incident are Long and Ponte (Miguel Sandoval), the same cops we encounter earlier in the film who show little respect or affection for the African Americans and Latinos in the neighborhood. Again, whether the officers are out-and-out racists is a tricky question, but they certainly manifest racist and prejudicial attitudes and behaviors. It is pretty clear, however, that they did not intend to kill Radio Raheem, because after he goes limp, they kick him and tell him to quit faking. Once they realize what they have done, they grab the body and quickly leave the scene—a black cop running alongside their squad car—exposing Sal and his sons to the anger of the crowd. However, in another example of art imitating life, the cops in the film use a choke hold on Radio Raheem that was later outlawed in the real world after several unnecessary deaths. Certainly, these "killer cops" were the *efficient cause* of Radio Raheem's death, but the film asks us to look to the deeper social and economic structural causes of their behavior.

So, who killed Radio Raheem? Although everyone discussed had a hand in it, the deepest answer is that Radio Raheem was killed by the culture of racism, violence, and materialism that is the ever-present flip side and constant shadow of the American dream.

Does Mookie or Anyone Else Do the Right Thing?

After the cops speed away, the enraged crowd, in search of catharsis, looks menacingly at Sal and his sons, at which point Da Mayor (Ossie Davis) steps forth to try to persuade them to "go home before anyone else gets hurt." The crowd calls Da Mayor an "Uncle," and indeed, we wonder throughout the film whether he is an "Uncle Tom" or just a good-hearted soul who ascribes to nonviolence and is doing what he thinks is right. We are also left to wonder, more generally, where the line between cowardice and principled nonviolence should be drawn. Da Mayor fails to subdue the mob, and Mookie hurls a trash can through the front window of the pizzeria while screaming "Hate"—doing to Sal's property what Sal did to Radio Raheem's boom box.

After Da Mayor sweeps Sal and his sons away to safety at his place, the crowd descends, stealing and destroying until finally the pizzeria is set ablaze. Sal's business becomes both symbolic of racial injustice and the vehicle through which the neighborhood vents its frustration and grief, rather than attacking Sal and his sons themselves. The last image in the scene is that of Smiley tacking up his photograph of King and X on the now ash-soiled "Wall of Fame," once again begging the central question of the film.

Does Mookie represent either X or King when, perhaps with forethought and calculation, he hurls the trash can through the pizzeria window, perhaps to draw the crowd's violent attention away from seeking revenge on Sal and his sons in a literal eye-for-an-eye retribution? Maybe Mookie represents neither King nor X but some middle ground, or maybe he represents black rage. No doubt, all these suggestions are too reductive in the end. Mookie is a well-developed and complex character of flesh and blood, not merely a vehicle for some ideological perspective or trope. However, the film's title certainly begs the question: has Mookie or anybody else done the right thing?

The film leaves this question open for the audience to contemplate. In terms of Mookie, perhaps the answer depends on whether he committed the act in anger to incite a riot or whether it was a calculated attempt to deflect the mob's anger away from Sal and his sons and toward the pizzeria—destruction of property over destruction of people. Either way, we need a conception of the kind of thing Mookie has done. His friend has just been killed by the police, and his employer Sal is implicated because of the circumstances. One question we might ask is whether Mookie's action is that of someone who has lost control, the way Sal did, or the action of someone who has carefully considered the situation before acting, in the hope of saving Sal and his sons? Regardless of Mookie's motive, his accomplishment is twofold. First, he diverts the crowd's violent attention away from Sal and his sons and onto the restaurant, leaving them unscathed. Second, Mookie exhibits solidarity with the rightfully enraged residents by initiating the riot on behalf of his dead friend. Regardless of Mookie's intentions, his action likely prevents the loss of more lives.

Spike Lee is on record as saying, "White people still ask me why Mookie threw the can through the window. Twenty years later, they're still asking me that. No black person ever, in 20 years, no person of color has ever asked me why." Lee says that Mookie is simply angry at the death of Radio Raheem and that questioning the riot's justification is implicitly valuing white-owned property over the life of a black man.[11] Of course, Lee is right that Mookie is acting out of anger, and his anger is more than justified. However, *why* Mookie does it and whether it is the *right* thing to do are separable questions in principle. Given the title of the film, one assumes that Lee does not want to dismiss the latter question. Again, these questions are related because the question of Mookie's motives bears on the question of rightness. How we evaluate Mookie's actions may turn, in part, on whether, in addition to being angry, he means to save Sal and his sons or whether he means to incite a riot that might lead to more than property damage.

Perhaps Lee is claiming that Mookie does not *intend* anything, he is merely expressing his justified rage. Maybe part of Lee's point is that, philosophical hand-wringing aside, if you treat people in a certain way, rage is going to be the default response, for better or for worse. That is factually correct, but after all, Lee's film is asking us to look beyond our rage and pain to try to figure out what is right and what might actually help defeat social injustices such as racism, prejudice, and discrimination. Maybe Mookie splits the difference between X and King by saving lives at the expense of property. This is likely too simple an explanation, but it is a hopeful thought.

Can King and X Be Reconciled?

Lee is clear that he never intended *Do the Right Thing* to force a choice between the views of X and King; rather, we should hope for some sort of synthesis or unity. As it turns out, a reconciliation of sorts was under way toward the end of their lives. Although X did not reject the possibility of violence and the need for self-defense, he did move closer to the views of King on a number of fronts after he left the Nation of Islam. He was willing to work with civil rights leaders but wanted to expand the movement to human rights and make it about downtrodden people of color all over the world. In a famous letter from Mecca, he wrote that his pilgrimage forced him to "rearrange" his thinking about race and "toss aside some of [his] previous conclusions." More specifically, after his hajj, X articulated a view of white people and racism that represented a significant change from his views as a minister of the Nation of Islam. Most important, he dropped his segregationist stance and became more open to working with white radicals and reformers. This was quite a change from his thinking about the descendants of Europeans as "white devils."

King, in contrast, became more focused on race in some ways because of the situation of many poor blacks and white resistance to integration. For example, he said, "I am sorry to have to say to you that the vast majority of white Americans are racist, either consciously or unconsciously. . . . We live in a confused. . . . , sick, neurotic nation," and "the judgment of God is on America now."[12] Toward the end of his life King favored what he called "temporary segregation," so that blacks could empower themselves to integrate from a position of strength rather than weakness. It was the Black Power movement driven by the conditions of inner-city blacks and the lack of support among most whites for sweeping integration that led him to this view. King was especially troubled by the Watts riot in 1965 because it made him realize that civil rights and voting rights do not necessarily change the socioeconomic conditions for blacks and that violence is an inevitable consequence of ghettoization or "internal colonialism." King learned that talk of turning the other cheek was not going to be effective here; many in Watts spoke of having "won," even though it was a Pyrrhic victory at best. He was also distraught by whites' law-and-order reaction to the riots, mostly driven by fear, anger, and paranoia. In short, King learned that economic and class concerns are even deeper than racial ones.

King also became profoundly disillusioned about the inherent goodwill of white people because of the Vietnam War. On April 4, 1967, King delivered a speech called "Beyond Vietnam" in which he accused the U.S. government of colonialism and called it "the greatest purveyor of violence in the world today." He also touched on issues beyond racism, such as the global inequality of wealth. He summed up by saying, "A nation that continues year after year to spend more money on military defense than on programs of social uplift is approaching spiritual death." That same year he gave another speech in which he decried the "cruel irony" of American blacks fighting and dying for a country that treats them as second-class citizens.

King's message became more and more focused on class issues and the distribution of wealth both at home and abroad. In 1968 King and the Southern Christian Leadership Conference organized the "Poor People's Campaign," which focused on issues of economic justice. It culminated in a march on Washington, D.C., demanding economic aid for the poorest communities of the United States. King also traveled the country to assemble a multiracial army of the poor that would march on Washington to engage in nonviolent civil disobedience at the Capitol until Congress created a bill of rights for poor Americans.

Although he never gave up on nonviolence, in all this we can see that King moved toward X's view in several respects. By the 1960s he moved away from the conception of white people as basically good, lashing out at both white southerners and northern liberals, the latter of whom he came to regard more and more as hypocrites. His increasing pessimism was again motivated by American colonialism in general, the Vietnam War in particular, and his growing sense that economic injustice is a deeper truth than racial injustice. He was frustrated at the inability of poor white southerners to see that they had more in common with blacks than with wealthy whites. Even early on, however, King cited Reinhold Niebuhr's "Christian realism" as an important approach to understanding human nature (*simul justis et peccator,* as Luther put it). At the very least, this implies that whatever his utopian influences, King thought the campaign for social justice should be based on a clear-headed assessment of facts about God, human beings, and the world. Toward the end of his life, King was often accused of sounding like a "nonviolent Malcolm."

Whatever realism King and X eventually shared about human nature and the sorry state of social justice in the present, they also shared a "theology of hope," which is to say a certain kind of divinely inspired telos about where the future is headed. A theology of hope holds that God's promise to act in the future is more important than the fact that he has acted in the past, and eventually all will be redeemed in the end. However, this focus on the future does not imply that one should withdraw from the world now because a better world is in the bag; rather, one must aid in the coming of that better world. For X, at least in the beginning, this theology of hope had a decidedly eschatological bent, as he thought white America was headed toward a likely doomsday judgment by Allah. And King was initially convinced that hope and love would ultimately win over fear and hatred: "Because the arc of the moral universe is long but it bends toward justice. How long? Not long! Because mine eyes have seen the glory of the coming of the Lord."[13] As we have seen, however, as time went on, King became more pessimistic about human nature and the immediate future, sounding more like an Old Testament prophet of doom. Malcolm X, though he never embraced nonviolence as such, became more optimistic and trusting of whites, focusing more on Black Nationalism than on the Black Muslim movement.

Thus, the ideologies of X and King appeared to be approaching a convergence near the end of their respective lives. Two later quotes from the two men bespeak the possibility of reconciliation. Malcolm X stated:

> Although I'm still a Muslim, I'm not here tonight to discuss my religion. I'm not here to try to change your religion. I'm not here to argue or discuss anything that we differ about, because it's time for us to submerge our differences and realize that it is best for us to first see that we have the same problem, a common problem. . . . Whether we are Christians or Muslims or nationalists or agnostics or atheists, we must first learn to forget our differences, let us differ in the closet; when we come out in front, let us not have anything to argue about.[14]

And King stated:

> There is a concrete, real black power that I believe in. I don't believe in black separatism, I don't believe in black power that would have racist overtones, but certainly if black power means the amassing of political and economic power in order to gain our just and legitimate goals, then we all believe in that. And I think that all white people of good will believe in that.[15]

Of all their convergences, perhaps the most important one for purposes of interpreting *Do the Right Thing* was their growing critique of the scourge of capitalism and the possibility of some sort of socialism as an alternative. King rejected unbridled capitalism and was a fan of Marx; however, he also rejected communism because of its "materialistic interpretation of history" that rejected religion and its "political totalitarianism." Although King did not want to be labeled a communist, for obvious reasons, he sometimes spoke in private of his support for democratic socialism. In one speech he stated, "Something is wrong with capitalism"; he observed, "There must be a better distribution of wealth, and maybe America must move toward a democratic socialism." Likewise, X made it clear that he thought socialism would be better for the black man. As he put it, "You show me a capitalist and I'll show you a bloodsucker."[16]

Both men were coming to see that racism was one symptom of a much deeper problem—namely, greed and economic injustice. The final moments of the film strongly suggest this as well. Following is the dialogue that ends the film, the day after the riot:

> [*Mookie walks up to Sal's Famous Pizzeria as it still smoulders in the morning light. Sal emerges from the wreckage; he looks like he might have slept there.*]
> SAL: Whatdafuck do you want?
> MOOKIE: I wants my money. I wants to get paid. [*Sal looks at Mookie in disbelief.*]
> SAL: Mookie, I always liked you. Not the smartest kid, but you're honest. Don't make me dislike you.
> MOOKIE: Sal, I want my money.
> SAL: Don't even ask about your money. Your money wouldn't even pay for that window you smashed.
> MOOKIE: Motherfuck a window, Radio Raheem is dead.
> SAL: You're right, a kid is dead, but Mook, this isn't the time.

MOOKIE: Fuck dat. The time is fuckin' now. Y'know I'm sorry 'bout Sal's Famous Pizzeria, but I gotta live, too. I gotta get paid.

SAL: We both do.

MOOKIE: We all know you're gonna get over with the insurance money anyway! Ya know da deal.

SAL: Do we now?

MOOKIE: Quit bullshitting.

SAL: You don't know shit about shit.

MOOKIE: I know I wants to get my money. [*Sal has had it.*]

SAL: How much? How much do I owe you?

MOOKIE: My salary. Two-fifty. [*Sal pulls out a wad and quickly peels off hundred dollar bills.*]

SAL: One, two, three, four, five. [*Sal throws the "C" notes at Mookie, they hit him in the chest and fall to the sidewalk.*] Are you happy now? That's five fucking hundred dollars. You just got paid. Mookie, you are a rich man, now ya life is set, you'll never have another worry, a care in the world. Mookie, ya wealthy, a fuckin' Rockefeller. [*Mookie is stunned by Sal's outburst. He picks up the bills.*] Ya just got paid, so leave me the fuck alone.

MOOKIE: You only pay me two-fifty a week. [*He throws two "C" notes back at him.*] I owe you fifty bucks.

SAL: Keep it.

MOOKIE: You keep it.

SAL: Christmas came early. [*Both look at the two hundred-dollar bills on the sidewalk and refuse to pick them up. It's a stalemate.*]

MOOKIE: This is the hottest Christmas I've known. [*Mookie counts his money.*]

SAL: It's supposed to be even hotter today.

MOOKIE: You gonna open up another Sal's Famous Pizzeria?

SAL: No. What are you gonna do?

MOOKIE: Make dat money. Get paid.

SAL: Yeah! . . . I'm goin' to the beach for the first day in fifteen years. Gonna take the day off and go to the beach.

This exchange between Sal and Mookie illustrates the possibility that racial and ethnic tensions are as much about wealth and its distribution as anything else. Along with other scenes in the film, it also illustrates that every ethnic group is infected by the virus of capitalism and becomes maniacally obsessed with the accumulation of wealth. Capitalism, once internalized by all, is a game that keeps the pawns at one another's throats while the kings and queens play for real money.

Curiously, the film concludes with Sal and Mookie tenuously making up. This reconciliation is crucial because it leaves the viewer with some sense of hope that people can, with some effort, get along with one another. As mentioned earlier, the last image we see is the photograph of King and Malcolm X shaking hands. The image both supports this hope and causes us to question its probability. The day after the riot, the neighborhood DJ, Mister Señor Love Daddy (Samuel L. Jackson), asks the only question that matters: "My people. My people. What can I say? Say what I can. I saw it but I didn't believe it. I didn't believe it what I saw. Are we gonna live together? Together are we gonna live? This is ya Mister Señor Love Daddy here on WE LOVE RADIO, 108 FM on your dial, and that's the truth, Ruth."

When thinking of King and X, it's important to remember that both were murdered—King by a white man, and X by his own people—and for all his talk, X never once used his fists, let alone a gun, when calling for "any means necessary." Señor Love Daddy's question, then, is not just for white and blacks or any other ethnic groups; it is for all humankind.

As for reconciliation, Cone's brilliant book has it right: "Martin's and Malcolm's movement toward each other is a clue that neither one can be fully understood or appreciated without serious attention to the other. They *complemented* and *corrected* each other; each spoke a truth about America that cannot be fully comprehended without the insights of the other. Indeed, if Americans of all races intend to create a just and peaceful future, then they must listen to both Martin and Malcolm."[17] Perhaps the greatest shared virtue of X and King, a virtue conspicuously absent today, was their willingness to die for the cause, to sacrifice themselves for something intangible and greater than their own lives. In their own words:

> Freedom is not free.
>
> If a man hasn't discovered something that he will die for, he isn't fit to live.
>
> If physical death is the price I must pay to free my white brothers and sisters from the permanent death of the spirit, then nothing could be more redemptive. (Martin Luther King Jr.)[18]

> The price of freedom is death.
>
> If you're not ready to die for it, put the word "freedom" out of your vocabulary.

It is a time for martyrs now, and if I am to be one, it will be for the cause of brotherhood. That's the only thing that can save this country. (Malcolm X)[19]

Notes

I would like to thank Elizabeth Newell, John Rohrkemper, Mike Long, and Mark Conard for their invaluable comments.

1. Quoted in Benjamin Schwartz, "What Jefferson Helps to Explain," *Atlantic Monthly,* March 1997, 61.

2. An absolute moral ethic advocates that certain moral principles be maintained no matter what the situation or context, whereas a situational ethic holds that what is morally right may change, depending on the situation or context.

3. According to natural law theory, the moral standards that govern human behavior are objectively derived from the nature of human beings and the world. Therefore, whether an action is good or not depends on whether it conforms to or abides by the relevant law. According to Aquinas for example, every law is ultimately derived from what he calls the *eternal law* (Thomas Aquinas, *St. Summa Theologiae,* trans. Fathers of the English Dominican Rovince [Westminster: Christian Classics, 1981], IaIIae 93.3, p. 20). The "eternal law" refers to God's providential ordering of all created things to their proper end. We participate in that divine order by virtue of the fact that God creates in us both a desire for and an ability to discern what is good (Aquinas calls this ability the "light of natural reason"). According to Aquinas, "it is this participation in the eternal law by the rational creature that is called the natural law" (ibid., 91.2; cf. 93.6). Thus, natural law is an extension of eternal law, for God implants within us both a general knowledge of and inclination for goodness. Notice that the natural law is not an external source of authority. Nor is it a general deontic norm from which more specific precepts are inferred (Ralph McInerny, "Ethics," in *The Cambridge Companion to Aquinas,* ed. Norman Kretzmann and Eleonore Stump [Cambridge: Cambridge University Press, 1993], 196–216; Thomas Hibbs, *Virtue's Splendor: Wisdom, Prudence, and the Human Good* [New York: Fordham University Press, 2001], 75). As Aquinas would have it, the natural law is a fundamental principle woven into the fabric of our nature.

4. Deontological moral theories judge the morality of an action based on the action's adherence to a rule or rules, such as rules pertaining to duties, rights, and justice.

5. Teleological moral theories judge the rightness of an action based on its consequences. The most well-known example is utilitarianism, which focuses on maximizing utility as a measure of consequences.

6. Just-war theory is a doctrine of military ethics originated by the Romans and Catholics and studied by theologians, ethicists, and international policy makers. It holds that a violent conflict can be justified if and only if it meets certain ethical, religious, and political criteria. Pacifism and other forms of nonviolence are typically construed as rejecting just-war theory.

7. 1963 *Playboy* interview with Alex Haley.

8. Ibid.

9. Mind you, there is no suggestion here that racism is a biological given.

10. James H. Cone, *Martin and Malcolm and America: A Dream or a Nightmare* (New York: Orbis Books, 1991), 247.

11. "Spike Lee's Last Word," special feature on the Criterion Collection DVD, 2000.

12. Quoted in Cone, *Martin and Malcolm,* 100.

13. Ibid.

14. Malcolm X, "The Ballot or the Bullet" speech delivered April 3, 1964, at Cory Methodist Church, Cleveland, Ohio.

15. Martin Luther King Jr., *The Autobiography of Martin Luther King, Jr.*, ed. Clayborne Carson (New York: Warner Books, 1998), 55.

16. Quoted in Cone, *Martin and Malcolm,* 175.

17. Ibid., 246.

18. Ibid., 150–55.

19. Ibid.

Fevered Desires and Interracial Intimacies in *Jungle Fever*

Ronald R. Sundstrom

Spike Lee's 1991 film *Jungle Fever* is one of several concerning American taboos against interracial intimacy and sex. The earliest film on the subject was D. W. Griffith's 1915 silent movie *The Birth of a Nation,* which condemns interracial sex or *miscegenation,* to use the term invented by opponents of black emancipation, as a threat to the nation. Every film on interracial intimacies since then has been a comment on Griffith's work, which also stands apart as a milestone of epic cinematography. Most of the subsequent films, such as Elia Kazan's 1949 film *Pinky* or Guy Green's 1965 film *A Patch of Blue,* deliver a contrasting antiracist message, but they focus on the tragedy of interracial romances and how social circumstances make them impossible. Stanley Kramer's 1967 film *Guess Who's Coming to Dinner* is notable for pushing this genre forward by featuring a relationship that is allowed to blossom, despite social opposition. Among these films and others, Lee's *Jungle Fever* stands out by questioning their optimistic trajectory (from hateful opposition to gleeful acceptance) and by giving equal time to African American opposition to interracial romance and sex. *Jungle Fever* puts the brakes on the chummy optimism of *Guess Who's Coming to Dinner* and turns up the volume on the black dissenting voices relegated to a supporting—and losing—role in these films. Moreover, Lee's films adds to this genre by portraying contemporary opposition to interracial intimacy in the context of other major American problems, such as sexism and domestic violence, residential segregation, police harassment and racial profiling, workplace discrimination, and notably the crack cocaine epidemic of the 1980s.

All the same, *Jungle Fever* has its shortcomings, such as Lee's pedantic style and, even more worrisome, Wesley Snipes's stiff acting and delivery as Flipper Purify.[1] *Jungle Fever*'s biggest flaw, however, is that it flinches in the face of honest and ordinary interracial intimacy. Lee does not shrink from dealing out painful criticisms of interracial sexual desire, nor does he duck the turmoil such relationships can ignite in families. He even provides a close-up of the lustful passions of an interracial affair. But, when confronted with the possibility of an interracial romance between a black woman and a white man marked by actual caring and love, Lee adopts a safely conservative tone that caters to the ambivalent attitudes of the black middle class his film gives voice to. Lee reverts to a desexualized romance—à la *Guess Who's Coming to Dinner.* Just as Kramer would not risk demonstrating passionate sexuality between a black man and a white woman on-screen, Lee similarly flinched in his film.

You Give Me Fever

The taboo against interracial romance and sex portrayed in Lee's drama is derived from the history of race in the West in general and in America in particular and from the role of sex in that history.[2] He covers two interrelated versions of this taboo. First is the taboo among white Americans against a wide variety of intimacies with blacks. Interracial romance, sex, and marriage were judged particularly despicable, and the general prohibition against lesser interracial intimacies, such as friendship, was a prophylactic measure against the greater "sin" of miscegenation. Second is the taboo among blacks against interracial romance and sex, especially with whites—a protective and prideful reaction against the first taboo.

More will be said about the second taboo later, but first let us review the basic elements of the taboo against white intimacy with blacks. The idea of race, as it developed in the West, involved the opinion that there were distinct groups of humanity separated by biology, culture, or God and that these groups were somehow meant to retain their distinctiveness by staying separate. Thus, defenders of segregation in the United States claimed that this was why God put innumerable barriers between them. According to Leon Bazile, the trial judge who convicted Mildred Jeter and Richard Loving of breaking Virginia law by marrying across the color line, the fact that God "separated the races shows that he did not intend for the races to mix."[3]

The individuals and groups who believed this also believed that, to ensure the health and well-being of the nation (as well as Western civilization), it was imperative that whites maintain their supremacy over the nation and their ethnic and racial purity. For example, in the years following the Civil War and the emancipation of blacks, the Alabama Supreme Court ruled in *Green v. The State* that the well-being and very existence of society depend on preventing racial mingling:

> It is through the marriage relation that the homes of a people are created—those homes in which, ordinarily, all the members of all the families of the land are, during a part of every day, assembled together; where the elders of the household seek repose and cheer, and reparation of strength from the toils and cares of life; and where, in an affectionate intercourse and conversation with them, the young become imbued with the principles, and animated by the spirit and ideas, which in a great degree give shape to their characters and determine the manner of their future lives. These homes, in which the virtues are most cultivated and happiness most abounds, are the true *officinae gentium*—the nurseries of States.[4]

This view, that interracial sex and marriage are a threat to the nation and civilization, is captured in the very word *miscegenation*. It is an American neologism that speaks volumes about race in the United States; the supporters of the Confederacy and opponents of emancipation in the United States invented it to negatively denote interracial sex. The word is derived from the Latin terms *miscere* ("to mix") and *genus* (as in the taxonomic category that ranks above species). Thus, for the opponents of interracial intimacy, sex between the races is as disordered as sex between different species—in fact, it may be worse because interracial sex involves mating between different genera. To add to the horrors of interracial sex, the mixed-race children "spawned" are monstrous and tragic. *Miscegenation,* then, delivers a theological, biological, and political threat in a clinical style.

The dark side of this taboo is inseparable from the evils of Jim Crow segregation, and the fear of black male sexuality as aggressive and bestial and the prurient judgments of black female animalistic promiscuity served as ideological justification for de jure segregation in housing, education, public transportation, business, and so on. Indeed, the terror of interracial sex was used to justify the lynching of thousands of black men by white mobs and the indiscriminate sexual violence and harassment directed at black women during the darkest days of Jim Crow.[5]

The stubborn legacy of this taboo and the evils it engendered serve as a starting point for *Jungle Fever.* The film begins with a dedication to Yusef K. Hawkins, a sixteen-year-old boy who was murdered by a white mob in Bensonhurst in 1989. Hawkins was in the neighborhood shopping for a used car when he was beaten with baseball bats and shot to death by local boys who were hunting for black or Latino boys they suspected of dating an Italian American girl.[6] This murderous attitude, full of vitriol and revulsion, is displayed in the film by the New York police officers who confront

Flipper and Angie Tucci (Annabelle Sciorra), in the anger of Angie's father Mike (Frank Vincent), and in the attitudes of the Italian American men who populate Paulie Carbone's (John Turturro) store.

At the heart of this taboo is the view that interracial intimacy—or "jungle fever"—is hardly a form of intimacy at all. Intimacy involves gentle and refined passions. Jungle fever, in contrast, is a diseased sexual passion. Like all bodily fevers, it is characterized by an abnormally high body temperature, delirium, and nervous excitement, but in this case, it is caused by sexual desire for the forbidden fruit of the racial Other. It is a "tropical" disease—hot, steamy, and of foreign, equatorial origin.

That description of jungle fever brings to mind the words of the song "Fever," popularized by Little Willie John and later by Peggy Lee:

> Never know how much I love you
> Never know how much I care
> When you put your arms around me
> I get a fever that's so hard to bear.[7]

The infectiousness of the original rhythm and blues song, which reached the impressionable ears of white youth through radio waves, was strong enough. Peggy Lee, however, added to its force when she, as a white woman, released her own sultry version, with added lyrics about the interracial romance between Captain Smith and Pocahontas.

Another aspect of the taboo is that jungle fever distorts the normal ordering of family, society, culture, and politics. Again, as observed in *Green v. The State,* interracial intimacy interferes with the *officinae gentium,* the nurseries of the state—namely, the white families that are the basis for other social institutions. For the segregationists and those invested in white racial supremacy, miscegenation is "hard to bear," as the song says. Of course, what is hard to bear for a racial supremacist is very different from the mad passions Little Willie John and Peggy Lee sang about. For the racial supremacist, jungle fever is not just a momentary indiscretion, not merely a one-night stand. It assaults the family and, from there, the whole structure of society.

As we reflect on these taboos and Lee's cinematic rendering of them, it is important to keep in mind, especially at the beginning of the twenty-first century, that although Americans have inherited the elements of this complex history, there has also been a significant change in attitude toward all forms of interracial intimacy. Americans generally believe that individuals have a high degree of autonomy over their intimate lives, and an increasing number of Americans, especially the youth (91 percent), approve of interracial intimacy. Yet taboos and informal family prohibitions against interracial intimacy remain: 77 percent of Americans report they do not have an immediate family member or close relative of a different race, and some 97 percent of marriages are monoracial.[8] American families and patterns of intimacy are changing and becoming more interracial, but old anxieties and fears persist.

Jungle Fever returns us to a time of anxiety and fear. Angie Tucci is Italian American and Flipper Purify is African American, and they meet at a firm beset by racial conflict and discrimination, where she works as a temporary secretary and he works as an architect. The friends and families of the couple are outraged over their relationship. On one side of the city are the families of Bensonhurst, a tough neighborhood in Brooklyn, and on the other side are the families of the Harlem neighborhood in Manhattan. Divided by ethnicity, race, and class, they are united in their turmoil over Flipper and Angie's affair and the havoc it unleashes in their lives.

Purity

The intimacy that jungle fever interrupts and damages is the marriage of Drew (Lonette McKee) and Flipper. Their family name, Purify, is richly suggestive, and with it, Lee offers a pun about the aspirations, pretensions, and frustrations of that family. Drew and Flipper seemingly have a great relationship, and they enjoy all the trappings of black, upwardly mobile young professionals, or "buppies"—the black version of yuppies. This family is more than upwardly mobile; with their brownstone home in Harlem, subscription to the *New York Times*, degrees from respected historically black universities, and professional careers, they belong to the black elite. Their status, however, is threatened by a number of negative social ills, and Flipper's infidelity is yet another assault on the integrity of this family.

In *The Birth of a Nation*, interracial intimacy, and especially sex, is presented as a threat to the United States as a white, civilized nation. In *Guess Who's Coming to Dinner*, interracial intimacy is modern, progressive, and characteristic of a new, optimistic nation that has benefited from the corrections of the civil rights movement. In contrast to both those films, *Jungle Fever* represents interracial intimacy as a threat to the stability and status of the black middle-class family. Although the black parents in *Guess Who's Coming to Dinner* are not happy with their son's surprise announcement that he is affianced to a white woman, they slowly recognize the authenticity of the young couple's love and offer their blessings. Flipper's parents do not go down so easily.

The Good Reverend Doctor Purify (Ossie Davis) and his wife Lucinda (Ruby Dee) are concerned with purity—expressly the sexual sort. With Mahalia Jackson's gospel music playing softly in the background, the Good Reverend Doctor announces his general worldview with his reading of 1 Corinthians 7:1–2, that it is good for "a man not to touch a woman," but to avoid "fornication," each man ought to be married to a woman.

For Reverend and Mrs. Purify, Flipper's wrong is not just fornication but fornication across racial lines, and it repeats a pattern of distorted racial-sexual relationships rooted in white supremacy. According to the Good Reverend Doctor, Flipper and Angie's tryst has a negative historical resonance; their fevered desire is due to racial, gender, and sexual ideals produced by the ideology of white supremacy and formed during the period of slavery and Jim Crow segregation. Roughly, these ideals impart an elevated and idealized status to white women (of the right class, of course), allow white men access to illicit and exploitative sex with black women, and deny black men access to white women. Thus, the Good Reverend Doctor reduces their relationship to this distorted pattern; he accuses Angie of "black adultery" and his son of being a "whoremonger" and "fishing in the white man's cesspool."

Of course, all is not well with the Good Reverend Doctor's self-righteousness purity. He is a preacher rejected by his congregation, and he has his own cesspools to deal with. Spike Lee is lampooning the figure of the African American preacher with the exaggerated portrayal of the Good Reverend Doctor, but he also makes him one of the mouthpieces—along with the so-called War Council and a waitress (Queen Latifah)—of one strain of African American opinion about jungle fever that perceives it as another threat to black family and community.

The Good Reverend Doctor's rebuke of Flipper is completed by the criticisms articulated by the women in the excellent War Council scene. It is tempting to see that council as offering a homogeneous condemnation of sexually straying black men, but that is not true. Some of the women enthusiastically support interracial romance and the broader benefits and opportunities it can offer black women. Other voices defend the principle of sexual autonomy for individuals, including black men and women, permitting them to date anyone they please whenever they please. This council reflects the heteronomy of African American communities on interracial intimacy. Despite the general anxiety and skepticism toward jungle fever in this film, the diverse voices of the council demonstrate that there is no clear consensus on this matter.[9]

That said, the War Council suspects that fever and distortion are at the heart of the trouble with Flipper. Their objections, however, are not driven by typical racist motives of inferiorization or antipathy. The women of the War Council do not express ill will toward whites in general; instead, their objections are informed by popular standards of black solidarity and roughly correspond to the themes of valuing black women, loyalty, and self-respect.[10] First, in a society that devalues African Americans in general and black looks in particular, loving and marrying black expresses care and respect for other blacks. When black men choose to love black women, they repudiate the devaluation of black looks and affirm the value of black women and black feminine beauty. Second, when black men choose white women, they appear to be acting opportunistically. Such men are engaged in racial-social climbing and are willing to cut ties with their families or communities for the sake of expedience. Third, when good black men marry black women, they demonstrate not only care for and loyalty to black women but also a healthy self-respect for themselves as black persons, because the standards that devalue black beauty derive from the general devaluation of blackness. By choosing to love black women, black men effectively demonstrate that they are comfortable with their identities and their communities. They exhibit healthy signs of pride despite living in a society that gives them every reason not to. In contrast, when black men—or, for that matter, black women—engage in interracial intimacy, they may be in the grips of self-hatred or self-loathing about their racial identity. Thus, for some African Americans, interracial intimacy, especially romance, is an outward display of a racial pathology.[11] Interracial love, according to this view, is pathological because it is the result of a "color" complex or, rather, an "inferiority" complex about skin color. White love for black, according to this view, is an expression of sexual adventurism and domination—an intimate version of colonialism. Black love for white is an attempt to escape blackness—the result of internalized racism. These three objections are closely interrelated and reflect the Good Reverend Doctor's stinging rebuke of Flipper.

A fourth objection is offered by Flipper, inspired by his anguish over how his affair has affected his family. He claims that interracial romances are confused and produce confused mixed-race children who are necessarily caught up with color complexes. Both Flipper and Drew see Drew's own multiracial status (her father is white) and Flipper's initial attraction to her, as a light-skinned woman, in this light; a color complex exists right below the surface of their healthy relationship, and Flipper worries that this complex will infect his daughter. The confrontation between Flipper and Vivien (Halle Berry), a light-skinned crack whore, dramatizes this fear. She calls him "Daddy" and offers to perform oral sex on him for a couple of dollars, an absurdly small amount of money. Although "Daddy" is a common sexually flirtatious name, in this context, its incestuous connotations are accentuated. For Flipper, the crack whore is an incarnation of the distorting forces of the fevers brought on by the color complex and the crack cocaine epidemic, both of which threaten his daughter.

Duty

The interracial intimacy between Angie and Flipper also disrupts Angie's home, which ignites and reveals further troubles within her network of friends and associates. In contrast to Flipper and Drew's world, Angie's is a working-class Italian American neighborhood. Searching for relief from that world, and needing to earn a living, Angie seeks employment in a Manhattan architecture firm.

Angie's existence in Bensonhurst is bound by the demands of her home life. Since her mother's death, she has inherited the duty of caring for the household, her father, and her two quarrelsome brothers. In addition to these ties, she has a relationship with Paulie Carbone, who runs a combination malt, candy, and newspaper store for his demanding and dependent father Lou (Anthony Quinn). Paulie's mother, like Angie's, is deceased, and the demands of their widowed fathers and the limited horizons of the neighborhood weigh them both down. They seek something bigger than their restricted lives in Bensonhurst, and as it turns out, their search for that something bigger inexorably tears them apart.

The men that populate Angie's and Paulie's lives are argumentative, explicitly bigoted, and unstable. The guys who while away their time in Paulie's store read the tabloid *New York Post* instead of the *New York Times.* They are scornful about blacks and are willfully ignorant of individuality among African Americans. For them, any individual black man is no better than the worst among them; Mayor David Dinkins of New York is no different from the notorious Mayor Marion Berry of Washington, D.C., or the "Central Park Five," the five black teenagers who were wrongly accused of beating and raping a female jogger.[12] Their antipathy toward blacks; the abruptness with which they turn on one another, screaming and punching; and the particular disdain they have for Italian American girls who date white Anglo-Saxon Protestants (WASPs) and, worse, blacks evoke the kind of paroxysm of violence that claimed Yusef Hawkins's life.

Regardless of their explicit prejudices, the lives of these guys are intertwined with African Americans. A central character in Paulie's store is Vinny (Nicholas Turturro), and he shows up blaring rap music from his car, wearing a jumpsuit and a gold chain, and sporting a high-and-tight haircut that evokes a high-top-fade—in another setting, he might pass as black. He and the other guys in the shop declare they would like to have sex with—but would never publicly date—the black woman Orin Goode (Tyra Ferrell), who lives in the neighborhood and stops by on weekdays to buy a paper. To top it off, his music of choice is Public Enemy's album *Fear of a Black Planet.* He seems completely unaware of the irony of enjoying the message and music of that album while expressing the racism it condemns. His contradictions are outrageous, but they are also indicative of America's ambivalence toward its interracial culture.[13]

What is more, Vinny's attitude toward Orin is not that far from his attitude toward all women and his treatment of his girlfriend. He and the guys have a double image of the women among them. Although they revere their dead mothers, they make use of the flesh-and-blood women around them and regard them with a degree of suspicion. Thus, when Angie's relationship with Flipper is revealed, she is mocked by the guys in Paulie's store, beaten by her father, and condemned all around for failing in her duties. She has failed in her obligations to her father and brothers, and she has failed to honor the values and taboos of her community. For this transgression, she, like Flipper, is rebuked by her father, who brutally beats her, calls her a disgrace to the memory of her mother, and proclaims that he would rather she be a murderer or a child molester rather than a good Catholic girl who goes bad by marrying a "nigger."

Mike Tucci's paroxysm recalls the brutal death of Hawkins, and it forcefully portrays the power of the American taboo against interracial romance and sex, especially between black men and white women. Although the toughs in Paulie's store can joke about their desire to fuck Orin, Angie is forbidden to make love to Flipper. At the heart of this injunction against Angie's miscegenation is sexism and racism. She is expected to express her sexuality in a manner consistent with her duties as a daughter, which includes abiding by her community's commonsense racial rules. Many in her neighborhood think blacks are inferior, and intermingling with them—Vinny's outrageous contradictions notwithstanding—is a target of antipathy. As one of Angie's friends puts it, echoing Mike Tucci's condemnation, "Personally, I think it's disgusting." The same forces confront Paulie. He falls for Orin, seeing in her a reflection of his own aspirations and open-mindedness, and he deliberately, instead of feverishly, asks her out on a date. With that, Paulie crosses a line and is assaulted by the guys from his shop.

Taj Mahal

Flipper and Angie' affair collapses under the weight of their guilt and isolation and the disapproval of their friends and families. It was a thin relationship to begin with, since it was hastily constructed from their dissatisfaction with their lives and built on the ruins of his marriage. Such materials do not make for a sturdy relationship, and theirs cannot withstand assault and rebuke. This is their fundamental problem, yet for the Good Reverend Doctor, Mike Tucci, the guys in Paulie's shop, and some of the War Council, the affair between Flipper and Angie is a token, a prime example of the fever and distortion of miscegenation.

Their fear of a mixed-up, mixed-blood world is brought to life in the fantastic scene in which Flipper searches for his brother, Gator, and ends up confronting him in the grandest of Harlem crack houses, the Taj Mahal. Gator Purify (Samuel L. Jackson) is a homeless crackhead and represents the devastating results of the crack epidemic that plagued U.S. cities, and in particular poor, urban African American communities, in the late 1980s. Flipper's procession through the Taj Mahal, accompanied by Stevie Wonder's affective sound track, becomes progressively more bizarre as he stumbles onto tableaus of interracial crack-addled fever and distortion: black hustlers and hookers, white businessmen and laborers, black and white couples, all in the grips of crack fever.

Those who agree with the Good Reverend Doctor, Mike Tucci, and the rest may see Flipper's procession through the Taj Mahal, with its racial and class commingling among squalor and addiction, as a depiction of the nightmare brought on by miscegenation. Lee, however, wants to show his audience that the place where dreams come to die is racially mixed. The worst corner of the dark ghetto is not just black; it is a black and white place. Just as *Taj Mahal* means "the abode of the chosen one," so we have built our own mausoleum and abode for the living dead. The Taj Mahal scene, filled with the sliding dance of crack zombies sucking on their pipes, is stunning.[14] Unlike Flipper's corporate office, the crack den is happily integrated, and it is here, in their desperation, that the denizens have realized a dystopia of interracial intimacy.

The nightmare summoned by the Taj Mahal scene is brought to a horrible end when the Good Reverend Doctor shoots Gator after he tries to wrangle yet more money from his elderly parents. The Good Reverend Doctor's despair is complete; he has been rejected by his congregation, and his sons are disobedient and godless—the successful son is a whoremonger, and his other son, possessed by the demon of crack, lies bleeding to death on his living room floor, shot by the Good Reverend Doctor out of an ambiguous mixture of self-defense and disgust. All he has left is his antiquated image of Jesus. And with that, Lee has made the backdrop of his film not only the frustration of racial discrimination and the damage of the crack epidemic but also the generational disappointment of the fathers, the men of the civil rights movement, as they confront old age and reconsider the goals for which they fought.

Love's Revolution

The negative emotions of the Good Reverend Doctor, Mike Tucci, and Lou Carbone are, paradoxically, a sign of hope. Their angry reactions stem from their fear and anxiety over generational shifts in behavior and customs. They see the social networks that give meaning to their existence fracturing as their children search for love and opportunity outside their neighborhoods. The cliché that there are no bloodless revolutions could be applied here. If interracial romance and other intimacies are "love's revolution," as Maria P. P. Root puts it, then the blood spilled is that of the fathers.[15]

To expect these men not to cry and scream or lash out at their children is plain silly. Their legacy, their hope that their children will carry on the family tradition, is dissolving. Therefore, whatever response can be given to the disapproving in Harlem and Bensonhurst, one should not pretend that all can or will be repaired. On the contrary, the feelings of betrayal that result from this or any form of elopement (leaping over family rules that govern romance) may be permanent. We should not expect love's warriors to be invited over for dinner as they busy themselves with the slow fracturing of their fathers' racially segregated social networks and heterosexist assumptions. These fathers are well within their rights to retort, "Well, guess who's *not* coming to dinner." That is the cost of cleaving from one's parents and community in the pursuit of romantic love, and it is sometimes the cost of pursuing same-sex or interracial love in our society.[16]

Moreover, it is important to keep in mind, especially when getting away from the narrative of *Jungle Fever* and thinking about the dynamics of particular families, that not every parental circumscription of an offspring's romantic choice is racist. That is, parental demands that children marry within some group may not be due to racial antipathy or a belief that outsiders are racially inferior. Certainly, such demands frequently have ethnic and racial overtones and may seem racist, especially in our society, where every racial incident, insensitivity, or conflict is quickly judged as an instance of racism. To make that leap, to assume that opposition to interracial romance, as a form of exogamy, is in every instance racist is a mistake that does not take many other relevant concerns seriously. For example, Paulie's father is upset at the news that his son is romantically interested in Orin, but what Lou really fears, as a lonely widower, is being left alone and suffering the consequences of Paulie's break with communal taboos.

Due to fears like Lou's, as well as long-term intergenerational goals, families put a significant amount of pressure on individuals to engage in homophily—that is, to select partners from within their familiar social network and hence those who reflect their own characteristics.[17] In the United States, homophily typically involves religion, class, and education, as well as the more controversial distinctions of ethnicity and race. Families that expect homophily in their children may be seeking assurance that the child's mate will fit in with, invest in, and otherwise cooperate with the family. They seek the security and pleasure of familiarity—a happiness and ease they may get from grandchildren that look like them and whom they assume will carry on their traditions and values.

This is not to say that such family demands must be obeyed. Individuals have the legal right to love and to marry whomever they please as part of their right to shape their own life plans. The U.S. Supreme Court, in *Loving v. Commonwealth of Virginia,* established this liberty. The Court held that denying interracial couples the right to marry or to engage in romance was unconstitutional, and that the freedom of individuals to marry whomever they please is "one of the vital personal rights essential to the orderly pursuit of happiness by free men."[18] The Court's legal position coincided with, and was clearly influenced by, standards of ethical and personal autonomy, which are deeply rooted in Western political and ethical traditions. To pursue happiness, we need the liberty to construct and follow our own life plans. As John Stuart Mill argues, individuals should be sovereign over their minds and bodies.[19] As long as we do not infringe on the rights of others, we do not have a duty to sacrifice our personal autonomy for the sake of others.

Moreover, even when such legal restrictions are not in place, and only social ones are in effect—what Mill calls the "tyranny of public opinion"—absurdities and tyrannies abound. Consider the extent of the naysayers' demands. For example, running through their objections to interracial intimacy is an assumption of mandatory heterosexuality. Heterosexuality is expected of the loyal member of the race, and no other possibility is even considered. This highlights how far the demands for ethnoracial sexual solidarity go. If we can be good members of the race only by dating and marrying opposite-sex members of that race, such visions of solidarity automatically cast gays and lesbians as disloyal to the community. One wonders as well about reproductive rights. Do we have an equal obligation to procreate? The end of such racial-sexual logic is an absurd and terrifying place.

In addition to the absurdity of the demand for racial-sexual loyalty, there is a problem with the assumption that loving or marrying someone outside of one's race or ethnicity is indicative of a lack of political or cultural solidarity or of internalized self-loathing. Just as it is a mistake to think that opposition to every instance of exogamy is racist, it is also incorrect to assume that endogamy is a clear and distinct sign of ethnic or racial loyalty and exogamy a sign of disloyalty.

Answers to the War Council

Given the preceding considerations, we're now in a position to provide answers to the War Council's objections to relationships between black men and white women. Their first objection—that successful black men who are intimate with white women fail to care for black women—is not a charitable or even a reasonable view of the intentions of black men involved in interracial relationships. Political or cultural solidarity is a poor basis for any romantic relationship; it is a form of objectification, reducing the partner to a prop or a tool for a personal political-cultural narrative. Second, plenty of the black men (and black women) who are involved in interracial relationships, whether gay or straight, care about their communities and the issues that affect them.[20]

This response goes right to the heart of the War's Council's second objection that interracial romance is a sign of disloyalty to the group. Interracial love and other forms of interracial intimacy are poor indicators of attitudes of solidarity or even a history of personal commitment and action on behalf of the group (this is also the case for those who choose endogamous relationships). Interracial intimacy can be perfectly compatible with group solidarity.

Moreover, one should be cautious about assuming whether and to what degree interracial intimacy is an issue for "the black community." Interracial intimacy may not be important, or it may be less of an issue, to different segments of the various African American communities. Like other issues concerning class, gender, and sexuality differences, interracial intimacy cuts across African American communities.[21] It matters a lot to the black middle-class and white working-class characters in Lee's film; indeed, Lee places it next to the crack cocaine epidemic in importance. But notice what is missing. In the late 1980s HIV and AIDS reached epidemic levels in the United States and other parts of the world, and an increasing number of African Americans had contracted HIV, were living with AIDS, and were dying of AIDS-related diseases. By 1991—Lee released *Jungle Fever* in June of that year—HIV/AIDS disproportionately affected African Americans.[22] Magic Johnson's public announcement of his HIV infection on November 7, 1991, helped bring much-needed public attention to the HIV/AIDS crisis and to the spread of HIV/AIDS among African Americans. *Jungle Fever*, even though it includes a depiction of the devastating effects of drugs on black urban communities, is absolutely silent about HIV/AIDS, right in the heart of that crisis. Why is heterosexual interracial intimacy a black "issue" that raises concerns about solidarity, while HIV/AIDS care and prevention are not?

The War Council's third objection—that blacks involved in interracial romance harbor an ethnic or racial self-loathing or self-hatred—reflects the Good Reverend Doctor's view that black and white romance is fevered and the result of racist, distorted patterns of behavior. Certainly, some segments of the American population have pursued interracial relationships based on questionable motivations, such as a belief in racial-sexual stereotypes or a desire for sexual experimentation. Likewise, some individuals use interracial relationships to escape their social conditions or rebel against an ethnic or racial identity. But to indiscriminately lay these charges at the foot of every man and woman involved in an interracial romance is ludicrous. These claims reduce the behavior of hundreds of thousands of couples to a single psychological explanation that has less to do with their actual motivations and feelings than with some politically convenient ideology. To make matters worse, this ideology that interracial relations are inherently distorted by the history of race and racism is based on spurious psychoanalytic theories of desire and identity. Such views are just as baseless as classically racist notions that miscegenation is theologically, naturally, and politically disordered. In contrast to all such speculation fueled by one or another ideology, actual evidence-based psychological research provides multiple ordinary motivations behind romantic attractions, including interracial ones.[23]

As for the concern about mixed-race children, it too is weak. Children face all sorts of claims on their identities, and all sorts of unions potentially have this problem. And as it turns out, there is ample evidence that multiracial children do just fine.[24] Moreover, as is evident in *Jungle Fever*, Flipper's concern about "mixed up" children is replete with contradictions. Flipper's wife is multiracial, and both Flipper and Drew avoid critiquing the morality or propriety of her parents' relationship or of their child's identity. After the trauma of Flipper's affair, it seems that Drew and Flipper try to manage the social and personal implications of their family's interracial history by defending racial purity as a bulwark against confusion and dissolution, even though their family is in no sense racially pure (which is an idea that makes no sense in the first place) or, for that matter, immune from social and personal confusion and crises.

Ordinary Love

Individuals who are intimate across the color line are not necessarily "fevered," nor are they "distorting" the basic elements of society. They are not sullying racial purity, nor do they have a perfect duty to obey family or community demands for homophily. Interracial relations, in this way, are just like every other relationship: they are subject to the desires and compromises of the couple and external pressures from friends and family. Interracial couples, and those involved in other intimate interracial relationships, may join with other families to serve, as Edmund Burke puts it, as the "ballast of society."[25]

The overwhelming ordinariness of interracial relationships is the best answer to the fantasies and fears of so-called jungle fever. The idea that interracial romantic attraction or lust is peculiarly feverish or outside the ken of normal human desire and experience is just wrong. The erotic passions of our species are biochemically, psychologically, and sociologically complex. It is absurd to think that the surprisingly wide range of normal human romantic feelings is bounded by race and ethnicity (and the very localized patterns of race and ethnicity in the United States, too!). Granted, there are social and cultural determinants involved, but those determinants do not absolutely control the chemical and psychological processes behind erotic attraction. Although we are not "color blind," or completely oblivious to the ethnoracial divisions in our society, the psychological, neurological, and biochemical processes of lust, attraction, and attachment are not at the absolute command of our racial rules.[26]

Just as interracial intimacies are not especially feverish, neither are they revolutionary. Claims to the contrary are hyperbolic. Take, for instance, Root's view that interracial marriages represent "love's revolution": "While hate, fear, and anger are common responses to interracial marriage and have powerful short-term effects, love has proved a formidable opponent. With stealth, persistence, and a few legal twists, love carves a more hopeful path for future race relations through the sacrifices of many who have made and make their commitments to love for better or worse."[27] This vision of love and reconciliation is sweet but false. Interracial relationships by themselves do not close racial disparities, resolve racial injustices, or banish racism. To think otherwise is to conflate instances of personal romance with vast social and political changes.

This is not to say that interracial relationships are socially meaningless. They are the results of changing laws, social trends, and the bold acts of individuals seeking love and friendship across the color line. Increased liberties have brought more contact and greater opportunity for interracial intimacies to form.[28] Friendships and relations from the casual to the professional have led to shifts in social networks and corresponding sexual markets. With integrated schools and other social spaces come more mixed marriages. Interracial relationships may actively contribute to this change as well. They provide examples to others and become the basis of new and growing multiracial social networks. Further, when and if these relationships become part of larger trends and are supported by institutions, laws, and customs, the reduction of stereotypes and discrimination is possible. All these developments may lead, in fact, to greater interaction, cooperation, and mutual trust among groups of people and dissolve the animosity and anxiety that sometimes result from ethnic and racial divisions.[29] The change that interracial intimacies may inspire, however, is incremental and localized. These marriages and relationships are ordinary things, caught up in the cycles of everyday life. We should not expect miracles, or revolutions, from them.

It is with a note of banality, rather than the ordinary, that *Jungle Fever* closes. Angie is silently admitted back into her father's home. Paulie, after being assaulted by the guys at his shop, goes to Orin, and the door closes on our vision of them. Flipper returns to Drew, and we witness them making love. The contrast between the final scenes with Drew and Flipper and with Orin and Paulie, in their respective homes, is interesting, and not just because the possibility of a successful interracial relationship—between a white man and a black woman, no less—is quietly slipped in at the end. The contrast comes from the respective visibility and public display of each couple. Drew and Flipper are seen half naked while making love, but the door closes on Orin and Paulie. We are not allowed to see into their home, much less their bedroom. For all the heat Drew and Flipper give off, there is something prudish about Spike Lee's view of interracial sexuality. We witness Drew and Flipper being passionate and having sex, but not Orin and Paulie; what happens with them will remain private. Lee seems to be communicating that a successful interracial relationship must not be public or fevered. Any signs of passion, like that displayed between Flipper and Angie, would bring about suspicions of jungle fever. Thus, on the topic of interracial intimacy, Lee's movie is oddly puritanical. On this point, *Jungle Fever* is more timorous than *Guess Who's Coming to Dinner.* Unlike the interracial couple in the latter film, Paulie and Orin have to be private and hidden. Lee has stuck close to the script of racial pieties and fails to provide an alternative artistic vision of interracial intimacy.

To break jungle fever, interracial intimacy must be exposed as ordinary. Interracial intimacies are imagined as fevered, distorted relationships, so displaying their ordinariness is absolutely not banal and may in fact offend and challenge those who perceive them as especially threatening. Moreover, one part of the wonderful ordinariness of our lives is passion. This of all things should not be hidden. Who does not want passion? It is, as Peggy Lee so wonderfully put it, "a lovely way to burn."

Notes

1. The names of the Purify brothers are an idiosyncratic feature of this film. Both names are suggestive of fictional animals that were main characters of popular television shows of the mid-1960s. "Flipper," of course, was the name of the heroic dolphin on *Flipper,* which ran on NBC from 1964 to 1967. "Gator" was a character on the Hanna-Barbera cartoon *Wally Gator,* which ran from 1962 to 1963.

2. For surveys of the social and legal history of interracial intimacy, see Randall Kennedy, *Interracial Intimacies: Sex, Marriage, Identity, and Adoption* (New York: Vintage, 2004); Rachel F. Moran, *Interracial Intimacy: The Regulation of Race and Romance* (Chicago: University of Chicago Press, 2001); and Renee Christine Romano, *Race Mixing: Black-White Marriage in Postwar America* (Cambridge, Mass.: Harvard University Press, 2003). I provide an analysis of interracial intimacy and related mixed-race issues in Ronald R. Sundstrom, "Being and Being Mixed Race," *Social Theory and Practice* 27 (2001); *The Browning of America and the Evasion of Social Justice* (Albany: State University of New York Press, 2008); and "Mixed-Race Looks," *Contemporary Aesthetics,* Special Volume 2 (2009), http://www.contempaesthetics.org/newvolume/pages/article.php?articleID=540 (accessed November 5, 2009). For a helpful and broad view of the diversity of the family across societies, see Gwen J. Broude, *Marriage, Family, and Relationships: A Cross-Cultural Encyclopedia* (Santa Barbara, Calif.: ABC-CLIO, 1994).

3. *Loving v. Commonwealth of Virginia,* 388 U.S. 1 (1967).

4. *Green v. The State,* 58 Ala. 190 (1877).

5. For a general history of the era of Jim Crow, lynching, and antiblack terror campaigns, see Leon F. Litwack, *Trouble in Mind: Black Southerners in the Age of Jim Crow* (New York: Knopf, 1998).

6. See Susan Sachs, "Recalling Yusef Hawkins and Hate that Killed Him," *New York Times,* August 22, 1999, http://topics.nytimes.com/topics/reference/timestopics/people/h/yusuf_k_hawkins/index.html?offset=0&s=newest (accessed November 3, 2009).

7. From the original version of the song "Fever," or, as it is sometimes called, "You

Give Me Fever." Otis Blackwell and Eddie Cooley wrote the song, and it was a rhythm and blues hit in 1956 for Little Willie John. Peggy Lee's version, with altered and additional lyrics, became a hit in 1958. Compare "Fever" to the 1972 hit song "Jungle Fever" by the Chakachas.

8. Paul Taylor, Cary Funk, and Peyton Craighill, "Guess Who's Coming to Dinner: 22% of Americans Have a Relative in a Mixed-Race Marriage," *Social and Demographic Trends* (2006), http://pewsocialtrends.org/pubs/304/guess-whos-coming-to-dinner (accessed November 6, 2009). For an analysis of current trends of interracial marriage, see Roland G. Fryer Jr., "Guess Who's Been Coming to Dinner? Trends in Interracial Marriage over the 20th Century," *Journal of Economic Perspectives* 21, 2 (2007). See also the U.S. Census Bureau's "Interracial Tables," http://www.census.gov/population/www/socdemo/interrace.html (accessed November 6, 2009).

9. For a fairly comprehensive review of African American objections to interracial romance, marriage, and sex, see Anita L. Allen, "Interracial Marriage: Folk Ethics in Contemporary Philosophy," in *Women of Color and Philosophy*, ed. Naomi Zack (Malden, Mass.: Blackwell, 2000); Charles W. Mills, "Do Black Men Have a Moral Duty to Marry Black Women?" *Journal of Social Philosophy* 25 (1994); Sundstrom, *The Browning of America*, 93–107; and Romano, *Race Mixing*.

10. The objections aired during the War Council are informed by the traditions of Black Nationalism and solidarity. For a philosophical analysis of Black Nationalism and group solidarity, see Tommie Shelby, *We Who Are Dark: The Philosophical Foundations of Black Solidarity* (Cambridge, Mass.: Belknap Press of Harvard University Press, 2005).

11. Frantz Fanon, *Black Skin, White Masks*, 1st ed. (1952; reprint, New York: Grove Press, 2008). Fanon's analysis of interracial romance, which was informed by psychoanalytic theory, existentialism, and phenomenology, influenced the development of this view. For an account of how this view functions among African Americans, see Romano, *Race Mixing*, chap. 3.

12. Timothy Sullivan, *Unequal Verdicts: The Central Park Jogger Trials* (New York: American Lawyer Books/Simon and Schuster, 1992). The attitudes and beliefs of the guys in Paulie's store are indicative of classic racism. They have an essentialist view of black bodies, society, and culture as being undifferentiated and distinctly inferior. Moreover, their feelings and beliefs match up with what current philosophical theories of racism identify as being racist. See Lawrence A. Blum, *"I'm Not a Racist, But . . .": The Moral Quandary of Race* (Ithaca, N.Y.: Cornell University Press, 2002). They display what Blum identifies as the "core" of racism—namely, attitudes of "inferiorization"; the idea that some race is in some way inferior; and "antipathy," an attitude or feeling that some group, because of its race, is the proper subject of disgust. The guys also display many of the psychological features of implicit bias, stereotyping, and discrimination. See Scott Plous, "The Psychology of Prejudice, Stereotyping, and Discrimination: An Overview," in *Understanding Prejudice and Discrimination*, ed. Scott Plous (Boston: McGraw-Hill, 2003).

13. For accounts of America's interracial cultural and social history, see Stephan Talty, *Mulatto America: At the Crossroads of Black and White Culture, a Social History*

(New York: HarperCollins, 2003), and Gregory Rodriguez, *Mongrels, Bastards, Orphans, and Vagabonds: Mexican Immigration and the Future of Race in America,* 1st ed. (New York: Pantheon Books, 2007). Lee's depiction of the inconsistency of racist attitudes is accurate. This phenomenon is called "selectivity." Racist attitudes or beliefs tend to be selective and inconsistent in terms of which groups, subparts of groups, or aspects of groups are targeted for disdain. See the discussion of selectivity in Blum, *"I'm Not a Racist."* Likewise, psychological research demonstrates that prejudicial attitudes are complex and selective. For a technical discussion of this phenomenon, see Catherine A. Cottrell and Steven L. Neuberg, "Different Emotional Reactions to Different Groups: A Sociofunctional Threat-Based Approach to 'Prejudice,'" *Journal of Personality and Social Psychology* 88, 5 (2005).

14. The idea of Lee's Taj Mahal as a view of hell comes from Peter Traver's review in *Rolling Stone;* see http://www.rollingstone.com/reviews/movie/5947337/review/5947338/jungle_fever (accessed December 15, 2009).

15. Maria P. P. Root, *Love's Revolution: Interracial Marriage* (Philadelphia: Temple University Press, 2001).

16. Compare the stories of family ostracism in James McBride's and Barack Obama's autobiographies. James McBride, *The Color of Water: A Black Man's Tribute to His White Mother* (New York: Riverhead Books, 1996); Barack Obama, *Dreams from My Father: A Story of Race and Inheritance,* 1st ed. (New York: Times Books, 1995).

17. Edward O. Laumann et al., *The Social Organization of Sexuality: Sexual Practices in the United States* (Chicago: University of Chicago Press, 1994). The findings of Laumann's sociological survey are presented for general consumption in Robert T. Michael et al., *Sex in America: A Definitive Survey,* 1st ed. (Boston: Little, Brown, 1994). An updated presentation of the theory of sexual markets is provided in Edward O. Laumann et al., eds., *The Sexual Organization of the City* (Chicago: University of Chicago Press, 2004).

18. *Loving v. Commonwealth of Virginia.* Compare the language of privacy in *Loving* to that in the decision of *Lawrence v. Texas,* 539 U.S. 558 (2003). Just as *Loving* decriminalized interracial sex, *Lawrence* struck down so-called anti-sodomy laws.

19. John Stuart Mill, *On Liberty,* in *Collected Works of John Stuart Mill,* vol. 18, ed. John M. Robson (Toronto: University of Toronto Press, 1977).

20. Romano, *Race Mixing.*

21. Cathy J. Cohen, *The Boundaries of Blackness: AIDS and the Breakdown of Black Politics* (Chicago: University of Chicago Press, 1999).

22. Ibid. See also the Centers for Disease Control and Prevention's fact sheet on HIV/AIDS among African Americans: http://www.cdc.gov/hiv/topics/aa/resources/factsheets/aa.htm#3 (accessed February 22, 2010).

23. Robert J. Sternberg and Karin Weis, eds., *The New Psychology of Love* (New Haven, Conn.: Yale University Press, 2006); Root, *Love's Revolution.*

24. Kerry Rockquemore and David L. Brunsma, *Beyond Black: Biracial Identity in America,* 2nd ed. (Lanham, Md.: Rowman and Littlefield, 2008).

25. Edmund Burke and L. G. Mitchell, *Reflections on the Revolution in France,* Oxford World's Classics (Oxford: Oxford University Press, 1999), 138–41.

26. For an accessible discussion of the science of romantic love, see Helen E. Fisher, *Why We Love: The Nature and Chemistry of Romantic Love,* 1st ed. (New York: Holt, 2004). For a technical account, see her paper "The Drive to Love: The Neural Mechanism for Mate Selection," in *The New Psychology of Love,* ed. Robert J. Sternberg and Karin Weis (New Haven, Conn.: Yale University Press, 2006).

27. Root, *Love's Revolution,* 1.

28. This account draws on intergroup contact theory in psychology. For an accessible review of contact theory, see Plous, "The Psychology of Prejudice, Stereotyping, and Discrimination." For a technical review of current research on contact theory, see the papers in John F. Dovidio, Peter Samuel Glick, and Laurie A. Rudman, eds., *On the Nature of Prejudice: Fifty Years after Allport* (Malden, Mass.: Blackwell, 2005).

29. Robert D. Putnam, "*E Pluribus Unum:* Diversity and Community in the Twenty-First Century," *Scandinavian Political Studies* 30, 2 (2007).

Bamboozled

Philosophy through Blackface

Dan Flory

Spike Lee is no stranger to controversy. Since the beginning of his career the director has used his films to confront audiences with difficult issues that need to be understood and thought about—for example, the genesis of riots (*Do the Right Thing* [1989]), the politics of interracial relationships (*Jungle Fever* [1991]), reasons for the existence of drug cultures (*Clockers* [1995]), xenophobia (*Summer of Sam* [1999]), and the importance of taking responsibility for one's actions (*25th Hour* [2002], *Inside Man* [2006]). Through his work, then, Lee seeks to compel viewers to face up to and reflect on matters of urgent importance that admit of no easy solution. Perhaps because of these significant cognitive demands, Lee's films frequently appeal most directly to a subset of the general moviegoing audience—namely, those viewers willing to be challenged by such issues and invest some effort in thinking about them.

With his 2000 feature *Bamboozled,* however, Lee touches a nerve that caused even many of his most loyal viewers to react in distaste. By suggesting that racist stereotypes that derive their power and strength from blackface minstrelsy continue to influence our thinking about and perception of African Americans, the filmmaker garnered some of the most deeply negative reviews of his career, even from critics who had previously championed his work, such as Roger Ebert, who stated that, in this case, "Lee misjudged his material and audience."[1] Despite some critics' claims that *Bamboozled* is one of the filmmaker's best,[2] audiences generally agreed with Ebert. Overall, reactions to the film have been decidedly negative and often filled with angry puzzlement or mystified shock at why Lee even made it.[3]

What I hope to show in this essay is that Lee had excellent reasons for making this film—and that he largely carried off his intentions successfully. In a 2001 interview with *Cineaste,* the filmmaker said, "I want people to think about the power of images, not just in terms of race, but how imagery is used and what sort of social impact it has—how it influences how we talk, how we think, how we view one another. In particular, I want them to see how films and television have historically, from the birth of both mediums, produced and perpetuated distorted images . . . and a lot of that madness is still with us today."[4] If we take these claims as keys to the artwork, the narrative trajectory of *Bamboozled* becomes clear. What this daring filmmaker hoped to do is get people to *think* about their own reactions to many examples of mass art and the degree to which they may be complicit with stereotypes and presumptions that owe their existence and vitality to blackface minstrelsy. In this sense, Lee's aim is overtly didactic, which isn't necessarily a bad thing; indeed, as Aristotle pointed out millennia ago, human beings by nature desire to know, especially when such information is about us.[5] In what follows I provide a description and explanation of *Bamboozled* that illuminates both what Lee aimed to do and how he sought to achieve it. In concluding, I also discuss some of the implications of this unsettling artwork.

Producing Blackface in the New Millennium

In many ways, *Bamboozled* is a movie lover's kind of film because it uses numerous cinematic predecessors to guide its audience to the appropriate response. For example, by framing his narrative in a way that explicitly references the classic *Sunset Boulevard* (1950),[6] Lee uses the familiar film noir technique of narrating by means of a dead man's voice as he reflects on the events leading up to his death. By employing the contemplative noir device of having a character tell his story from beyond the grave, *Bamboozled* encourages viewers to mull over ongoing difficulties faced during the past two centuries by African Americans, even while acknowledging that those difficulties have evolved into different forms. Through this device, Lee aims to emphasize how the images and ideas that constitute a legacy of blackface minstrelsy must still be recognized as amazingly enduring and damaging entities, even though they have become submerged from our consciousness or evolved to the point that most people no longer recognize them or their influence. As the first homegrown form of American popular entertainment, and one whose popularity dominated the nineteenth century and lasted well into the twentieth,[7] blackface minstrelsy remains a crucial part of the ongoing cultural background for antiblack racism. Lee wants us to grasp that minstrel images and their related scenarios, songs, and jokes, and the presumptions that support them, constitute a pervasive, albeit latent, aspect of American popular culture.

Lee brings these minstrel elements to our attention by having Pierre Delacroix (Daman Wayans) broodingly narrate the events leading up to his demise. The young man, a token black television writer who is unhappy with his job, decides to propose the most racist idea for a TV show he can imagine, in the hopes of being fired and receiving a comfortable severance package. Delacroix's idea is to present an unapologetic, unironic, and unrepentant blackface minstrel show, disingenuously titled *Mantan: The New Millennium Minstrel Show,* complete with "coon" routines, tap dancing, pickaninnies, Aunt Jemimas, Sambos, Rastuses, shucking and jiving, watermelon patches, and the whole litany of racist images, gags, and routines that owe their existence and strength to this theatrical form.

To Delacroix's astonishment, his boss, the appropriately named Dunwitty (Michael Rapaport), a white producer who thinks he knows more about being black than Delacroix himself, loves the idea and fast-tracks it into production. In stunned horror, Delacroix sees all the outrageous, hateful images he thought would get him fired paraded before his eyes, accepted and lovingly embraced by audiences, critics, and peers alike. *Mantan* and its blackface imagery become "the newest sensation across the nation," he sullenly observes. As its creator, Delacroix skyrockets to fame aboard a fad he cannot control, and rather than dying the immediate death he envisioned, the program arises vampire-like to a voracious and frightening vitality. Like small-time Broadway producer Max Bialystock (Zero Mostel) in *The Producers* (1968)—another admitted influence on Lee here[8]—Delacroix watches in shock and disgust as an idea he thought would guarantee failure (while assuring himself a small profit) achieves astounding success at the expense of personal catastrophe.

Self-Deception and Minstrel Stereotypes

For a while, Delacroix attempts to control the ugly, racial "Frankenstein's monster" he has created. Seduced by the adulation that accompanies being the creator of a huge television hit, he looks forward to receiving awards "for all my hard work, my talent that had been previously overlooked," and becoming what he describes as "Hollywood's favorite Negro." But the show is so powerfully racist that it eludes his ability to guide it, and his sardonic voice-over conveys to us that he has struck a racial "mother lode" buried deep in the American psyche, including his own. Audiences, both black and white, laugh at the coon routines and stereotypes in which the show trades, not realizing that in doing so they reveal racialized aspects of their expectations and thinking about African Americans that extend far deeper than almost any of them realize. By bursting into laughter when one of *Mantan*'s characters evinces a slow-wittedness or infantile desire worthy of Stepin Fetchit (whose real name was Lincoln Perry), "Hollywood's favorite Negro" of the early 1930s, audiences reveal that they find such stereotypes enjoyable objects of pleasure and mirth.

In laughing at such sequences, audiences also reveal that they find such characters comforting and nostalgic of a past that never existed, except in films like *The Birth of a Nation* (1915), *The Littlest Rebel* (1935), and *Gone with the Wind* (1939) or their televisual descendants such as *Amos 'n' Andy* (1951–1953), *Beulah* (1950–1953), *Calvin and the Colonel* (1961–1962), or their more contemporary equivalents in the form of certain cable television programming.[9] What *Mantan* re-creates for viewers is "a simpler time when . . . nigras knew they place," as Sleep-and-Eat (Tommy Davidson) tells the audience in minstrel dialect during the show's first taping. Current racial stereotypes, such as those of urban welfare recipients and professional athletes, may be forgotten, as he deftly points out. His partner Mantan (Savion Glover) picks up on this theme and advises the audience, "Cousins, I want you to go to your window, yell out, scream with all the life you can muster up inside your bruised and battered and assaulted bodies, 'I'm sick and tired of niggers and I'm not gonna take it anymore!' "

The implication of these remarks, of course, is that minstrelsy permits the audience to dismiss present-day stereotypes in favor of ones that are more comforting and reassuring. Yet the comfort and reassurance that audiences find in these nostalgic racial images reveal their willingness to accept and think in terms of them, their eagerness to turn from existing racial realities—or racist delusions—and indulge in the consoling fantasies offered by blackface minstrelsy. The humorous, entertaining dimensions of this theatrical form thus mask the fact that such fantasies necessarily presuppose the inferiority of an entire class of human beings, and that this presupposition causes nearly unimaginable damage to them by refusing to recognize, let alone acknowledge, their full humanity.[10]

One of the most noteworthy and daring features of Lee's film is that he presses home the idea that such unquestioned presuppositions exist in the minds of not only whites but blacks as well. He makes this point by showing members of both groups responding with uninhibited laughter to coon routines and generally enjoying the outrageously racist sequences of *Mantan*. Nearly everyone in the story finds them funny and pleasurable, in spite of the harm they cause.

Self-Deception and the Epistemology of Ignorance

Another way Lee explores the acceptance of blackface minstrelsy is by probing the psyche of his main character. As the narrative proceeds, viewers see that in relation to his blackness, Pierre Delacroix is a figure attempting the impossible. He seeks to escape this aspect of his identity that American culture has imposed on him. We discover that in order to evade it, Delacroix has changed his name; adopted a baroque, pretentious, and very "white" way of speaking; and generally eschewed dealing with anything stereotypically black. After witnessing a particularly garish audition by a group that hits all the crudest base notes of gangsta rap, for example, Delacroix distastefully remarks, "I don't want anything to do with anything black for at least a week," as if he could escape his existence and live unracialized for a time. Although the narrative plays his comment as an amusing exaggeration from the foppish Delacroix, viewers come to realize that he also speaks from the heart in expressing this disdain for blackness, including his own.[11] His consistent use of the outmoded term *Negro,* instead of *African American* or *black,* further symbolizes his need to distance himself from the United States' demeaning forms of racialization by displacing them into a past that he sees himself as having escaped.

Once the show becomes a hit, Delacroix, deluded by the fame and success within his easy grasp, protectively argues in favor of the televisual monster he has created. He makes the case for its aesthetic, moral, and expedient justification on the shifting grounds of free speech, aesthetic freedom, and social necessity. Opportunistically, Delacroix employs any strategy he can to seek exoneration for the show and his actions in creating it. During a radio interview soon after his program becomes a sensation, he asserts a thoroughgoing, simple-minded moral relativism: "Who is to judge? Who is to say that 'this is right' and 'this is not'?" Like many people who have thought only superficially about morality, he espouses the stance that anything goes, even racist presentations of African Americans, because no one has the right or authority to determine what is moral. In making such a claim, Delacroix fails to realize that such a position also implicitly endorses the idea that the determination of morality would then be left to nodes of power that he himself can never control, influence, or possess, to say nothing of the havoc it would wreak on everyone's lives.

He also argues that *Mantan* is "art, and that is what it should be called." Citing former New York City mayor Rudy Guiliani's 1999 rejection, sight unseen, of African art in the Brooklyn Museum, Delacroix asserts, on the contrary, that, in the name of art, all must be permitted. Art may in no way be either censored or criticized on the grounds that it is immoral or promotes the injury and distress of others. Rather, it must be allowed to express freely and without criticism whatever it will, regardless of the consequences. Here, Delacroix equates any sort of moral examination of art with its censorship, thereby failing to distinguish between two very different critical stances—one condemnatory of an artwork's particular features, and the other condemnatory of its very existence.

Mantan's creator also dismisses the issue of racialized slavery as a quaint historical problem that occurred, as he says, "400 years ago." "We need to stop thinking that way, stop crying over 'the white man this, the white man that,'" he lectures the talk-show host. "This is the new millennium and we [meaning all blacks] must join it," presumably by "getting over" all past racial injustices, ignoring their legacies, and going on from where current circumstances have left African Americans—however unfair those circumstances may be. When the host points out Delacroix's faulty arithmetic and the fact that he is excusing the black Holocaust that racialized slavery represents, the television writer dismisses it as "talking numbers . . . it doesn't matter. What matters . . . is slave mentality, and that is what must be broken." He goes on to tell a story about an aunt who refused to believe that anyone had ever walked on the moon, comparing her unreasonable skepticism to those who feel that past racial injustices have some meaningful impact on the present. "We must adapt to the times," he declares in his florid and overarticulated way. "Otherwise we will be left behind."

Delacroix's defenses of *Mantan* incorporate many of the standard arguments whites have employed to defend the idea that blacks are too sensitive about race in these postmodern times. His arguments in defending his televisual creation presuppose that all major problems having to do with race have been resolved and that blacks need to "wake up," as he declares, and recognize the dawning of a new era, one in which racial injustice has been overcome. Sliding without conscience or scruple from one defense to the next as they are criticized and refuted, Delacroix argues that blacks should simply "get over" slavery, "white privilege," and long-enforced racial hierarchies because they happened a long time ago and have no relevance to current circumstances; their memory imposes unfair obligations on the "freedoms" and advantages of others. And he implies that it must be morbid preoccupation with the past, mental instability, or excessive bitterness that causes blacks to remain so obstinately concerned with the oppressive dimensions of race and its consequences.

These strategies are typical ploys mobilized to defend what philosopher Charles Mills calls an "epistemology of ignorance," an inverted pattern of social cognitive norms that, though psychologically and socially functional, dysfunctionally and systematically misidentify other human beings as superior or inferior with regard to their moral value. Such a mode of believing and thinking thus provides "an invented delusional world" for whites that fundamentally distorts their sense of who they are and their conception of social placement, such that they become oblivious to problems related to race. In other words, these commonly held norms cast whites' experience in a way that unfairly presumes advantages for them and disadvantages for nonwhites and, at the same time, renders this shaping of experience invisible.[12]

One might think, then, that the best solution would be to eliminate *any* use of favored treatment as quickly as possible. Yet as Mills explains, if, upon recognizing such epistemological problems, one immediately and universally imposes nonracialized moral ideals on current racialized reality, this has the ironic effect of masking that reality and blocking the actual achievement of those very ideals.[13] Racial injustice would be rendered undetectable because the cognitive tools for doing so (e.g., historically important conceptions of race and racial hierarchy) would be perceived as unfair and unjust to use, while racial advantages (such as those due to "white privilege") would seem more appropriately attributable to dumb luck or good fortune. Whatever solution to the epistemology of ignorance we devise must therefore first recognize existing racial injustices and move to resolve them before we can achieve the full measure of our ideals—a truly color-blind ethics.

Self-Loathing and the Inconsistencies of Racialized Thinking

At a deeper level, Delacroix's defense of his television show illustrates his own internalized racism, his inner self-hatred.[14] As someone who is forced to admit unwillingly that he constitutes a devalued and denigrated member of the society in which he lives, Delacroix shows profound discomfort over his blackness. Like philosopher and social revolutionary Frantz Fanon's famous struggle to confront his own racialization,[15] Delacroix finds himself at odds with what Mills refers to as "a depersonalizing conceptual apparatus . . . through which nonwhites must learn to see themselves" if conceptions of white supremacy and "white privilege" are to be either explicitly or implicitly accepted by them.[16] But rather than struggle against this denigrating way of thinking, as Fanon did, Delacroix gives in to it. At a certain level, he embraces the social devaluation of blackness even as he must admit that he himself is black. This conflict creates self-loathing, as it does for other blacks who similarly accept this white supremacist conception and thus consent to think of themselves, at least on some level, as inferior and therefore undeserving of the regard and advantages typically granted whites.[17]

Understanding Delacroix's thinking in this manner clarifies that his justifications for the show—that it is somehow satirical, an expression of moral or aesthetic freedom, or offers insight into the new millennium for blacks—are desperate self-deceptions. These claims presume an acceptance of beliefs that undergird ongoing white privilege and racial hierarchy, even as they violate the internal sense that most blacks—including Delacroix, at some obscure and subterranean level—have of themselves as fully human. While acceptance of white supremacist beliefs typically causes soul-destroying conflict over African Americans' sense of self, the depersonalizing conceptual apparatus that makes acquiescence with white supremacy possible also provides powerful tools for dealing with difficulties of inconsistency, such as "scientific" studies alleging blacks' inferiority on cultural, social, or genetic grounds, and their overall entrenchment and consistency with other historically embedded beliefs regarding race.[18]

One way Lee's narrative depicts Delacroix's self-deception as well as his self-hatred is by having him interact with the "Jolly Nigger Bank," a toy from the turn of the twentieth century. This toy "reminds [us] of a time in our history in this country when [blacks] were considered inferior, subhuman, and we should never forget that," says Delacroix's assistant Sloan (Jada Pinkett Smith) when she gives him this collector's item as a symbol of his ambivalent success. Within the context of the story, the bank functions as what T. S. Eliot calls an "objective correlative" for Delacroix's background assumptions, the beliefs he must accept if he is to advance, promote, and protect *Mantan*. Eliot defines his term as identifying something, such as an object, that represents a particular emotion or, by extension, belief.[19] Here the Jolly Nigger Bank represents the racist presumptions necessary to create Delacroix's hit TV show. Eventually, objects like the bank take over the television producer's office, literally colonizing his workspace, just as their intellectual counterparts come to dominate his thinking. He begins to imagine the Jolly Nigger Bank as having a life of its own, just as these presuppositions do, and just as his television show does. This second correlation between *Mantan* and the bank further symbolizes the way racist presumptions take over Delacroix's psyche and put him wildly at odds with himself. It shows how some parts of his thinking are out of his control and he is losing the battle to coordinate all these disparate, racially inflected elements of his mental and emotional life.

Moral Centering, Education, and Cognitive Reformation

Sloan is the narrative figure who serves as the major conscience, the moral center, of the film. Lee has described her as "the most sympathetic and the most intelligent" character in the story,[20] for she realizes from the start that a television show such as *Mantan* could easily become unadulterated racist minstrelsy. Time and again she calls viewers' attention to its egregious stereotyping by indicating its use to other characters in the narrative or through occasional voice-overs, such as when she describes the proper methods of burning and using cork to create blackface makeup.

Other characters function narratively to morally orient viewers as well. For example, Tommy Davidson's character Womack, who plays Sleep-and-Eat in *Mantan,* eventually quits the show because acting the coon becomes too much for him. "It's the same bullshit! Just done over," he exclaims in frustration to the unbelieving Manray, who plays Mantan and is the show's star. Womack initially went along with *Mantan*—its shucking and jiving, blackface, and cooning—because it put a roof over his and Manray's heads, got them off the streets, and gave them something to eat. But eventually Womack realizes there is nothing ironic, satirical, or positive about it. *Mantan* is just a straight-up racist minstrel show, doing the same damage to humanity that its predecessors had been doing since the 1830s. Womack's sense of humiliation at putting on the coon act becomes so intense that he can no longer force himself to do it. He walks away from a show that offers him all the security, fame, and money he could ever want because he is overwhelmed by its racial degradation. After some earlier uncertainty, the character realizes that the shame and humiliation of portraying a subhuman stereotype throw into question not only his own humanity but also the humanity of all blacks.

Even the minor character of Delacroix's mother provides a crucial moment of moral centering for the audience. "You disappoint me," she sadly but firmly tells him when he tries to milk her for some comforting maternal approval of his blatantly demeaning television program. The show's star Manray eventually sees the truth about *Mantan,* too: "This buck dancing, this blackface shit—I'm not doing it," he finally tells Delacroix after much soul-searching. Refusing to black up or don his minstrel costume, he appears in front of the television audience one last time before he is fired and thrown off the set to tell them, "Cousins, I want you all to go to your windows, go to your windows and yell out, scream with all the life that you can muster up inside of your bruised, assaulted, and battered bodies, 'I am sick and tired of being a nigger and I'm not gonna take it anymore!'" In doing so, he echoes verbally (but this time, without the minstrel dialect) the earlier scene played to introduce and justify the television show, as well as echoing in both instances Peter Finch's famously fed-up newscaster in *Network* (1976). By using some of the same camera shots, blocking, and gestures as the earlier scene—except in this instance to stress its seriousness—Lee and his collaborators further underscore Manray's change of heart, his realization that, as Womack put it, *Mantan* is simply "the same bullshit," just done over.

Linked with these characters' realizations about the truth of *Mantan,* Lee features a character who explicitly emphasizes education and learning. Earlier in the film, Sloan tells Manray, "You should start reading," when he confesses a complete ignorance of past minstrel shows and their racist dimensions. But he is disinclined to learn because, he says, reading "makes my head kind of hurt." The importance of knowing the past and reflecting on its effects in the present, as well as its likely influences on the future, are thereby underscored by Sloan's explicit emphasis on reading and learning, as well as her implied message that it is crucial to think things through. Even though she facilitates the show's creation and production by doing research for Delacroix, and even though she goes along with *Mantan* because it promotes her career, time and again she emphasizes "telling the truth" about the program rather than sugarcoating it as alleged satire or allowing the other characters' historical amnesia to pass unremarked. Through Sloan's repeated endorsement of education, learning, and the implied need to think, Lee provides his audience with a partial antidote to what he sees as the poisonous toxicity of blackface minstrelsy.

Paying the Piper: From Satire to Melodrama

Another feature of the narrative that shows how deeply blackface has been internalized by more than just the primary characters is that not only the fictional television audience finds the coon routines funny; these scenes in the film prompt laughter from its *own* audience as well. One of the most audacious, courageous, and upsetting aspects of *Bamboozled* is that Lee allows some of these minstrel sequences to be humorous and entertaining to his viewers. Even Sloan, the character who provides the central moral orientation for the film, laughs during one of the classic coon routines, and Delacroix points this out so that its occurrence is not lost on viewers. We also see one of the Maumaus, the self-righteous rap group led by Sloan's brother Big Black Africa (Mos Def), laugh at one of *Mantan*'s minstrel-derived sequences. These narrative details push audience members to reflect on why they would laugh at such racist humor, which violates beliefs about equality and justice that most of them would otherwise explicitly uphold. Again, Lee urges his audience to seriously contemplate troubling dimensions of contemporary life in America by encouraging self-reflection about one's presuppositions concerning race, specifically by reflecting on the psychological conditions that make such laughter possible.

To further underscore these points, Lee makes a tonal shift in mid-narrative from biting comic satire to melodramatic seriousness. Some critics have complained that this shift is where many viewers become lost or alienated,[21] but the change in tone crucially highlights what Lee aims to achieve in *Bamboozled.* The shift, which he refers to as "paying the piper" for the events that preceded it,[22] functions to emphasize the negative aspects of the film's characters, which were played for laughs earlier. It shows the other side of Delacroix's acquiescence to the presumptions of blackface minstrelsy, Manray's ignorance of his blackface predecessors, and the Maumaus' unknowing mimicking of that which they profess to reject. Like *Network, Sunset Boulevard,* and, for that matter, *Do the Right Thing,* the narrative of *Bamboozled* turns from the comic pleasure of satirizing its characters, their weaknesses, and their gaps in knowledge or insight to showing the more serious consequences of such traits, which it does through violence (as did its antecedents) because Lee seeks to forcefully bring home their gravity. The director and his fellow filmmakers here transform those features that earlier made us laugh into the cause of several characters' downfall.

Consonant with this goal, and like many of Lee's earlier narratives, *Bamboozled* provides a way for its audience to see the actions of morally complicated characters as explicable and understandable but not justified. *Bamboozled* thus operates as a companion piece to *Do the Right Thing,* in that its amusing preceding events also aim to explain the subsequent violence. One strength of the later film is that, as in the earlier work, Lee does not allow viewers to avoid the ugly, hateful consequences of racism, here in the form of blackface minstrelsy and its damaging ongoing legacy. To drive home the impact of that phenomenon and the price of acquiescing with it, Lee feels the need to depict violent ends for Delacroix, Manray, and the Maumaus.

Viewers may readily comprehend why Delacroix and Manray have to pay for promoting and maintaining minstrel imagery in the new millennium; why, from the perspective of our conventional morality, their actions require significant penalty. Both characters commit self-centered and seriously injurious acts toward others through either ignorance or willful self-deception, and this part of the film's moral structure implies, in agreement with the typical values of most viewers, that their transgressions should be punished. As film theorist Murray Smith explains, classic Hollywood storytelling offers an implicit system of values, such that the moral structure of a narrative is relatively clear. One option is a "Manichaean moral structure" through which the virtuous are rewarded and the evil are punished, just as most of us hope happens in real life.[23] Lee invokes these conventional presuppositions here: narratively speaking, then, it should make sense to most viewers that Delacroix and Manray are punished for what they have done to themselves and to blacks in general because audience members presumably hope and expect that evildoers will be punished for their transgressions. The violence of that punishment drives home Lee's point that their transgressions against humanity are severe. Here, some might argue that Lee's narrative morality borders on Old Testament harshness, but I think Lee would respond that the impression of harshness may be due to a certain racial insensitivity or underappreciation of the dehumanizing effects of minstrel images.[24] The degree of harm and injury caused by such imagery is, Lee hopes to show, profound—a point he presses home by means of the serious consequences visited on these fictional characters.

Similarly, the Maumaus' anger at Manray for propagating minstrel stereotypes is justified, even if their actions are not. Like Mookie's (Spike Lee) actions in *Do the Right Thing*, the Maumaus' televised torture and execution of Manray may be seen, from the moral perspective presumed by the narrative, as actions that understandably grow from preceding events, even as they remain unjustified and unfair. Even though Manray deserves to be punished for his feckless actions, what the Maumaus do to him is far worse than he deserves, particularly when one considers his belated realization that Womack was right. Some of the ways the Maumaus torture Manray are racialized in precisely the manner they seek to criticize, because due to their lack of knowledge and insight about the past, they fail to recognize that what they are doing is simply another version of blackface minstrelsy, a point the filmmakers emphasize by intercutting a cartoon version of their actions that stresses their congruity with those portrayed on *Mantan* itself. In these ways, *Bamboozled* makes Manray out to be something of a tragic figure, even as it implies that he deserves serious retribution for his earlier complicity. But because Manray has seen the error of his ways and sought to make amends, the Maumaus' literal and metaphorical blackface execution of him is that much more unjust, even if it remains explicable in terms of the film's narrative contours.

The Maumaus themselves are then summarily massacred by the police while resisting arrest. All but the one member who appears phenotypically white die in a hail of bullets as the police raid their hangout just after they execute Manray. Their surviving member, One-sixteenth Black (MC Serch), cries that he too should have been killed because he is black, since all it takes in America is "one drop of black blood."[25] Viewers see narrative retribution visited on these characters not only for their treatment of Manray but also for the misguided ways they ignorantly reenact aspects of minstrelsy themselves, such as their silly rejection of the letter *c* in the word *black*, on the grounds that it is an instance of white oppression, or the ways they enact the worst excesses of gangsta rap, which Lee has argued in interviews "has evolved to a modern day minstrel show, especially if you look at the videos."[26] Although the Maumaus' rejection of *Mantan* and their anger at its demeaning imagery are justified, their gangsta-inspired vigilantism is not, for the narrative depicts their actions as unfair, excessive, and ignorant rather than judicious, proportionate, and wise.

Delacroix's Self-Assessment and Viewer Reflection

The narrative analogously explains Sloan's anger and her killing of Delacroix without justifying it. Unhinged by the events that have just occurred, she shows up at his office in her bedroom slippers carrying a gun because she knows that his actions were a factor in both her brother's and Manray's deaths, as well as playing a role in the denigration of blacks generally by creating a profoundly racist television show. She feels that the only way she can get him to understand "what [he has] contributed to" is to force him, at gunpoint, to watch a compilation tape of demeaning minstrel images that show *Mantan*'s continuity with America's racist past. The noirishly unbalanced, off-kilter shots of this sequence underscore her hysteria.

Once Sloan compels Delacroix to pay attention to the results of her research, he seems to realize his complicity. As he walks toward her, asking her to put the gun down, she warns him not to come any closer, and there is a sense that the gun just goes off in her hand as he tries to wrench it from her. As she screams at the gun's report, it goes off once more, and her reaction to the second shot indicates she is surprised by it as well. When she apologizes for having shot him, he replies gently, "It's okay," as if he were comforting a child who was not responsible for some harm she had caused. Delacroix's forgiveness softens and to some extent exonerates Sloan's action within the fiction, as does the blocking of the shooting as accidental. These narrative elements still do not justify what Sloan has done, any more than the film justifies the Maumaus' actions against Manray. Again, the narrative offers reasons for Sloan's shooting of Delacroix without absolving her. The film makes it clear that, like her brother's rap group, she has acted excessively rather than in accordance with justice, even while it offers more comprehensive and mitigating reasons for her disproportionate act with respect to the circumstances.

This question of what Delacroix deserves is further underscored by his dying soliloquy: "As I bled to death, as my very life oozed out of me, all I could think of was something the great Negro James Baldwin had written. 'People pay for what they do and still more for what they have allowed themselves to become, and they pay for it very simply by the lives they lead.'"[27] Through these words and subsequent shots, the film explicitly prompts viewers to think about the kind of life Delacroix has led and what an appropriate judgment for it would be. These elements also more subtly prompt viewers to contemplate what kind of lives they themselves are leading in terms of the themes just presented, as well as what would be an appropriate consequence for living such a life. Is it a life that somehow acquiesces with the sort of imagery promoted by *Mantan* or its real-world counterparts? Is it one intermixed with feelings of self-hatred and internalized racism, or one in which unthinking acceptance of stereotypes has facilitated harm and injury to others? How free are we of background assumptions that make possible the unfair treatment of African Americans? Are there really adequate justifications for laughing at or finding pleasure in the images of blackface minstrelsy, such as those with which the film ends? Just as Joe Gillis (William Holden) bitterly sums up his wasted, deluded life from the grave in *Sunset Boulevard,* so Pierre Delacroix assesses his own. By distancing himself from blackness and selfishly living in ways that seriously damage the lives of others, he has been bamboozled into making human existence worse for everyone, including himself, as he belatedly realizes.

The Baldwin quotation likewise underlines several other themes. One is a sort of noir deterministic fatefulness that *Bamboozled* directs at the consequences of going along with stereotypical images of blackface or its modern-day equivalents. Another is the need for education so that viewers might know the thoughts and insights of individuals such as Baldwin and thereby have some hope of avoiding past mistakes. A third is that of taking seriously the Socratic need for contemplation and analysis of the lives we lead and what our actions say about ourselves and our stance toward humanity in general. A fourth is that of remaining properly attuned to ongoing versions of racialized thinking and the damaging effects such thinking may have. As a clip of Farina (Allen Clayton Hoskins) from the 1930s *Our Gang* serial mockingly tells the viewer, "Brother, this certainly gonna be a lesson to me!" Delacroix additionally tells us to "always leave them laughing" and follows with his own forced, bitter chuckling that merges into an obviously canned laugh track and Terence Blanchard's melancholic film score.

Delacroix's acidic irony forces onto viewers an acrid aftertaste from having found amusement and pleasure in the images presented earlier. Given the film's structure and the careful way it presents its tale of self-deception and casual dismissal of racism gone horribly wrong, Lee and his collaborators intend for their audience to thoroughly experience that bitterness. In the end, *Bamboozled* is a scathing, angry satire that wishes to explicitly convey its fury over these matters, so that viewers might have some reason to think and act differently. By carefully considering the film's narrative, they might grasp that Lee's aim here is a lesson that will make them turn inward to contemplate what made their earlier laughter possible, as well as motivate them to actually do something about what they find within themselves.

Spike Lee as Philosopher

As an artist and a filmmaker, Spike Lee aims to provoke emotional responses in his viewers ranging from anger and outrage to compassion, laughter, sadness, empathy, and recognition. Frequently, he courts these responses to make his viewer *think* about the issues presented—he wants us to mull over the role and importance such issues have in our lives. When Lee incites controversy, he does so because he wants people to reflect seriously and discuss the matter at hand—whether it be misunderstandings of race and xenophobia or the need to take responsibility for one's actions—and come to a better understanding than they previously have had. One technique he regularly employs is the arousal of anger over injustice, or righteous indignation at the way some people uncomprehendingly fail to appreciate the full humanity of others. As Aristotle noted long ago, being *appropriately* angry or righteously indignant at undeserved good or ill fortune is sometimes the proper response.[28] In the right amount, at the right time and place, aimed at the right things or the right people, for the proper length of time, and expressed in the proper way, anger can serve as a motivating force in getting us to eliminate injustice.[29] In this sense, Lee is being a good Aristotelian by getting the ball rolling and compelling us, through our anger, to thoughtfully consider how injustice might best be addressed.

Moreover, coupled with the deep compassion, sympathy, and empathy with which he invests so many of his characters, Lee aims to compel his viewers not only to think but also to *act* differently as a result of their serious and thoughtful consideration of these matters. Again, this conception of reflection agrees with Aristotle, who tells us that when we contemplate philosophically, we use our best intellectual capacities to achieve some truth, knowledge, or understanding of what we contemplate. Ideally, our reflections will yield a conclusion of sorts, although such a result is by no means necessary, even if it is the most desirable outcome. Our intellectual concentration on some topic thus achieves the level of philosophy if our considerations are sufficiently theoretical, abstract, or general, even if a resolution does not immediately result.[30] Many of Spike Lee's films thus qualify as artworks that encourage us to philosophize, to think deeply and intensely about fundamental human questions in ways that could potentially change our lives because, as a result of our reflections, our sense of the world and our place in it could change as well.[31]

Lee's use of satire, film noir, discomforting themes, and narrative shocks thus function, especially in *Bamboozled,* to urge us not only to think but also to do so philosophically. Like Socrates' description of himself as a "gadfly" who goads the Athenians to think about virtue in the *Apology,*[32] Lee goads us to think about the role of minstrel stereotypes in determining how we gauge others' humanity as superior or inferior to our own. And as a result of that philosophical thinking, Lee's aim is to get us to see how we must change—think, act, and perceive our world and our place in it differently—if we are to fully live up to our professed ideals of justice and equality. In this sense, *Bamboozled* is by no means an anomaly in Spike Lee's oeuvre. Rather, it lines up consistently with his other work, from *Do the Right Thing* to *When the Levees Broke* (2006).

Sadly, America still has not put to rest the damning litany of stereotypes that black film historian Donald Bogle used as the title of his famous book more than thirty-five years ago: "toms, coons, mulattoes, mammies, and bucks," all of which owe their existence and strength to blackface minstrelsy.[33] Sprinkled throughout the history of film and television are shockingly uncritical uses of these stereotypes, which ultimately do no one any good, for they demean not only those they malign but those doing the demeaning as well. "White privilege" dehumanizes not just blacks and other nonwhites but also whites themselves; it cuts off their access to the full range of human possibility and flourishing that would be within their grasp if only they could recognize and acknowledge the full worth and dignity of *all* their fellow human beings—a point that Martin Luther King Jr., James Baldwin, and others have made again and again.[34] For whites who embrace their "white privilege," whole dimensions of human interactions, lifestyles, languages, gestures, and relationships are surrounded by a racial *cordon sanitaire* that forbids transgression, on the pain of being ostracized as "race traitors," "renegades," or worse. For nonwhites, it becomes a psychological concentration camp where neither work nor conformity makes one free. Spike Lee desperately wants us to appreciate these insights, which is why *Bamboozled* aims to show us how blackface continues to exert a profound influence on our thinking, perceiving, and acting. Such insights, of course, can be agonizingly humbling and distressing to face, which may well explain why so many recoiled from Lee's presentation of them in this film.

As with any artwork, these elements exist for us to perceive or not, to accept or reject as we deem appropriate. The first of these alternatives, I would argue, also make available a much richer, caring, and just world; the latter alternatives, almost too sad to contemplate, are much closer to our current state of affairs, but they are by no means necessary or inevitable. The choices are up to us.

Notes

I would like to thank the Pennsylvania State University Press for permission to use materials from my *Philosophy, Black Film, Film Noir* (2008) for this chapter. I would also like to thank Susan Kollin and Mark Conard for helpful comments on earlier versions of this essay.

1. Roger Ebert, "*Bamboozled* [review]," *Chicago Sun-Times,* October 6, 2000, rogerebert.suntimes.com (accessed September 13, 2009).

2. For example, listen to the interviews of Clyde Taylor, Jack Newfield, and Stanley Crouch in "The Making of *Bamboozled*" on the *Bamboozled* DVD (New Line Home Entertainment, 2001).

3. For a sampling of negative responses, see Armond White, "Post-Art Minstrelsy," *Cineaste* 26, 2 (2001): 12–14; Tavia Nyong'o, "Racial Kitsch and Black Performance," in *The Spike Lee Reader,* ed. Paula J. Massood (Philadelphia: Temple University Press, 2008), 212–27; Jamie Barlowe, "'You Must Never Be a Misrepresented People': Spike Lee's *Bamboozled,*" *Canadian Review of American Studies* 33, 1 (2003): 1–15; Beretta E. Smith-Shomade, "'I Be Smackin' My Hoes': Paradox and Authenticity in *Bamboozled,*" in *The Spike Lee Reader,* 228–42. For examples of more positive responses, see Michael Rogin, "Nowhere Left to Stand: The Burnt Cork Roots of Popular Culture," *Cineaste* 26, 2 (2001): 14–15, and Michael H. Epp, "Raising Minstrelsy: Humour, Satire, and the Stereotype in *The Birth of a Nation* and *Bamboozled,*" *Canadian Review of American Studies* 33, 1 (2003): 17–35. See also the "User Comments" for *Bamboozled,* which run the gamut from positive to negative, on the International Movie Database, www.imdb.com/title/tt0215545/usercomments (accessed September 5, 2009).

4. Gary Crowdus and Dan Georgakas, "Thinking about the Power of Images: An Interview with Spike Lee," *Cineaste* 26, 2 (2001): 9.

5. See Aristotle, *Metaphysics,* book I, trans. W. D. Ross, in *The Basic Works of Aristotle,* ed. Richard McKeon (New York: Random House, 1941), esp. 689ff.

6. Crowdus and Georgakas, "Thinking about the Power of Images," 9; Spike Lee commentary, *Bamboozled* DVD.

7. According to American historians Alexander Saxton and Robert Toll, blackface minstrelsy began roughly around 1830; by the beginning of the next decade, it had become the dominant form of theatrical entertainment in the United States and remained so for most of the rest of the nineteenth century. Alexander Saxton, *The Rise and Fall of the White Republic: Class Politics and Mass Culture in Nineteenth-Century America* (London: Verso, 2003), 165–81; Robert C. Toll, *Blacking Up: The Minstrel Show in Nineteenth-Century America* (New York: Oxford University Press, 1971). Moreover, its influence persisted well into the twentieth century, as seen in films such as *The Jazz Singer* (1927), *Babes in Arms* (1939), *Dumbo* (1941), *Holiday Inn* (1942), *Song of the South* (1946), and *Jolson Sings Again* (1949). For more on this dubious Hollywood blackface legacy, see Michael Rogin, *Blackface, White Noise: Jewish Immigrants in the Hollywood Melting Pot* (Berkeley and Los Angeles: University of California Press, 1996).

8. Lee commentary, *Bamboozled* DVD.

9. For more on the older television programs mentioned here, see Thomas Cripps, "*Amos 'n' Andy* and the Debate over American Racial Integration," in *American History/American Television,* ed. John O'Connor (New York: Ungar, 1983), 33–54; Aniko Bodroghkozy, "*Beulah,*" http://www.museum.tv/archives/etv/B/htmlB/beulah/beulah.htm (accessed February 7, 2005); and Wil and Ron Kurer, "*Calvin and the Colonel,*" http://www.spudtv.com/features/primetimecartoons/calvinandthecolonel.html (accessed September 15, 2001). For more contemporary versions of such programming (such as *The Secret Life of Desmond Pfeiffer*), see Crowdus and Georgakas, "Thinking about the Power of Images," 6–7, 9, and Lisa Jones, "Slave TV: Defending *Pfeiffer* Is the Most Offensive Sitcom of All," *Village Voice,* November 10, 1998, http://www.villagevoice.com/content/printVersion/213223 (accessed September 8, 2009).

10. For more on the importance of recognizing and acknowledging other human beings as well as narrative characters in film, see Stanley Cavell, *The Claim of Reason: Wittgenstein, Skepticism, Morality, and Tragedy* (New York: Oxford University Press, 1979), esp. 372ff, and *The World Viewed: Reflections of the Ontology of Film,* enlarged ed. (Cambridge, Mass.: Harvard University Press, 1979).

11. See also Lee's comments on Delacroix in Michael Sragow, "Black Like Spike," in *Spike Lee: Interviews,* ed. Cynthia Fuchs (Jackson: University of Mississippi Press, 2002), 193.

12. Charles W. Mills, *The Racial Contract* (Ithaca, N.Y.: Cornell University Press, 1997), 18–19.

13. Ibid., 75–78.

14. Sragow, "Black Like Spike," 193; see also Damon Wayans interview in "The Making of *Bamboozled,*" *Bamboozled* DVD.

15. Frantz Fanon, "The Lived Experience of the Black" (1951), trans. Valentine

Moulard, in *Race*, ed. Robert Bernasconi (London: Blackwell, 2001), 183–201. The essay has also been translated as "The Fact of Blackness," in *Black Skins, White Masks*, trans. Charles Markmann (New York: Grove Press, 1967), 110–41.

16. Mills, *The Racial Contract*, 87–88.

17. Ibid., 89.

18. Sadly, scientific studies alleging black and other forms of nonwhite inferiority are legion; for a summary and analysis of some historical versions, see Stephen Jay Gould, *The Mismeasure of Man*, rev. ed. (New York: W. W. Norton, 1996), and Elazar Barkan, *The Retreat of Scientific Racism* (Cambridge: Cambridge University Press, 1992). For examples of more recent versions, see Charles Murray and Richard J. Herrnstein, *The Bell Curve* (New York: Free Press, 1993); J. Philippe Rushton, *Race, Evolution, and Behavior* (New Brunswick, N.J.: Transaction Books, 1995); Seymour W. Itzkoff, *The Decline of Intelligence in America* (Westport, Conn.: Praeger, 1994); Michael Levin, *Why Race Matters: Race Differences and What They Mean* (Westport, Conn.: Praeger, 1997); and numerous articles in the peer-reviewed journals *Mankind Quarterly* and *Intelligence* or the more popularly aimed *American Renaissance*. For a scary reminder of how persistent these allegedly scientific claims can be, see the remarks of 1962 Noble Prize winner James Watson (who discovered the structure of DNA) in Helen Nugent, "Black People 'Less Intelligent' Scientist Claims," *Times Online* (London), October 17, 2007, www.timesonline.co.uk/tol/news/uk/article2677098.ece (accessed November 19, 2009).

19. T. S. Eliot, "Hamlet and His Problems," in *The Sacred Wood: Essays on Poetry and Criticism* (London: Methune, 1921), 100.

20. Crowdus and Georgakas, "Thinking about the Power of Images," 6.

21. For example, Sragow, "Black Like Spike," 190; Crowdus and Georgakas, "Thinking about the Power of Images," 8.

22. Sragow, "Black Like Spike," 192; Crowdus and Georgakas, "Thinking about the Power of Images," 8.

23. Murray Smith, *Engaging Characters: Fiction, Emotion, and the Cinema* (Oxford: Clarendon Press, 1995), 205–14. Smith argues against interpreting Hollywood melodrama *strictly* in terms of Peter Brooks's conception of melodrama as a Manichaean moral structure; see Peter Brooks, *The Melodramatic Imagination: Balzac, Henry James, Melodrama, and the Mode of Excess* (1976; reprint, New Haven, Conn.: Yale University Press, 1995), esp. 28ff. Instead, Smith argues for a "graduated moral structure" for typical Hollywood films, especially melodramas. I agree with Smith that Hollywood melodrama provides a range of possible moral structures; I merely point out here that in the case of Delacroix and Manray, Lee invokes the Manichaean *option* of giving immoral or blameworthy characters their comeuppance.

24. See, for example, Spike Lee interview in "The Making of *Bamboozled*" and Lee commentary, *Bamboozled* DVD.

25. For more on the complicated history of what counts as "blackness" in America and its relation to the "one drop rule," see F. James Davis, *Who Is Black?* (University Park: Pennsylvania State University Press, 1991).

26. Sragow, "Black Like Spike," 195; Crowdus and Georgakas, "Thinking about the Power of Images," 5. Presumably, this collapse of rap excess into modern-day minstrelsy is due to some artists not understanding the use of criminality as a pose for rejecting the status quo rather than an actual identity to adopt, or due to their belief in their own hype.

27. Lee is quoting here from Baldwin's "The Black Boy Looks at the White Boy" (1963), in *Collected Essays* (New York: Library of America, 1998), 386.

28. Aristotle, *Nicomachean Ethics,* trans. David Ross, rev. J. L. Ackrill and J. O. Urmson (Oxford: Oxford University Press, 1980), 96–98, and *The Rhetoric of Aristotle,* trans. Lane Cooper (1932; reprint, New York: Appleton-Century-Crofts, 1960), 98, 101–2, 123, 126.

29. Aristotle, *Nicomachean Ethics,* 96; *The Rhetoric of Aristotle,* 93–102, 123–27.

30. For more on philosophical contemplation and reflection, see Aristotle, *Nicomachean Ethics,* books VI and X, 138–39, 263–69.

31. For more detailed arguments concerning how film can function as philosophy by spurring our reflection on fundamental human questions, see Stanley Cavell, "The Thought of Movies," in *Themes Out of School* (Chicago: University of Chicago Press, 1984), 3–26; Stephen Mulhall, *On Film,* 2nd ed. (London: Routledge, 2008), 3–11, 129–55; Dan Flory, *Philosophy, Black Film, Film Noir* (University Park: Pennsylvania State University Press, 2008), 1–3, 58–62, 168–83, 315–22; and Noël Carroll, "*Memento* and the Phenomenology of Comprehending Motion Picture Narration," in *Memento,* ed. Andrew Kania (London: Routledge, 2009), 127–46.

32. Plato, *Apology* 30e-31b, in *Five Dialogues,* 2nd ed., trans. G. M. A. Grube, rev. John M. Cooper (Indianapolis: Hackett, 2002), 35.

33. Donald Bogle, *Toms, Coons, Mulattoes, Mammies, and Bucks: An Interpretive History of Blacks in Americans Films* [1974], 4th ed. (New York: Continuum, 2001).

34. Martin Luther King Jr., "Letter from Birmingham City Jail" (1963), in *African-American Philosophy: Selected Readings,* ed. Tommy L. Lott (Upper Saddle River, N.J.: Prentice-Hall, 2002), 247; James Baldwin, *The Fire Next Time* (New York: Dell, 1964), 127–37; Lewis R. Gordon, *Bad Faith and Antiblack Racism* (Atlantic Highlands, N.J.: Humanities Press, 1995), 183–84; Cavell, *The Claim of Reason,* 372ff; Mulhall, *On Film,* 33–39; Flory, *Philosophy, Black Film, Film Noir,* 98, 116–17, 301–2, 320–21.

Part III

Time, the Subject, and Transcendence

Transcendence and Sublimity in Spike Lee's Signature Shot

Jerold J. Abrams

In most of his films, Spike Lee includes a shot of an individual silently floating forward toward the viewer. Lee calls this his "signature shot."[1] Before the signature shot, the on-screen world appears interconnected and real. But then suddenly realism fades and the character enters a different mode of space-time as if temporarily removed from gravity and the present. The character appears to leave the film and traverse the boundary between screen and viewer like an object in a 3-D movie or like the viewer's imagination itself, which also traverses this boundary to immerse itself in the film. In this twilight space between viewer and film, the suspended character in the signature shot faces the viewer and projects forward in slow motion or with superhuman speed, depending on the character's state of mind and the mood of the scene. The effect of the signature shot is mildly shocking to the viewer and sufficient to suspend for a moment the viewer's immersion in a continuous cinematic narrative. In this way, Lee injects a moment of phenomenological complexity into the film, recasting the view of the film as a whole because this moment throws into relief the relation between the viewer and the film viewed. In the moment of the signature shot, the viewer is thrown clear from her unconscious immersion in a cinematic world as she is faced with an individual character who looks out of the film at the viewer in a transcendent, silent, detached, individuated state, apparently looking into another world—like the individual in the theater. The viewer now finds herself faced with her cinematic mirror image in the form of the character in which she was previously immersed.

Transcendence in Film Experience

In cinematic experience, the viewer engages in two forms of imaginative transcendence: immersion and anticipation. Immersion is spatial because the viewer forgets her spatial location in the theater and enters a representation of a three-dimensional space or world. Anticipation is temporal because the viewer forgets time in her own world and projects the future of the world within the film. The same experiences of immersion and anticipation occur when a reader "gets lost" in a novel: the words and the pages disappear and the world of the story unfolds and takes the reader into it. The reader loses track of time in her own world and forgets the spatial relation of the book in her hands. The capacity to lose oneself in another world is a natural feature of the aesthetic imagination, as philosopher George Santayana writes in *The Sense of Beauty:*

> There seems to be a boundless capacity of development in each of us, which the circumstances of life determine to a narrow channel; and we like to revenge ourselves in our reveries for this imputed limitation, by classifying ourselves with all that we are not, but might so easily have been. We are full of sympathy for every manifestation of life, however unusual; and even the conception of infinite knowledge and happiness—than which nothing could be more removed from our condition or more unrealizable to our fancy—remains eternally interesting to us.[2]

All good literary and cinematic fiction is transcendent, insofar as it takes the viewer to another world. In the case of film immersion, the experience can be greater than novel immersion because film presents a realistic set of givens in moving images on a massive screen with color and sound and dialogue. The screen and the sound envelop the individual's visual and auditory fields while the darkness of the rest of the theater isolates and makes the viewer forget her seated position. The architecture of the theater is built for this purpose of actualizing the natural capacity of immersion in another world. The viewer in the dark theater immerses imaginatively in the character and lives for a time in the world portrayed.

Of course, in film experience, as in literary experience, the immersion is never absolute. The imagination divides itself: the viewer projects her identity into the film through immersion, but she also remains vaguely (but foundationally) aware that she is not actually *in* the world portrayed. Film experience is complex. Philosopher of aesthetics Arthur Danto describes this power of film to maintain the viewer in two positions at once, inside the theater and inside the film:

> In a way, I think the kinetification, if you will, of the camera goes some way toward explaining the internal impact films make on us, for it seems to overcome, at least in principle, the distance between spectator and scene, thrusting us like movable ghosts into scenes that a kinetic photography locates us outside of, exactly like disembodied Cartesian spectators. We are within scenes that we also are outside of through the fact that we have no dramatic location, often, in the action that visually unfolds, having it both ways at once, which is not an option available to the audiences of stage plays.[3]

As a *nonimmersed* viewer, the moviegoer examines the on-screen world as a *filmed world* (an object), with a closed future, causally determined from beginning to end, and a set running time. Cinematic determinism is fully apparent, and the viewer judges the aesthetic unity of the film as temporally extended toward an end. As an *immersed* viewer, the moviegoer experiences the filmed world as her own (as "mine"), with an open future. The fact of cinematic determinism is suspended. Yet in both forms of cinematic experience, the viewer cannot but project transcendentally and transcendently forward what is given on the screen into the future. All cinematic viewing (and all thought, for that matter) depends on this forward projection (or transcendence) of the present into the future, as German philosopher Martin Heidegger writes in *Being and Time:* "Anticipation makes Da-sein *authentically* futural in such a way that anticipation itself is possible only in that Da-sein, *as existing,* always already comes toward itself, that is, is futural in its being in general."[4] (*Da-sein* is Heidegger's term for the human being—literally, "being there.") One projects one's being beyond the *now* of the present into the *then* of the open future. This transcendence is mostly unconscious. For example, whenever I begin saying or writing a sentence, I seem to race ahead of the words (even as the words come out) to see how the sentence should go on or to see how best to shape the next sentence. Thought does not go on without this fundamental (and unconscious) assumption of being thrust forward into the future in anticipation of things to come. The same applies to viewing a film. The viewer anticipates the action of the film by transcendental extension of the patterns of previous scenes, such as the persistence of forms of characters and causal relations of actions.

There is also a dialectical dimension of this structure of transcendence within cinematic experience, as philosopher Noël Carroll writes in *Mystifying Movies.* Film narration works by question and answer. One scene asks a question (implicitly), and a later scene answers that question (again, implicitly): "The basic connective—the rhetorical bond between the two scenes—is the question/answer."[5] For example, in Lee's *25th Hour* (2002), early scenes establish the question of how drug dealer Monty Brogan (Edward Norton) will face his prison sentence. Monty's friend Francis Xavier Slaughtery (Barry Pepper) presents the three possible answers: "Man, he's got three choices and none of them are good. One, he can run. Two, catch the bullet train. . . . His third choice is he goes to prison, and that's it." No matter what, Monty will be gone. If he runs or commits suicide, his friends will never see him again. If he goes to prison, his friends will never see him again either—at least not as he is now, because prison will break him. As the film unfolds, the dialectic narrows: suicide disappears as an answer, and the other two possibilities play out.

Lee establishes a similar type of dialectic in *Inside Man* (2006) as bank robbers take hostages. Questions arise. Will Detective Frazier (Denzel Washington) catch Russell (Clive Owen)? Will the bank robbers execute hostages? Will Frazier kill Russell? Will Russell kill Frazier? From the beginning of the film, with the raising of these questions, the viewer remains in a relational tension between the presentness of the empirical given of the moving images and what the mind projects. The viewer remains immersed in these dialectics and anticipates future scenes as answers to early questions—until Lee introduces the signature shot. This shot dissolves immersion and throws the film into relief as a self-reflexive film.

Signature Shot in *Malcolm X*

In *Malcolm X* (1992) the signature shot appears near the end of a long and well-executed film. Lee immerses the viewer in the world of Malcolm X (Denzel Washington). The entirety of his life unfolds, and the viewer knows ahead of time that Malcolm X will die, but not how Lee will portray this death and not what experiences Malcolm X will have before his death. Malcolm X knows that he is facing death as he drives to the auditorium for his last speech. He sits in his car. He considers his life as a whole and its end. Everything still appears real at this point. Then Lee introduces the signature shot. It comes from below, looking up at Malcolm X with the sky behind him. He floats forward. He floats toward the viewer. He is silent. His eyes look transcendent, ethereal. The viewer does not see his feet lift off the sidewalk. Rather, Lee implies levitation by the smoothness of his movement. Malcolm X hovers above the ground in slow motion. He looks into himself and beyond himself, and he looks beyond this world. He is in a transcendent state. He feels peace.

In this moment, as Malcolm X detaches from immersion in his world, the viewer's imagination also detaches from its immersion in the world of the film. The viewer effectively follows the character out of the film itself to arrive back in the theater in a reflective state of viewing the character from an objective perspective. In this moment, Lee's realism becomes magical; the viewer becomes aware of her own immersion in the world of film achieved by the magic of cinematic realism, and she becomes strikingly aware of her position in the theater. The viewer's projected identity has been ejected from the film and thrust back into self-awareness. Now the relational structure of a subjective viewer watching a film as an object from a distance is thrown into relief for the viewer. Danto describes a similar effect achieved by master filmmakers as among the most important advances in the history of cinema:

> I think the chief innovation of the moving camera is to make the mode of recording part of the record, which in turn thrusts the art of cinema into the image in a singularly intimate way. This happens when, for instance, the swinging of the image through an abrupt angle is to be read as a movement not of it but of the camera, as in a mob scene, where the camera is, as it were, "jostled," or when, more archly, the camera literally climbs the stairway with an eye and a lubricity of its own and pokes into one bedroom after another in search of the lovers, as in one of Truffaut's films. In such cases, the movement of the camera is not our movement, and this has precisely the effect of thrusting us outside the action and back into our metaphysical Cartesian hole.[6]

In Lee's signature shots, the camera does not float with lubricity or an eye all its own so much as it captures the individual floating with lubricity, but the effect achieved is the same. Like Truffaut, Lee thrusts the viewer out of the film and back into an awareness of herself as a spectator in a theater who was immersed and then ejected from the narrative.

Once the viewer is thrust back into her Cartesian viewing hole, the experience of the film becomes phenomenologically self-reflexive. The viewer becomes aware of herself *as a viewer.* But she also becomes aware of the film as metaphorically aware of itself as a film to be viewed. The film is effectively *about* being viewed. That is its content. Danto writes that such images (those achieved by Truffaut's floating camera or Lee's floating character) render films "self-conscious." By self-conscious, Danto means that the films no longer take as their subject matter the world they imitate; the subject becomes the very activity of filming itself. So the film *Malcolm X,* before the signature shot, is about the man Malcolm X. But with the signature shot, the film *Malcolm X* changes phenomenologically. Nothing material about the actual light and sound of the film has changed. But insofar as *Malcolm X* contains the possibility of a relation to the viewer, insofar as its ontological nature is to be viewed phenomenologically by a viewer who immerses within it, the film changes because the relation to the viewer changes. And the change in the relation to the viewer changes the viewer's experience of the film. Danto again explains this cinematic phenomenon in relation to Truffaut: "When this happens . . . the subject of the film changes; the story is no longer one of young lovers, rather, it is about their being observed and filmed as though the story itself were but an occasion for filming and the latter is what the film itself is about. Film becomes in a way its own subject; the consciousness that it is a film is what the consciousness is of."[7] In other words, the film changes from a representation of a world that actualizes the imagination's capacity for immersion to a new kind of film that seems to portray the very activity of watching a film (in the film). The ejected viewer now looks *at* the film as an object rather than looking *through* the film as a transparent lens into a world, an object that forces the understanding to consider the nature of cinematic representation.

What appears before the mind, once ejected from the *unconscious* transcendent state in cinematic experience, is the *conscious* awareness of the previous (unconscious) state of cinematic experience. The film *Malcolm X*, then, is about the film *Malcolm X* (as well as about the man) because the signature shot thrusts the viewer out of the film and back into the theater to examine phenomenologically the viewer's relation to the film and, more specifically, how the film invites the viewer to examine her relation to the film. The viewer has a strange experience of looking at herself, as though in a mirror, at the same moment she looks into the screen and sees Malcolm X looking out of the screen. Lee then completes the experience by showing Malcolm X (after the signature shot) looking into a mirror and contemplating his own transcendent state. As he sits in front of the mirror, he says, "It's a time for martyrs now." As Malcolm X experiences his new illumined self-consciousness, the viewer of *Malcolm X* simultaneously experiences her own newly illuminated self-consciousness, caused by the experience of seeing her cinematic mirror image in the film.

Signature Shot in *25th Hour*

In *25th Hour* Monty spends his last night of freedom with his girlfriend Naturelle Riviera (Rosario Dawson) and his two old friends Francis and

Jacob (Philip Seymour Hoffman). They get together at a nightclub to listen to music, drink, and have one last good night together before Monty goes to prison for seven years for dealing drugs, after which time he knows he will no longer be the same man. Outside the club they run into Jacob's seventeen-year-old student Mary D'Annuzio (Anna Paquin), who is waiting with her friends to get in. Monty invites Mary into the club (without her friends), where she drinks and dances with Naturelle. She feels at home in the loud and darkly lit nightclub, whereas her teacher feels estranged from his quiet, protected world of poetry. The classroom is *his* world. The nightclub is *her* world. She is immersed in this world, and the viewer immerses with her. But Mary disappears from view for a scene as Monty and Francis discuss Monty's sentence and how he might be able to manage his first night in prison. The scene is lit in cold blue. In his commentary on *25th Hour,* Lee sets up the signature shot.

> You know after this scene goes, ends, excuse me, we go back to the dancing, and another one of the Spike Lee dolly shots coming up as we see Anna, Anna Paquin ride in. The reason why we use the shot there is that we want to show what her mind state is. . . . She's been drinking champagne, drinking that Cristal, and she's taken some Ecstasy. . . . She's flying. And she's feeling sexual too. Right here. Here's the shot.[8]

Mary emerges slowly from behind tall, dark curtains, as if from a different world. Her eyes look transcendent, and her whole body floats forward. She looks up. Light shines on her face. Her face glows. She smiles. She feels the Ecstasy take effect. She feels light, like nothing holds her firm to the world. She does not move side to side as one moves when walking. Her shoulders do not move because her arms do not swing. Then she sees that she is floating. She does not question her transcendence. Her experience is epistemologically self-justifying. Nothing further is needed to know that she is in this transcendent state right now. She embraces it. She does not wonder whether others have this experience. She knows some do and some do not. But they do not matter right now. She has entered an individuated state. The openness around her individuates her form. Now she rolls her shoulders slowly. She dances through this transcendent space slowly. The curtains she walked through earlier now appear to be an ontological threshold she crossed, taking her into a new and higher dimension. She hovers in a transcendent state outside of this world.

As in *Malcolm X,* Lee's shot of Mary in *25th Hour* achieves what Danto describes in the films of Truffaut. The shot detaches the viewer from immersion in the film, just as Mary detaches from the world of the club. Mary projects forward and outward from the film, toward the viewer, and the viewer detaches from projection into the metaphysical Cartesian viewing hole. The shot of Mary ejects the immersed viewer from the film, and the relation between viewer and film appears before the viewer. Now the viewer examines the film as an object and sees in Mary a mirror image of the viewer in the theater. Mary is a viewer—silent, individuated, and detached from her world, like the theater viewer. She is surrounded by darkness and looks forward into the light, again like the theater viewer. In looking into the light, she looks beyond her world and into another world, like the viewer in the theater looking into the film's world. But Mary looks directly out of her world at the viewer, as if she knows a viewer is there to see her. She almost appears to emerge from the screen. The signature shot almost has a 3-D effect. She seems to hover just in between the screen and the viewer. The source of the light on Mary is not seen (by the viewer) as she traverses the ontological boundary between the screen and the viewer, like a mirror image of the activity of the imagination that also traverses this distance from metaphysical Cartesian viewing hole to cinematic immersion. In this twilight space, the light thrown all around her no longer appears to be the means of her portrayal on the screen; rather, it is additional light she experiences as if suspended beyond the screen in front of the film projector and above the heads of the moviegoers in the theater. She smiles into the light and knows she is being watched. The viewer looks into this light and knows that Lee has portrayed the viewer herself on-screen in the image of Mary.

Signature Shot in *Inside Man*

In *Inside Man,* Dalton Russell and his crew take a bank full of hostages and dress them in uniforms identical to their own, with face masks, so no one can be identified. Detective Keith Frazier tries to negotiate the safe release of the hostages and learn about Russell. Frazier enters the bank and talks with Russell. He wants to know his opponent. He attacks Russell, but Russell's assistant steps in and ends the situation at gunpoint. Russell lets Frazier go, but this tells Frazier that Russell is not violent, and that is too much for Frazier to know. Frazier has crossed the line, and Russell tells him so. Frazier returns to the mobile command center outside the bank and reviews the situation with Captain John Darius (Willem Dafoe):

FRAZIER: I gave him every excuse to blow my brains out. . . . He doesn't bite. Why? He ain't the type. Let's just step back and think about this for a second. We know that they planned this whole thing. The tape, the cameras, the costumes. There was a game plan, but it never included airplanes. He's up to something, but it ain't violence. [*Phone rings. Frazier answers.*]

RUSSELL: How's the reception?

FRAZIER: Excuse me?

RUSSELL: The camera on the truck. Give me a close-up on the second floor window. [*Russell executes a hostage.*]

In his commentary on *Inside Man,* Lee says of these scenes: "Oh wait a minute. Let's see the guy get shot in the head. Boom. Now comes the signature shot right here. Denzel on the dolly. Right here."

Frazier and his crew watch the execution of the hostage from the mobile command center. The execution is a fake, but Frazier and the other officers think it is real. Before the (staged) execution, Frazier is a man in control, confident, and intelligent. But at the moment of the execution, Frazier changes. The sight of the execution dissolves the ontological foundations of the world around him. Frazier stares directly into the camera at the viewer. Detective Mitchell (Chiwetel Ejiofor) yells after Frazier: "Keith! Keith! Keith!" Frazier cannot hear Mitchell. He cannot hear anything at this point. Frazier moves through the air with superhuman speed for the length of a block toward the viewer, facing the viewer, inflamed with anger. His movement is more superhuman than the movement of Malcolm X or Mary. They also float, but the signature shot of Frazier is superhuman in two ways: he floats *and* he accelerates beyond the capacity of any human being. Policemen sprint behind Frazier, but they cannot match his pace even though he does not run at all. Frazier looks monstrous, dangerous, like he could kill someone. He appears to be both superhuman and inhuman, like the monsters of nineteenth-century novels. Bram Stoker's vampire in *Dracula,* for example, moves with monstrous and superhuman speed: "There was something so panther-like in the movement—something so unhuman, that it seemed to sober us all from the shock of his coming."[9] So does Mary Shelley's monster in *Frankenstein:* "I suddenly beheld the figure of a man, at some distance, advancing towards me with superhuman speed."[10] But unlike Dracula and the monster of *Frankenstein,* who leap and bound with animal grace and power, Frazier's superhuman movement looks mechanical, almost robotic; it is vibrating and bumpy, unsteadied by what he thinks is a hostage negotiation gone sideways.

Like the signature shots of Malcolm X and Mary, this shot throws the viewer from her immersion in the film. At one moment the viewer lives within Frazier's world. He is rational, emotionally interesting, strong, and more capable than his rank reveals. And, like the viewer, Frazier wants to know what Russell has planned. Lee makes the viewer identify with Frazier from the beginning. But with the signature shot, the viewer detaches as realism disappears and Frazier appears to project out of the film toward the viewer, as if he might traverse the ontological boundary separating viewer and viewed—again, just like the imagination, like Danto's "ghost," who traverses the distance from theater to screen. At this point, the viewer sees in Frazier a potential mirror image of the viewer (like Mary): once immersed in a world, but now detached, individuated, silent, observing, and looking out of his world and into another. The viewer reconsiders the scene. Frazier is also a kind of viewer projecting forward into another world. At one moment, he sits calmly in his chair inside the enclosed room of the command center, as if in a very small theater. Russell tells him to look at his monitor. He does. He watches a broadcast of a hostage execution. But Russell has staged the scene to evoke an emotion and alter Frazier's perception of the real world (not unlike a filmmaker). As Frazier watches the scene, he projects forward and toward that world, silent and focused, like a theater viewer. Russell's own broadcast actualizes Frazier's capacity to become part of that screened world. He does not need to move his body to become part of this world. He simply projects forward without physical motion by an act of apparently superhuman power. But as Frazier thrusts forth *into* the screened world of the broadcast, the experience of those in the theater is that he appears to thrust forth *out of* Lee's film, *Inside Man,* and toward the audience. The viewer sees a strange and ghostly scene of Frazier projecting out of the screen. In this projected state, Frazier appears as a representation of the activity of the imagination, which also traverses the distance between the theater and the filmed world, as Danto describes that phenomenon.

Signature Shot as Sublime

The signature shot is also aesthetically sublime. Philosophers contrast the sublime with the beautiful. A natural object such as a rose or an artwork like Leonardo da Vinci's *Mona Lisa* is beautiful if it has form and shape and reasonable magnitude and if its ordered diversity as complexity delights the imagination, gives free play to the faculties, and draws the mind into a passive aesthetic contemplation (this combines elements of definitions by Aristotle in *The Poetics* and Kant in *The Critique of the Power of Judgment*). In the sublime, by contrast, sheer magnitude of power and size overwhelms the imagination, and the sheer genius and godlikeness of the author and the character the author portrays overwhelm the imagination as well. The sublime inspires awe both at the world beheld and at the imagination within that beholds that world. Longinus (a first-century Greek critic) makes this point in *On the Sublime:* "In dealing, then, with writers of genius, whose grandeur is of a kind that comes within the limits of use and profit, we must at the outset observe that, while they are far from unerring, yet they are above all mortal range. Other qualities prove their possessors men, sublimity lifts them nearer the mighty mind of God."[11]

Good writers and good filmmakers make *beautiful* and moving works of art. Great writers and great filmmakers make *sublime* and moving works of art. Geniuses make sublime works of art. Longinus highlights Homer of *The Iliad* (*The Odyssey* is less sublime); Plato of *The Republic,* with the powerful dialectical voice of reason; and Demosthenes, the great orator of antiquity, as sublime writers and thinkers. The beginning of Genesis is also sublime: "God said, 'Let there be light' and there was light."[12] The essence of the experience of the sublime in the reader or listener of these works is always a feeling of transcendence of the natural limits of humanity and a vision of the superhuman. Longinus makes this point about sublime poetry and philosophy in contrast to beautiful sculptures: "Also we expect a statue to resemble a man, but in literature, as I said before, we look for something greater than human."[13] We look for a vision of the superhuman or a world that only the superhuman could understand, a world without bounds.

In cinema, Stanley Kubrick's *2001: A Space Odyssey,* with its visions of space and the star child, is a sublime film. Steven Spielberg's *Jaws,* with its images of the vast ocean, is also sublime, as is Ridley Scott's *Alien.* These filmmakers overwhelm the viewer's mind with objects so vast and beings so powerful and so Other that the sensation and the imagination must struggle to grasp them. Lee is not one of these filmmakers. He is not a sublime filmmaker, not in the way Kubrick and Spielberg are sublime filmmakers. Lee's settings are often urban and hardly reveal the infinite in nature or humanity. His characters are very human, and their experiences are not (on the whole) transcendent or superhuman. But his signature shot *is* sublime, and in this shot he reveals his genius. The signature shot is sublime in two ways. First, the shot is sublime as an image. The shots of Malcolm, Mary, and Frazier are sublime because they portray these characters as superhuman. Second, these shots are sublime because they portray characters in transcendent states in which they also experience sublime transcendence. The signature shot is an image of what it is like to experience the sublime from the inside. It portrays the experience of aesthetic and emotional transcendence and elevation, a sense that one is beyond one's own limitations and beyond all human limitations. This sense of transcendence and elevation, Longinus writes, is the essence of the sublime: "For the true sublime naturally elevates us."[14] Of course, when Longinus says that the sublime elevates the individual, he does not mean that the individual is literally elevated off the ground. But Lee portrays the individual in the sublime state as elevated off the ground to represent the experience of emotional elevation. The elevation of the character is an objective image of the subjective experience of sublime transcendence, and the superhumanity of the elevation renders the objective image sublime as well. With these sublime and transcendent signature shots, Lee signs his work not only as a great filmmaker but also as a serious philosopher. He signs his films with phenomenologically self-reflexive and sublime moving images that present cinematic mirror images of the viewer to the viewer in her own cinematically transcendent state.

Notes

I am very grateful to Elizabeth F. Cooke and Mark Conard for comments on this essay that greatly improved the final version. Any mistakes that remain are my own.

1. Commentary, *Inside Man* DVD. Lee discusses the signature shot with Erich Leon Harris in "Spike Lee Speaks, Demystifying the Man," *MovieMaker Magazine,* March 2, 1997. Harris remarks, "One of your most interesting shots is a dolly shot that gives the effect of walking on a moving sidewalk." Lee says, "The first time I used it was in *Mo' Better Blues* with my character Giant" (www.moviemaker.com/directing/article/spike_lee_speaks_demystifying_the_man_3171/).

2. George Santayana, *The Sense of Beauty: Being the Outlines of Æsthetic Theory,* critical ed., ed. William G. Holzberger and Herman J. Saatkamp Jr. (Cambridge, Mass.: MIT Press, 1988), 115–16.

3. Arthur Danto, "Moving Pictures," in *Philosophizing Art: Selected Essays* (Berkeley: University of California Press, 1999), 229. I discuss Danto's thesis on the Hegelian self-consciousness of film in "Hitchcock and the Philosophical End of Film," in *Hitchcock as Moralist,* ed. R. Barton Palmer and Steven Sanders (Albany, N.Y.: SUNY Press, forthcoming).

4. Martin Heidegger, *Being and Time,* trans. Joan Stambaugh (Albany, N.Y.: SUNY Press, 1996), 298.

5. Noël Carroll, *Mystifying Movies: Fads and Fallacies in Contemporary Film Theory* (New York: Columbia University Press, 1988), 171.

6. Danto, "Moving Pictures," 230.

7. Ibid.

8. Later she talks in the club with her teacher. He asks, "Are you drunk?" She says, "Yeah. And I had some 'E' earlier."

9. Bram Stoker, *The Illustrated Dracula* (New York: Penguin Books, 2006), 312.

10. Mary Shelley, *Frankenstein: or, The Modern Prometheus,* ed. Maurice Hindle (New York: Penguin, 1992), 95.

11. Longinus, *On the Sublime,* trans. W. H. Fyfe, rev. Donald Russell (Cambridge, Mass.: Harvard University Press, 2005), 277–79.

12. Ibid., 191.

13. Ibid., 279–81.

14. Ibid., 179.

Economies of Time in *Clockers*

Richard Gilmore

> Art is more moral than moralities.
> —John Dewey, *Art as Experience*

Clockers (1995) begins with signs of violence: still shots of brutally shot people, all young, all black, all apparently inner city.[1] On the sound track Marc Dorsey sings a cool jazz "People in Search of a Life" (written by Raymond James). Capitalism is an extremely violent social system, but that violence is mostly symbolic in the bourgeois boardrooms and in the middle-class experience. In the inner city, where poverty is extreme, the violence is literal and very real. It is the dark side of the American way, of the American dream. But it is, essentially, the same system. The literal violence on the inner-city streets is just the desymbolized corollary to the symbolized violence of the system as a whole.

Very early in the movie *Clockers,* the nose of a black Chrysler Gran Fury glides its ominous way through a mostly black neighborhood of Brooklyn, New York, like a predatory shark. It represents the law, but the law in this neighborhood is not about protection so much as it is about oppression. The Gran Fury is on the prowl, in search of prey. Its prey are those who defy the law. The law is a function of the system, and the system is, among other things, deeply racist.

American Racism

The name of Spike Lee's production company, 40 Acres and a Mule, nicely captures the deep systematic ambivalence about race in the United States. It refers to the U.S. government's initial attempt to provide reparation to freed slaves after the Civil War. Under the First Freedman's Bureau Act, each freed slave would have received forty acres, but the act was defeated by Congress in 1866. General Sherman ordered that forty acres and a mule be allocated to the freedmen who marched with him, but that order was rescinded by President Andrew Johnson. Therefore, 40 Acres and a Mule also refers to the failure of those initial gestures toward reparation. As Spike Lee says, "the name of my production company is really a reminder of a broken promise."[2] It is a reminder of a broken promise by the U.S. government and a reference to the perpetuation of systematic racism in the United States.

"White"[3] Americans hate racism and embrace racism—the former overtly, the latter covertly, but both sincerely. If the Gran Fury signifies an element in the great system of American racism—racism in so concentrated a form that it has become a physical object—and if that object also signifies the system as a whole—a kind of microcosm of the macrocosm—then why the *fury*? The fury the car represents would be the fury of white people toward black people, but why, in a racist society that favors white people, would white people feel such fury toward black people?

Since the fury cannot be based on any sense of systemic injustice the white people experience, it must be based on fear. That fear, presumably, is of the loss of something. It is the result of a sense of vulnerability, a fear, perhaps, that the system itself, a system on which they feel dependent, may fall apart. It is the fear, I would say, of losing their status as "white." In any event, the fury this fear gives rise to is a fury to maintain the system, expressed through the laws enacted by a largely white federal government and judicial system, and enforced by the police forces of our cities, which may not be mostly white at all.

There are two ways of understanding racism. There is personal, individual racism, which anyone can manifest. Then there is systemic racism, the racism inherent in the U.S. cultural and economic system as a whole, so that all white people receive some advantage within the system for being white, and all black people receive some disadvantage for being black. In this latter way of understanding racism, it is appropriate to say that all white people are racist and no person of color can be racist. As it was phrased by the National Education Association: "In the United States at present, only whites can be racists, since whites dominate and control the institutions that create and enforce American cultural norms and values . . . blacks and other Third World peoples do not have access to the power to enforce any prejudices they may have, so they cannot, by definition, be racists."[4] This was written in 1973, and even though we now have a "black" president, insofar as "white" people continue to "dominate and control the institutions that create and enforce American cultural norms and values," it is still true today. What this means is that the system—the education system, the police system, the system of government, the economic system—looks radically different, depending on whether one is a person of color (disadvantaged by the system) or a "white" person (advantaged by the system). This is the insidious doubleness of the American system as a whole.

Ironies of Time

"Clockers" are the drug dealers on the streets selling drugs 24/7; hence they are always on the clock. The ironies are legion. "On the clock" is an expression denoting hardworking Americans at work. The clockers are also hardworking Americans at work, except they have no time clock and they work outside the legal system. It is as though they accept the values of the larger (legal) social system, but that system does not accept them, so they feel compelled to work outside it. What they sell is a form of relief from the oppression of the system. One way of describing this relief is in terms of time. The system enforces a strict notion of chronological time, time by the clock, *kronos* time. Drugs provide a release from that kind of time into something akin to what the ancient Greeks called "heroic time," or *kairos* time.

The movie opens with temporal jump cuts of Strike (Mekhi Phifer), the central protagonist. Strike surveys the scene. He appears to be a very alert, healthy young man, but we will learn that he suffers terribly from what appear to be ulcers. Ulcers are supposed to be the affliction of white middle-management men, men with a lot of responsibility and very little power, men so taxed by this combination of responsibility and powerlessness that their bodies take on the stress; their worry and frustration become internalized, and their bodies attack themselves, causing ulcers. This combination of responsibility and powerlessness is not, of course, the sole prerogative of middle-management white men. It is clearly the situation in which Strike finds himself, and he is suffering horribly from it.

The plot of *Clockers* involves two brothers, a murder, and a cop intent on solving the murder and bringing the murderer to justice. Strike seems to be the bad brother, and Victor (Isaiah Washington) seems to be the good brother. Rocco Klein (Harvey Keitel) seems to be a racist cop, although his persistence in pursuing justice rather than making an easy arrest complicates his character. The murder occurs at a fast-food fried seafood restaurant called Ahab's, complete with a neon white whale on top of the restaurant and a black whale with a saddle for children to ride by the front door. There does not seem to be an actual fast-food chain by this name, so I presume this is

Lee weighing in on the great subject of Melville studies: the symbolism of the white whale in *Moby Dick*. I read the white whale as, ironically enough, a symbol of the legacy of racism in the United States. The neon whale on top of the restaurant has several pink harpoons stuck in its side. As a nation, we have taken some shots at this specter of evil lurking under the surface of American life, but we certainly have not killed it.

There are various strands to the plot of the movie. The central strand is Rocco's conviction that it was Strike and not Victor who shot Darryl Adams (Steve White) outside Ahab's, even though Victor has confessed. Rocco is convinced that Strike is the killer and Victor is trying to cover for his brother, and Rocco is determined to pressure Strike into confessing. One way he tries to do this is by arresting Strike's street boss, the older local drug dealer Rodney (Delroy Lindo), and making Rodney think Strike set him up. The general idea seems to be that either Rodney will kill Strike, which would be one kind of justice, or Strike will have to ask the police for protection and thus confess to the shooting, which would be another kind of justice.

A subplot of the movie has to do with the friendship between Strike and the young boy Tyrone (Pee Wee Love). The scenes between Strike and Tyrone reveal how Strike himself is caught between childhood and the ugly realities of adulthood. They also reveal how easily the sins of adults get passed on to the next generation, even when the adults are well-meaning, as Strike seems to be toward Tyrone. Tyrone's mother, Iris (Regina Taylor), is ferociously protective of her young son, but to little avail. Strike's own mother, it is suggested, fought a similar battle to protect her sons; she lost the battle in the case of Strike and, in a way, of Victor as well, although she may have the power to redeem Strike, or even both her sons, in the end.

Similarly, Iris represents an option of redemption to Strike. There is a certain erotic tension in Iris's fury at Strike. Iris is not much older than Strike, and each may be precisely what the other needs. Strike needs a commitment to something real, as opposed to his unreal and unrealistic commitment to selling drugs and making money. Iris would probably like (I won't say "needs") a partner, a father for her son, and a companion who is her equal in intelligence, compassion, and even idealism. Strike, in his way—or at least in his potential—is all these things. Both Strike and Iris could probably really use, and would probably really enjoy, an erotic embrace and skirmish. That there is not even the slightest gesture toward this possible development is further testimony to the extreme duress imposed by the circumstances they are living under.

Gift Economies versus Commodity Economies

Lewis Hyde, in his book *The Gift: The Erotic Life of Property,* contrasts two very different kinds of economic systems: gift economies and commodity economies. Gift economies work by means of the circulation of gifts, whereas commodity economies work by the circulation of capital (money) and commodities (things that have a price). Both economies produce a surplus, a kind of remainder that results from the act of exchange. In gift economies, the surplus is human relationship, which entails certain social responsibilities. In commodity economies, the surplus is called "profit," which is the extra money generated by the exchange.[5] Profits can be saved up (in a bank) in a way that the surplus from gift exchanges cannot.

Tribal societies tend to be based on gift economies. Hyde specifically talks about gift economies among, for example, the North Pacific tribes such as the Kwakiutl, the Tlingit, and the Haida,[6] but Native Americans now living on reservations also function (mostly) according to gift economies. The official systems of most industrialized Western countries, like the United States, function according to the commodity economy known as capitalism. In commodity economies, everything is capable of acquiring a price, and the central working principle of capitalism is that the acquisition of profit is a good thing. Gift economies can work within commodity economies, as little eddies of counternarratives to the larger official narrative of the official system, which is capitalism. Churches, social groups, and family groups all tend to operate more according to the logic of the gift economy than that of the commodity economy. Various forms of gifts are exchanged, and various forms of social responsibility are formed as a result of those exchanges. Commodity economies exist, for the most part, in accordance with the logic of chronological time. Gift economies exist, for the most part, in accordance with the logic of *kairotic* time; they are more responsive to the movement of the sun and the moon than to clocks and calendars. In commodity economies, clocks are essential; in gift economies, there is no real need for clocks. Gift exchanges work in temporal patterns more attuned to the rhythms of hours, days, months, and years rather than seconds or minutes.

Double-Consciousness

Two kinds of economies, two forms of time, two forms of racism, two systems of values—the reality of these dualities are precisely captured in W. E. B. DuBois's description of a "double-consciousness" in his important book *The Souls of Black Folk:* "It is a peculiar sensation, this double-consciousness, this sense of always looking at one's self through the eyes of others, of measuring one's soul by the tape of a world that looks on in amused contempt and pity. One ever feels his twoness—an American, a Negro; two souls, two thoughts, two unreconciled strivings; two warring ideals in one dark body, whose dogged strength alone keeps it from being torn asunder."[7] DuBois is talking about the experience of African Americans here, but it is so poignant a description and so powerful a concept precisely because it is something everyone experiences to some degree.[8] It is a feature of our "thrownness," to use a phrase from Martin Heidegger—the fact that we find ourselves thrown into a world we did not choose, saddled with a gender, an ethnicity, a nationality, a socioeconomic status, and a family we have not chosen and cannot fully escape.

There are two sequences early in the movie that capture this idea of double-consciousness, which I interpret as being about inhabiting a space where the dualities of commodity economy and gift economy, chronological time and *kairotic* time, individual racism and systemic racism, and a value system oriented around human relations as well as one oriented around money simultaneously obtain. In the first scene, the clockers are, in a phrase used by Zora Neale Hurston, "playin' de dozens"[9]—that is, they are engaged in a kind of competitive verbal play on the subject of whether a hip-hop artist can be authentic if he doesn't do what he raps about. They are arguing about the hip-hop group Public Enemy and its front man Chuck D, who "ain't shot nobody." This scene is about pure gift economy, *kairotic* time, and establishing social relationships. As they talk they move around, physically enacting the realignments in social relationship that develop through the game. From the commodity economy perspective, this activity is a waste of time, and since time is money, it is also a waste of money, which means a total perversion of the appropriate sense of values. It is Strike, he of the tormenting ulcers, who enforces a return to the other consciousness, the consciousness of the commodity economy of market values. He says, "We got to be about business."

Following is a sequence of scenes in which a drug deal goes down. The drug deal is amazing. The whole process is like a military operation: complexly organized, well disciplined, precisely executed. What is bitterly amusing in this scene is how orthodoxly capitalistic it is. What they are doing is illegal, but the way they do it conforms to what Jean-François Lyotard calls "the logic of maximum performance,"[10] the logic of efficiency, which is the central principle of a capitalistic economy. They are not fighting the system so much as imitating it and re-creating it as accurately as they can, but outside the official system itself.

This homage to the system, this reproduction of the system, means nothing to the system itself. Or, alternatively, it is seen as a threat to the system since, among other things, it puts capital into the hands of those who should not have capital. In the film, representatives of the official system immediately descend on this mini–capitalist system to crush it. All those complicated maneuvers of evasion are, ultimately, pointless. The police can shake the whole lot of them down at any time, and they do.

This situation is even more complicated than it initially appears. Slavoj Žižek identifies what he calls the "politics of drugs." He asks the question, "Was it really an accident that, at the very moment that a strong self-organized collective of those outside the law emerged, it was soon corrupted by hard drugs—from African American ghettos after the rebellions in the 1960s and Italian cities after the workers' unrests of the 1970s up to today's *favelas*?" He answers his own question by stating, "Those in power knew full well when to use drugs as a weapon against self-organized resistance."[11] This answer is anticipated in the "action manual" of the National Education Association: "What white Americans have never fully understood . . . is that white society is deeply implicated in the ghetto. White institutions created it, white institutions maintain it, and white society condones it."[12] The logic of why they do so is obvious enough: the ghettos maintain a social structure that favors "white" dominance. The logic of how they do so is more complicated and obscure, but it is reflected in the way Lee represents the relationship between the police and the clockers. Their relationship is characterized sometimes by tolerance, sometimes by arbitrary raids, and sometimes by covert and illegal bribery or coercion. It is out of this complicated mix that the social institutions "manage" and control the status quo of the ghettos.

The Ethics of Anguish

The next sequence makes explicit the reality of DuBois's concept of "double-consciousness." There is a police raid. The police are shaking down the clockers, looking for drugs or cash, looking just to harass the drug dealers. They are especially thorough in their shakedown of Strike, insisting on examining his private body parts. The scene re-creates a slave sale, in which a human being, a slave, was examined thoroughly to determine his or her worth—the mouth was examined, the haunches were slapped, and so forth.[13] The pretense is to search for hidden drugs, but the indignity, the disrespect, and the values reflected indicate that Strike is the equivalent of an object, and he can be examined like any other object.

This humiliating, intrusive examination is simultaneously juxtaposed and intercut with shots in slow motion, which seem to indicate different worlds. The juxtaposition is between Strike in the street, dealing with the police, and Strike looking over his shoulder and up at a window in the tenement building behind him, where his mother stands. She grimly watches it all happen, witnessing the humiliation and oppression of her son. This scene enacts and makes manifest DuBois's concept of the double-consciousness that people of color are forced to maintain. Our identification with Strike, however, complicates this simple interpretation. The way the scene is shot from two perspectives—that of an observer of the shakedown and that of Strike himself—leads the audience, both white and black, to actually experience this sense of double-consciousness. Not everyone can see the workings of systemic racism, but everyone has a mother and can feel, from the inside, the poignancy of a mother watching the degradation of her son and of a son being humiliated in front of his mother. This, it seems to me, is Lee's ultimate goal. It is not simply to show that systemic racism is still going on or to make us think that racism is bad. It is to get us to feel the anguish these people feel. It is to make us feel like we are watching a human drama that we all have an investment in because, in some sense, it could be about any of us. We all share, I think, in DuBois's double-consciousness to some degree. It is precisely for that reason that we can empathize with the characters in Lee's movie. Once we can see and feel their anguish, and see that their anguish is caused by an unfair system—a system we had not previously seen as unfair—then what Lee is doing becomes not just ethical but political. Dan Flory puts Lee's achievement into a larger context of the development of black political filmmaking. He says, "Black film's artistic development illustrates more generally how *film noir,* by virtue of its capacity to urge audiences to question the validity of assumptions that guide their moral judgments, may function to criticize the unfairness of existing social orders."[14]

Music, Irony, and Philosophy

These point-of-view shots from Strike's perspective get us into the movie. The cool jazz score accompanying the scenes of real violence that begin the movie and recurring throughout it lets us step out of the movie. The musical score allows us to detach from the violence, the humiliations, and the tensions of the movie and think about what we are seeing. It is essential for our appreciation of a tragedy, according to Aristotle, that we know it is a fiction, that we know it is only a play. If we think it is really happening, we will be horrified. We need a certain amount of detachment to receive the moral lessons tragedies have to teach. We need some detachment to do the *philosophical* work of understanding what we are seeing and experiencing.

It is Richard Rorty's project in *Contingency, Irony, and Solidarity* to clarify the pragmatic project with respect to certain forms of social injustice. Rorty accepts that human beings are essentially tribal and hence prone to racism, exclusionary behaviors, and insider-outsider thinking, but he thinks the solution to these perhaps genetically instilled dispositions is simply to renarrativize who is on the inside, who is part of the group. As Rorty puts it, the project is "a shared, social effort—the effort to make our institutions and practices more just and less cruel."[15] This, as a matter of fact, is precisely what has happened in the melting pot of America. The concept of being "white" is a social construct. It is a narrative of who is what. It is a narrative that can be renarrativized. The book *White Privilege*, for example, contains essays about which ethnic groups living in the United States have had their status changed from that of nonwhite dangerous minority to "white." Italian immigrants were not "white" and then they became "white," as did Irish immigrants, eastern European immigrants, and Jews. Outsiders become "white" when the system stops identifying them as Other and starts accepting them as members of the system.[16] This is not done individually; it emerges as a kind of consensus. What is necessary for this consensus to emerge is some kind of narrative that makes the experience of *those* people seem familiar to people like *us*. This is the project in which I see Lee engaged.

The Sorites of Love

There is an ancient logical paradox called the sorites paradox, or the paradox of the heap (*soros* means "heap" in Greek). The inventor of the sorites paradox is Eubilidies, a contemporary of Aristotle.[17] The way the paradox works is to consider a heap, say a heap of sand. If you remove one grain of sand, it is still a heap. If you remove another grain of sand, it is still a heap. There seems to be no condition under which you could remove a single grain of sand and thereby convert a heap of sand to a nonheap, and yet, after the removal of a sufficient number of grains of sand, there will be no heap there.

The area of maximum vagueness is called the penumbra.[18] The penumbra is the area along the continuum between heap and nonheap that is most ambiguous, where the judgment could go either way. Some might call it a heap; some might not. There is a sorites paradox at the core of racism: how many racist thoughts does a person need to have to be a real racist? I would say that having one racist thought inadvertently pass through your head does not make you a racist. But what about two racist thoughts? Three? There is no set number, but at some point, if a person is having racist thoughts all the time, you would want to say, "Well, he's a racist." Most "white" Americans, it seems to me, live in the penumbra, the area of maximum ambiguity. They have too many racist thoughts to be totally innocent on the issue of racism, but their intentions and commitments are decidedly antiracist, so they are stuck in a sorites paradox. It is hard to say precisely what term applies to them.

The great American philosopher Charles Sanders Peirce, one of the original pragmatists, described what I will call a sorites of love. He developed the paradox by preaching what he called a countergospel, the gospel of hate. In his essay "Evolutionary Love," Peirce says, "self-love is no love," and he adduces a quotation from Henry James Sr. that he claims effectively solves the theological problem of evil: "It is no doubt very tolerable finite or creaturely love to love one's own in another, to love another for his conformity to one's self: but nothing can be in more flagrant contrast with the creative Love, all whose tenderness *ex vi termini* [from the force of the term] must be reserved only for what intrinsically is most bitterly hostile and negative to itself."[19]

The sorites of love is that there is a continuum between love and hate. In some sense, according to this conception of authentic love, there can be no real love without hate. Love without hate is just self-love, which is no love at all. Here, *hate* just means an encounter with an Other, an encounter with something or someone in whom one can find no traces, or few traces, of oneself. To transform the sense of repellence we feel toward such Otherness into affection, connection, affirmation—which is to say, real love—takes a new way of seeing the Other, a new perspective, a new narrative of what *they* are doing and of what *we* are doing. That is the work Lee is doing in *Clockers*. He is working with people's perspectives, attempting to renarrativize what we see and transform people's hate and fear into love and compassion.

There is a scene in *Clockers* in which Rocco is questioning Victor in an interview room at the police station. The room is dark, except for a bright interrogation light, and the walls are bare, except for a darkened mirror on the back wall. Rocco is convinced that Victor is lying or at least hiding something. Specifically, Rocco is convinced that Victor is not responsible for the shooting he has confessed to and is covering up for his brother Strike. Rocco is convinced of this because of his own self-trust (his own self-love). He believes he can tell a "bad one" from a "good one," and he believes Victor is one of the good ones and Strike is most assuredly one of the bad ones. There is a beautiful, subtle, powerful moment during this interrogation when the camera focuses on an image on the surface of Victor's right eyeball: it is the reflection of Rocco in Victor's eye. It is an amazing shot. As I understand it, what we are seeing is an image of what Rocco is seeing—namely, his own reflection.[20] When Rocco looks into Victor's eyes, Rocco does not see Victor; he does not see into Victor's soul. What Rocco sees is Rocco. What Rocco sees, in other words, is precisely, and only, what Rocco wants to see, what Rocco is looking for, what Rocco *knows* is there. This is self-love (which is not really love) expressed as racism.

What would Rocco see if he could look into Victor's soul? If he could really see Victor at all, he would see how "tired" Victor is. "Tired" is Victor's own self-description. He says several times, "I was just so tired." What he is tired of is the oppression of the double-consciousness he is forced to live with and maintain day in and day out. He is tired of having to restrain his feelings of anger and frustration, which such double-consciousness demands. He is a smart, competent, inner-city black man trying to play by the rules of the system, and it is wearing him down. One thing the system is very afraid of, one thing the system will not tolerate, is anger from such men, yet their anger is justified. Cornel West says of Malcolm X: "The substance of what he said highlighted the chronic refusal of most Americans to acknowledge the sheer absurdity that confronts human beings of African descent in this country—the incessant assaults on black intelligence, beauty, character, and possibility. His profound commitment to affirm black humanity at any cost and his tremendous courage to accent the hypocrisy of American society made Malcolm X the prophet of black rage."[21]

"Intuitions" versus "Deepest Moral Commitments"

In the book *Living High and Letting Die,* Peter Unger distinguishes between our "intuitions" and our "deepest moral commitments."[22] This is just another form of double-consciousness. Our intuitions are the habits of judgment with which we have been inculcated by the system. They are judgments that serve the system, and if one is of the group privileged by the system, they are also self-serving. They seem to be moral judgments, but they are really ideological judgments. Our deepest moral commitments, in contrast, are just that: our real, authentic, deepest moral values. "White" people's intuitions tend to be racist, whereas their deepest moral commitments are horrified by racism. Our intuitions constantly present us with rationalizations for the "justice" of our racist beliefs, votes, and actions. It takes a very specific confrontation with the humanity of the people who are the subject of our racist intuitions to bring forth our deepest moral commitments.

Our intuitions say, "Those clockers should stop clocking and get *real* jobs." Victor is Lee's answer to these moral intuitions. His situation engages our deepest moral commitments. We can see and feel the soul-deadening sacrifices he makes to try to work within the system as it is. We can see that getting a legitimate job does not necessarily, or even possibly, make the system work for you. We can see his anguish.

This conflict between one's intuitions and one's deepest moral commitments is precisely the experience Rocco has by the end of the movie. He has been directly confronted with the fallaciousness of his intuitions about Strike and Victor. He has become aware of the immense complexities of both these men and of their anguish. In a sense, though more indirectly, he has been confronted with the anguish of all the people he has been dealing with who are connected to the two men: their mother, Victor's wife, the drug lord Rodney, little Tyrone. In the last scene of the movie, Strike asks Rocco why he pursued the case so long and so far. Rocco gives him no answer, but one of Louis Farrakhan's Nation of Islam workers selling *The Final Call* brings a copy of the paper up to Rocco's car window. The headline reads, "Justice in Black and White." Rocco just nods his head. It is not the justice he thought he wanted, but it is justice sure enough.

Hate KO'd by Love: The Way Out of the Double-Consciousness

Peirce says, "The movement of love is circular, at one and the same impulse projecting creations into independency and drawing them into harmony."[23] This movement of what Peirce calls "love" is meant to apply to the way evolution works in the world as well as in society and in human relationships. The idea is that the way to understand the world is to think of it as being in a constant process of evolution, and evolution is the process of forming new creations and simultaneously establishing some kind of harmony among the things that already exist.

This evolutionary process has its own logic, which is, according to Peirce, the logic of Firstness, Secondness, and Thirdness. In terms of human experience, Firstness is the experience of being in a kind of bubble of unawareness. This is pure self-love (which is nonlove). It is the condition of the unreflective racist. It is the condition that our "white" social institutions want to maintain in us. Secondness is the state of sudden awareness. It is experienced when we become aware of an element that does not fit our assumptions, does not fit into our working narratives. It is the experience of pure Otherness. Thirdness is achieved when we see how this Otherness can be renarrativized into a consistent whole. Only when we move beyond the narrative we have been using, which has no place for this new element, and recognize a new narrative in which this new element has a place and a function and a purpose, can we understand. Thirdness is the way out of the doubleness of the "double-consciousness" that DuBois identified.

This understanding of the way the world works is one that Spike Lee, as a good American pragmatist, as an inheritor of the wisdom of the American pragmatists, well appreciates. It is stated as explicitly and comprehensively as it could be in any philosophical text in the speech by Radio Raheem (Bill Nunn) to Mookie (Spike Lee) in *Do the Right Thing* (1989):

> Let me tell you the story of "Right Hand, Left Hand." It's a tale of good and evil. Hate: It was with this hand that Cane iced his brother. Love: These five fingers, they go straight to the soul of man. The right hand: the hand of love. The story of life is this: Static. One hand is always fighting the other hand; and the left hand is kicking much ass. I mean, it looks like the right hand, Love, is finished. But, hold on, stop the presses, the right hand is coming back. Yeah, he got the left hand on the ropes, now, that's right. Ooh, it's the devastating right and Hate is hurt, he's down. Left-Hand Hate KOed by Love.

"Hate KOed by Love" is Peirce's whole philosophy of evolutionary love summed up in a phrase. It describes the way art works, the way art narrativizes the struggles of love and hate, conflict and overcoming, with love triumphing, if only in the work of art itself, which holds the various strands of the narrative together. This is love as a Peircean Thirdness, the way of renarrativization, of interpretation and mediation. The mediation itself is full of tensions, which are themselves potentially generative—of new meanings, new interpretations, new understandings, and even new artworks.

John Dewey, a student of Peirce's, says, "Art is more moral than moralities."[24] I understand him to mean that art manifests this evolutionary process of self-overcoming that dogmatic moralities, more or less, deny. Insofar as moralities are about moral rules and judgments, they are fixed, dogmatic, and inflexible. Insofar as moral improvement is possible, it takes an understanding that is open, responsive, and flexible. This kind of art, then, becomes an opportunity, first, for individual self-critique (and hence of self-overcoming), which in turn becomes an opportunity for social critique (critique of the society that created the self that needs overcoming). These processes of overcoming are driven by a desire for something better, a "love" for a better self and a better society, and they are versions of what

Peirce calls "evolutionary love." This is the most moral activity of all, and art is its primary source.

This spirit of evolutionary love, this idea of the ongoing struggle between love and hate, with the ultimate triumph of love, is well captured by the word Charles Darwin used to describe the way evolution works, by "adaptation." *Adaptation* refers to the creation of new species and to the process of various species changing to fit together within a given ecosystem. We do this in our interpersonal lives: we change, and we change those we live with, in ways that make it possible to live together. This is precisely the process Peirce calls "evolutionary love." This is the process Spike Lee is devoted to in the creation of his movies. It is the process that most specifically underlies the film *Clockers.*

Notes

1. These shots are re-creations of actual crime photos. As Spike Lee explains, "We reenacted these crime-scene pictures for the opening credits, as we felt it would be disrespectful to the families of the dead to show the real bodies." Spike Lee, as told to Kaleem Aftab, *Spike Lee: That's My Story and I'm Sticking to It* (New York: W. W. Norton, 2005), 240.

2. Ibid., 4.

3. I am using this term stipulatively, to designate not a racial group but a social construct. I discuss this idea at length later.

4. "Education and Racism" (National Education Association, 1973), 12.

5. Lewis Hyde, *The Gift: Imagination and the Erotic Life of Property* (New York: Random House, 1983), 47.

6. Ibid., 33.

7. W. E. B. DuBois, *The Souls of Black Folk: Essays and Sketches* (1903; reprint, New York: Fawcett, 1961), 17.

8. James C. McKelly addresses DuBois's concept of "double-consciousness" in Spike Lee's films in "The Double Truth, Ruth: *Do the Right Thing* and the Culture of Ambiguity," in *The Spike Lee Reader,* ed. Paula J. Massood (Philadelphia: Temple University Press, 2008), 58–60.

9. Zora Neale Hurston, *Their Eyes Were Watching God* (New York: J. B. Lippincott, 1937), 96. My thanks to Affi Ingberg for this observation.

10. Jean-François Lyotard, *The Postmodern Condition: A Report on Knowledge* (Minneapolis: University of Minnesota Press, 1979), xxiv.

11. Slavoj Žižek, *Organs without Bodies: On Deleuze and Consequences* (New York: Routledge, 2004), 201.

12. "Education and Racism," 9.

13. As Keith M. Harris puts it, "The housing-project block becomes the slave block." "*Clockers:* Adaptation in Black," in *The Spike Lee Reader,* 131.

14. Dan Flory, *Philosophy, Black Film, Film Noir* (University Park: Pennsylvania State University Press, 2008), 1–2.

15. Richard Rorty, *Contingency, Irony, and Solidarity* (New York: Cambridge University Press, 1989), xiv.

16. Paula S. Rothenberg, ed., *White Privilege: Essential Readings on the Other Side of Racism* (New York: Worth Publishers, 2002). See all four essays in Part 2 of this edited collection. The essays are James R. Barrett and David Roediger, "How White People Became White"; Karen Brodkin, "How Jews Became White Folks"; Neil Foley, "Becoming Hispanic: Mexican Americans and Whiteness"; and George Lipsitz, "The Possessive Investment of Whiteness."

17. Roy Sorensen, *A Brief History of the Paradox: Philosophy and the Labyrinths of the Mind* (New York: Oxford University Press, 2005), 83–99.

18. Bertrand Russell, "Vagueness," in *Australasian Journal of Philosophy and Psychology* 1 (1923): 84–92, reprinted in *Vagueness: A Reader*, ed. Rosanna Keefe and Peter Smith (Cambridge, Mass.: MIT Press, 1999), 63–64.

19. Charles S. Peirce, *The Essential Writings*, ed. Edward C. Moore (New York: Prometheus Books, 1972), 238.

20. This interpretation is different from the one offered by Harris in "*Clockers:* Adaptation in Black," 131. Harris's interpretation is that we are seeing what Victor is seeing. I cannot disagree with that, but this seems to be an insufficient explanation for such a complex shot.

21. Cornel West, *Race Matters* (New York: Vintage Books, 1993), 135–36.

22. Peter Unger, *Living High and Letting Die: Our Illusion of Innocence* (New York: Oxford University Press, 1996), 10–11.

23. Peirce, *Essential Writings*, 238.

24. John Dewey, *Art as Experience* (New York: Perigee Books, 1980), 348.

Rethinking the First Person

Autobiography, Authorship, and the Contested Self in *Malcolm X*

David LaRocca

> Language, for the individual consciousness, lies on the borderline between oneself and the other. The word in language is half someone else's.
>
> —Mikhail Bakhtin, "Discourse in the Novel"

Can someone else write my autobiography? The question challenges the conventional meaning of autobiography. And since writing an autobiography—in America, after Benjamin Franklin—often occurs with an awareness that the status of the work is bound up with the authority of its author, the notion of authorship also becomes troubled.[1] For instance, because an autobiography appears to be direct communication from its author, the very conditions of its presentation may suggest we are reading a true story, a mere record of what happened. Yet, like the life it aims to account for, autobiography is fashioned, a literary artifact, necessarily created and fictitious. If this is so, how important is it that the author write his own story? Also latent in these considerations is the substantive problem at the heart of autobiographical practice since antiquity: an autobiographical work is supposed to be at once a work written and constituted by oneself—like a cartoon drawing itself. *The Autobiography of Malcolm X* gives us occasion to reconsider our understanding of these beliefs and practices, since the work is both autobiographical and not written by its subject. If writing an autobiography is taken to be continuous with self-creation, what is the status of a work—and its named subject—if the work is authored by someone else?

Malcolm X did not write his autobiography. Instead, the autobiography is "as told to" Alex Haley. Yet the implication that X spoke and Haley wrote down what he said is misleading. Haley didn't take dictation from X, so he was neither a stenographer nor an amanuensis, much less a ghostwriter.

Haley authored Malcolm X's autobiography. But how is that possible? And what happens when a filmmaker—in this case, Spike Lee—uses *The Autobiography of Malcolm X as Told to Alex Haley* as the basis for a film biography? Does the adaptation necessarily draw Lee into the practice and art of writing someone else's autobiography? Because Lee bookends his film biography—admittedly altered "for the purposes of dramatization"[2]—with documentary footage, *Malcolm X* (1992) pushes an already extensive theoretical debate in philosophy and literature to a new degree of complexity and urgency. We are now dealing with layer upon layer of creation and influence: from X's telling to Haley's "as told to" autobiography to Lee's screenplay to Denzel Washington's performance to the final edited film. The project at hand is to critically evaluate how Spike Lee's film contributes to an understanding of film biography's philosophical impact on theories of autobiography, authorship, and personal identity. To do so, I consider some attributes of Lee's film: how it reinforces an already established literary account of historical lives transformed by an actor's filmed performance and a director's editorial interventions; reflects the enterprise of individual identity defined through literacy, the coextensive process of reading and writing; undertakes a genre-mixing experiment that produces both contradictions and insights; offers a provocation to our understanding of fact and truth, documentary and fiction, narrative unity and narrative fragmentation, self-understanding and how we are understood by others; and, to these ends, enfolds diverse media—literary works, photographs, newspaper clippings, surveillance video, filmed reenactment, archival documentary footage, stylized dramatization, and choreographed documentary.

Since a film biography proposes to render an account of a life first by embodying the life in the form of an actor and then by selecting and organizing discrete elements—editing them—to create a story or narrative of the life, it is a genre particularly well suited to elucidate what is at stake in the millennia-old debate over the nature of personal identity, especially how we account for it representationally.

When viewed from the landscape of contemporary academic disciplines, autobiography and biography appear to be strictly under the purview of history and literature, but there is a long tradition of both genres informing, and being informed by, the history of philosophy. Plato created literary works featuring Socrates as a provocateur of philosophical reflection.[3] Boethius wrote a literary fantasy while incarcerated, liberating himself to consider philosophical problems from an imagined alternate reality.[4] Montaigne engaged the history of philosophical skepticism and the works of the ancient Stoics in a novel literary mode—the essay—and said of his work: "I am myself the matter of my book."[5] In these instances, the forms of autobiography and biography have become vehicles for philosophical reflection. Just as important, and perhaps even more pertinent to the activity of philosophy, is the way autobiography and biography demonstrate myriad enduring philosophical conundrums: defining the nature of personal identity (or selfhood); description as interpretation; truth, and its effect on self-understanding; the authority and legitimacy of self-generated accounts of oneself versus those made by others; the validity of data and documents, and their use in the development of theories, accounts, or stories of the self; the logical relationship between argument (as rhetorical) and narrative (as literary); how writing about one's self can be understood as a process of self-generation, self-justification, and defense or declaration of one's status as a self.

When philosophers discuss the self, they must necessarily make claims about how they understand the nature of personal identity. John Locke, in a chapter entitled "Identity and Diversity," offers what would become an influential theory of individual persistence, stating that a person is "a thinking intelligent being, that has reason and reflection, and can consider itself as itself, the same thinking thing, in different times and places."[6] Earlier, René Descartes, in *Discourse on Method,* proposed that it is precisely the thinking subject that makes our existence possible.[7] Contrast these views with that of David Hume, who hypothesizes in *Treatise on Human Nature* that an individual is "a bundle of perceptions," thereby diminishing the effect (or even the possibility) of a unified and enduring personhood.[8] Likewise, Ludwig Wittgenstein, in *Tractatus Logico-Philosophicus,* says, "There is no such thing as the subject that thinks or entertains ideas."[9] More recently, Slavoj Žižek said: "One of the commonplaces of today's theory is that transcendental subjectivity is *passé:* if one is to assert the notion of the subject, one has to displace it with regard to the standard Cartesian *cogito;* that is, the new subject has to be a divided, finite subject, a subject 'thrown' into a non-transparent, contingent life-world."[10] Still other challenges to a defense of transcendental subjectivity appear in contemporary theories of neuroscience, artificial intelligence, and biosemiotics, many of which alter long-standing accounts of how we come to know ourselves as individuals with discrete identities.[11] Žižek, interestingly, turns the other way: "From my perspective, the celebrated postmodern 'displacement' of subjectivity rather exhibits the unreadiness to come to terms with the truly traumatic core of the modern subject."[12]

As a genre, autobiography presumes one point of view, and the subject and the author are believed to share it. It appears self-evident that an autobiography is an account of one's life written by oneself. Yet as Spengemann and Lundquist note, "conventional autobiography, which grew out of a very special idea of individuality . . . is unfit in its traditional form to examine new possibilities of being . . . new ideals must seek new forms appropriate to them."[13] The genre of the "as told to" autobiography complicates the definition of conventional autobiography: in an "as told to" autobiography, another person helps the subject see himself. The other acts as guide, critic, interlocutor, editor, curator, and literary stylist and is in a position to check the subject's hubris and self-delusion, delete the tedious and tiresome elements, and emphasize what is resonant and potentially enduring. As a result, the "as told to" autobiography is a challenge to our philosophical understanding of the self as something singular, fixed, or transcendental. In this case, the notion of the self—and self-understanding—is widened at least to a community of two. In this relation, the subject is suddenly accountable to the other for his stories, truths, elisions, deceits, disclosures, and what remains unseen, forgotten, and distorted.

The conceit at the heart of autobiography remains that one person has endeavored to account and be accountable for his experience. What if it turns out that a person isn't very good at doing this? What if he needs another—one who wasn't "there"—to be an aid to his reflections? Film biography seems like a genre that parallels the "as told to" autobiography: it is a form that depends on writers, directors, actors, cinematographers, set designers, and film editors to figure out how to portray someone else's life. But isn't that just biography? Why are we calling "as told to" autobiography *autobiography* at all? Why not just label it biography that has the input and cooperation of the subject? The specifically philosophical aspects of these questions, and their implications for our understanding of the self, self-understanding, and personal identity, are now explored in relation to Spike Lee's film biography *Malcolm X*.

Camera and Consciousness

I want to emphasize three filmmaking techniques Lee employs in *Malcolm X* that seem to be philosophically significant, and suggest how such techniques enrich the art of accounting for a life on film.

First, using the sound of actual gunshots during scenes that do not involve guns—in which pointed fingers replace guns—creates a startling disconnection between what is in the film and what seems to be outside of it. For the viewer, the sound of the gunshot becomes a meronym for what we already know (or will know) is X's destiny.[14] The sound, in its separation from what takes place on-screen, registers the unexpected and extreme violence of actual gunshots. Each time we hear the sound, our habits of viewing assure us that a gun has been fired, but each time we are relieved by the artifice of Lee's sound effect. At the end, when the sound of gunshots aligns with the slain X, his body falling back from the force of the bullets' impact, the meronym is no more. The man is dead.

The gunshots are even more affecting when viewing the film a second time, when they become signs of inevitability—and, worse, a warning that only we can truly hear what is to come. X thinks Shorty is just playing with him in the park as they frolic in their zoot suits, reenacting James Cagney movies.[15] And West Indian Archie is being ferocious but somehow still friendly when he points two "guns" across the room, aims, and "fires."[16] But upon pulling the triggers, Archie's look reveals his suspicion and his caring admonition: go on like this, and soon enough the bullets will be real. On a third occasion, in the hours before X enters the Audubon Ballroom in New York City, where he will be executed, we hear the gunshot again in the context of X declaiming black-on-black violence.[17] "Brother, we don't want black people killing each other, alright . . . alright?" he sternly tells an associate keen to avenge the recent attempt on X's life. "Peace be unto you. Peace be unto you," X says emphatically, without irony. A gunshot punctuates the sentence and the sentiment.

Lee's use of realistic sounds of gunfire, wholly nondiagetically, functions as Haley's asides do in the *Autobiography,* or as any comment would that gives the reader or viewer more information and insight than the subject ever had. As a result of our special knowledge, the actions of the protagonist become even more weighted. Knowing what we know—or think we know—we are invited to feel more and care more about his fate. Yes, this is a form of editorializing, but it is precisely how Lee as a director and cocreator of X's film biography can register his reading of this life and explore and exploit film's technical possibilities for this purpose.

The second technical element is a camera roll or spin: we see X's face turned around, upside down, and spinning.[18] The rotating camera—centered and pivoting about his face—gives an outer image to match the internal "turning" in X's thinking. He is being reoriented in the wake of his rejection by Elijah Muhammad, his trip to Egypt, and the bombing at his home. Lee makes sure we know X is undergoing something severe and life-altering. And as viewers, our sense of the screen—and the usual rules that govern what it contains—is also turned around. We experience an alternating figure-ground reversal, not quite sure whether we are moving or X is moving. Because films so commonly operate on a lateral, horizontal axis (with familiar pans and tracking shots), this revolving camera offers a novel perspective from which to consider X's condition and our relation to it.

The third technical aspect I want to emphasize comes very late in the film, when X is alone on the day of his death. Lee films him driving to the Audubon Ballroom, and before he enters the building, X appears to be on a sidewalk—brownstones on either side, leafless trees framing his torso, wearing a hat and his distinctive spectacles—while on the sound track we hear Sam Cooke singing plaintively "A Change Is Gonna Come." But we can see that X is not walking; he is gliding.[19] Lee has used this technique in several films, including *Do the Right Thing* (1989). The actor stands on a wheeled platform, which is pulled in sync with the camera; as a result, the camera and actor remain at the same distance, and the background slides past. The effect seems to be a filmic reply to Emerson's sentiment that "ghostlike we glide through nature, and should not know our place again."[20] The technique seems to capture something remarkable about human introspection—a kind of deep, inner perception—that is not possible when we are walking, making contact with the earth, step after step. Here, on Lee's slightly elevated platform, the character has evolved, as it were, to a higher state of consciousness. In this moment of radical self-reflexivity, he appears calm and acquiescent in the face of his imminent demise. The gliding motion enhances the sense—in his face, in his eyes—that he registers the strange inertia, the unstoppable fate he is being drawn toward. He looks as if he sees everything clearly yet reluctantly, with the mournfulness of a man who will never see his children again, but also dutifully and bravely, as a man who knows who he is at last. On that roving platform, Malcolm X looks like the eye that can finally see itself.[21]

Character and Performance

"There's an art to listening well," Malcolm X told Alex Haley. "I listen closely to the sound of a man's voice when he's speaking. I can hear sincerity."[22] Did Haley share this talent when listening to X? And could Spike Lee and Denzel Washington hear X "through" Haley? I suggest that Lee's film biography illustrates how an actor does precisely what Haley did: listen, select, and then perform someone else's autobiography. This can be done with varying degrees of success. Lee and Washington, working from Haley's manuscript, reenact a life in order to give it shape and sense. To what extent, though, are these autobiographies-by-others original visions of a life and not truly referential to the life lived by the historical Malcolm X? Lee's film and Haley's book are compelling, skillfully made, creative artifacts. Yet treating them as autobiographies may complicate our better sense of what autobiographies do and what they are for.

Lee, like most film biographers, aims to create the illusion of facticity, for example, by encouraging the viewer to think he is watching a historical event (in this way, suppressing the actor and revealing the character).[23] Once the viewer sufficiently suspends disbelief, the film becomes a window through which he looks onto historical phenomena. Because the viewer doesn't know where dramatization begins and fact ends, the whole field of vision blends together into a fantasy of projected reality. On such a reading, the viewer is lured into believing that there is a connection between Denzel Washington and the historical Malcolm X. This impression creates a "rangefinder effect," a phenomenon in which our idea of the historical Malcolm X is mapped isomorphically over our image of the actor playing him. But there are crucial layers of mediation between the historical X and the images we see in Lee's film. Lee, then, does not "blur the line" between the historical and the written; instead, he aims to sharpen the line to the point where we no longer see the actor but see *through* him to the real Malcolm X. We are left to ask, though, which Malcolm X is he trying to show us: Haley's X, or some historical X? Some viewers may say that Washington's achievement as an actor is the way he "dissolves" into his role and "becomes" Malcolm X. That's not it, though: what the viewer sees on film is the fictional or rather the literary Malcolm X. When we watch Washington, we get Haley. It is reasonable to expect that Washington studied documentary footage of X and is, in some way, imitating him—his manners, his moods, his postures, the inflections of his voice—to say nothing of the lengths the costume designers and makeup artists go to finishing off the illusion of isomorphism. But in *Malcolm X,* this isn't what is happening.

It's crucial to understand that Denzel Washington is not enacting a performance of the historical Malcolm X; actually, he is performing Haley's text, or even Lee's understanding of Haley's *Autobiography.* The conceit of film biographies, illustrated by Lee's film, must be that the "real" Malcolm X is richer than the concept "Malcolm X." Yet it is just the other way around: the concept (or ideal) is richer because of the details, because it is built from extremities. We get the ideal Malcolm X because of the world in which we know these details, and it is a writer who delivers that world full of details. When we have a literary, interpretive version/vision, we have more than we thought we had (in "real life"). A world is built, and it is only when we have a world that we have a concept. The ideal is not the distilled, simplified version but the richer, detailed, overflowing, superabundant version.

When Malcolm X visited Haley in Greenwich Village, Haley tried to create an atmosphere in which X would feel comfortable talking to him or, more importantly, not just chatting but telling stories that could be used in the book. It took a while. "For perhaps a month I was afraid we weren't going to get any book. . . . He would bristle when I tried to urge him that the proposed book was *his* life."[24] As Haley says in the epilogue: "Malcolm X gave me a startled look when I asked him if he would tell his life story for publication. It was one of the few times I have ever seen him uncertain."[25] As Haley tells it, Malcolm X's "writing" of the *Autobiography* began largely as "scribbles" on scraps of paper, on index cards, and in newspaper margins. Once Haley caught on to X's habit, he supplied white napkins whenever he served coffee, hoping to transform a casual napkin jotting into the beginning of a book manuscript.[26] One of the notes Haley found after X left stated: "There is nothing more frightful than ignorance in action. Goethe."[27] Eventually, the epigrammatic notes gave way to rambling confessions: "from this stream-of-consciousness reminiscing I finally got out of him the foundation for this book's beginning chapters."[28] And X continued to talk to Haley for two more years.

Still, there are indications that neither X nor Haley were clear about what they wanted from this relationship, and they were not sure of the nature of their roles and responsibilities. "After signing the contract for this book, Malcolm X looked at me hard," Haley recounts, "and said: 'A writer is what I want, not an interpreter.' " Haley ends his epilogue by saying: "I tried to be a dispassionate chronicler."[29] X wanted someone to stylize what he said, not judge what he said. But what can be called Haley's modesty gets in the way of our sense of his self-consciousness about his work as creator: He was no mere "chronicler"—someone arranging historical data in useful ways. He undersells his achievement and mischaracterizes his contribution if he does not admit that he failed at his attempt to be a dispassionate chronicler. We can say for him, then, that in this failure lies his success. He did not take dictation from X; he made X into a literary character.

The glimpse Haley offers the reader into the development of the manuscript shows that merely compiling a book of facts is not going to build a world or deliver an intelligible story of a self. As they were negotiating the book contract, X wrote to Haley: "Nothing can be in this book's manuscript that I didn't say, and nothing can be left out that I want in it."[30] Here we must take stock of X's desire for creative control and put it in the context of the difficulty he had trusting people. (He tells Haley at one point that he trusts his wife 75 percent and Haley 25 percent.)[31] From a literary point of view, though, X's demand doesn't make any sense. Haley isn't taking dictation. He's not creating a day-by-day sequence of life events. Haley was hired to create not an appointment book but a work of literary merit. And that means Haley will have to write things X didn't actually say—but would say as the character in this autobiography. And it means Haley will have to leave things out that X wants in—because part of writing requires making choices about what constitutes the life of the subject, and this requires throwing some drafts on the floor. If Haley is going to write a book worth anything—for example, one revelatory of X's life and one that conveys a sense of its interest for readers—he must violate X's two stated conditions. The literary understanding of a life is the true understanding, and it is not something one finds in a book of facts.

A quick recollection of film biographies based on literary understandings of people's lives reveals how much truer they are than "factual" films. A bunch of facts do not add up to insight into a life; such films merely show life as one thing after another. Some of Oliver Stone's film biographies—*JFK* (1991), *The Doors* (1991), *Nixon* (1995), *W.* (2008)—illustrate the point rather well. Stone creates his screenplays from facts and bold conjecture, not from a literary understanding of his subject. Compare his approach with Tom Hooper's *John Adams* (2008), based on a biography by David McCollough; Michael Mann's *Ali* (2001); and Milos Foreman's *Amadeus* (1984), based on a play by Peter Shaffer. The contrast between these approaches to using facts suggests something unexpected about the nature of truth: the literary treatment of facts reveals truth better than the accumulation and display of facts. In Stone's films, we get closer to what he thinks of his subjects; with Hooper, Mann, and Foreman, we get closer to the subjects themselves. The work of these three directors suggests that to inhabit reality, one has to go through fictitious, constructed details. The way to get to the "real" Malcolm X is not by validating a series of facts, much less all the facts of his life, but rather by encountering the fabricated details.

Most readers of *The Autobiography of Malcolm X* quickly forget that Haley created a fictional, literary voice for X; almost at once, the reader believes in this voice as authentically X's own. Haley's presence is thoroughly suppressed (as it is in Lee's film), so the transformation of X's oral history should be counted as a profound literary achievement, even as it is acknowledged as a work of fabrication.[32] Lee drew from the *Autobiography* to help create the dialogue and circumstances of the action in X's life. As a result, Washington's performance as Malcolm X is an interpretation of a literary phenomenon, not a reenactment of a historical phenomenon.

Empiricism and Biography

One of the most compelling and confounding aspects of Lee's film is the way it makes us rethink the nature of the first person—in philosophy, autobiography, and film biography. Who exactly is speaking when we hear Denzel Washington in *Malcolm X?* A reader of the *Autobiography* will recognize in the film lines drawn from the book. And since Lee makes clear that some aspects of the film have been changed for the purposes of dramatization, at any point we may be hearing Haley's rendering of X's speech, Lee's transformation of Haley's text, or, presumably, even Washington's ad-libbing away from Lee's screenplay. Somewhere along the way, the ideas of biography and autobiography have been muddled, the nature of first-person authorship put into question. The terms should be fairly straightforward: a biography is a work written by one person about another person's life (e.g., James Boswell's *Life of Samuel Johnson*); an autobiography is a work written by one person about his or her own life (e.g., Goethe's or John Stuart Mill's autobiography). In the present case, however, we have a person writing someone else's autobiography. Do we learn anything from this use of the term *autobiography*? For instance, is it possible that the revelation of subjective truths can be better realized when characterized by someone else? Why not just call that biography?[33] The achievement of Haley's book, however, suggests that writing a biography of X wouldn't have yielded nearly as engaging—or as truth-revealing—a book. In Haley's hand, X becomes a literary creation. But then, importantly, wouldn't X be a literary creation even if he had penned every word in the book himself? In this way, biography and autobiography involve the invention of literary identities that do not correspond to the empirical, factual, historical elements of a life, what I referred to earlier as a "book of facts."[34]

Professional historians, it seems, fear that "literary" concerns will obscure the empirical facts of a historical account of a person's life.[35] An empirical historical biographer is guided by "a strictly empirical methodology" and thus focuses on documentary evidence as the basis for any inferences.[36] As Stephen Davies points out: "This means that much of the traditional content will frequently be dismissed as mythical or speculative. Such matters as the psychological state of the subject cannot be addressed unless there is some empirical warrant for it in the shape of such sources as letters, diaries or an autobiography, and even then only with great caution."[37] Empirical biographers may worry, though, that letters, diaries, journals, and autobiographies are compromised by their "subjective quality," preferring instead artifacts of the public record, which are taken to be "objective."[38] Do we suppose there is more reliable knowledge contained in a political stump speech than in a midnight confession written in a private notebook? In some sense, doesn't the empirical biographer's assumption run counter to common sense and perhaps even to actual experience? A journal entry may be more manipulative than a political speech, but it seems, in general, that it would also be more revealing (if only of one's private manipulations!). Therefore, it is worth retaining some degree of skepticism about how the writer conducts himself in private: Is he being candid or distorting, revealing or delusional? Is he writing for posterity instead of for himself and thus guarding or misleading with lies and omissions, inadvertently or even purposefully? As Davies notes: "Autobiographies are commonly written for purposes of self-justification. In fact, their greatest use for the historian frequently is to provide a guide to the author's view of themselves [*sic*] rather than the facts of their life."[39] And yet it is precisely that—the author's view of himself—that autobiographers seem in the most danger of obscuring, confusing, or forfeiting. For this reason, empirical biographers would clarify an important aspect of their craft if they defended the idea that autobiographers are not in a position to write about themselves with knowing self-revelation. It would seem that the person best equipped to write an autobiography is a biographer.

Historians, claims Davies, produce "a more critical but more accurate view" than literary authors.[40] In the context of the present discussion, is this what we mean by "critical" and "accurate"? What exactly are we trying to view: facts or truths? Here, it may be useful to distinguish between the fact and truth of empirical history and the truths made possible by a literary reading of history. Davies notes that "a strictly empirical approach to biography can lead to deeper knowledge and understanding of the individual and their [*sic*] place in history."[41] What kind of knowledge is this, though? Is it something that literary, philosophical, and filmic biography cannot achieve? Haley and Lee are decidedly not empirical biographers. What, then, is their contribution to our understanding of Malcolm X? Given what the empirical biographer claims, do their portraits of X have any relation to X's life whatsoever? The question may resonate for anyone who has ever wondered about the extent to which an author's or a filmmaker's work is "based on a true story."

Even though Haley and Lee do not qualify as empirical biographers, we may ask the following questions: Is there really any such thing as an empirical biography? Would a "strict empirical approach to biography" render a story merely by way of dates, times, GPS coordinates, and the like—in short, a biography by numbers? The claim to "objective" knowledge of a subject's life seems odd no matter how one describes it and regardless of the *source* of that knowledge (whether public or not). The bandwidth of empirical biography is necessarily very narrow. Moreover, the selection, arrangement, emphasis, and content of facts change the story such biographers tell. All "empirical facts" are also potentially interpreted and interpretable, thus not simply or merely descriptive. The literary biography may be said to take interpretation further, but it may also be said to acknowledge the necessity of interpretation in any biographical project. Despite differences in degree, empirical biography and literary biography are both interpretive.

Document and Narrative

Spike Lee's *Malcolm X* illustrates the continuity I'm claiming between empirical biography and literary biography because it employs documentary footage (what empirical biographers would call "objective," or part of the public record) in the service of an invented narrative scheme—namely, the story of Malcolm X that Lee wants to tell or imagine, given all the data available to him. In the nearly three-minute-long opening credits sequence, we hear Denzel Washington as Malcolm X for the first time; he is giving an outraged speech about the injustices suffered by blacks in America. Names register against the backdrop of a draped American flag, which eventually begins to burn, leaving the initial "X" charred at its edges. Intercut, we see documentary footage of inverse surveillance video of Los Angeles police officers beating Rodney King on March 3, 1991, in an effort to arrest him.[42] The clip is not contextualized or editorialized but simply appears as a prologue to the film. But what is the viewer supposed to think about it? Is it possible to generate a reading of the clip, in the context of the film's release on November 18, 1992, that is useful to the remainder of the film? Lee parallels X's indignant speech about the brutality of whites toward blacks, but the viewer would have to *already know* this footage as an icon of such violence, since the figures cannot be made out as white or black and we are given no sense of the offense committed or the nature of the beating. Or maybe Lee uses the footage to signal another episode in which one's race informs one's point of view about the meaning of an event. Like the title sequence itself, is the clip meant to be incendiary, to enflame the passions of the viewer? But to what end? Is Lee's entire film meant to be a response to the attack on Rodney King? Generating such questions from the presence of the apparently unrelated documentary footage signals to me that Lee's use of this footage is of great consequence to the meaning of his narrative. For instance, the documentary footage conveys the idea that the King beating is "real." Lee trades, then, on the credibility we ascribe to empirical video footage. Oddly, the very indecipherability of the scene—the graininess, the darkness, the lack of detail—enhances the sense of reality, fact, and truth. Partly, the illusion of facticity is bound up with the viewer's knowledge of technology: the look of video from a handheld camera becomes a sign of a person's proximity to a real event and of the credibility of the event itself (even if wholly decontextualized). When the King footage ends and we enter the feature-film world of Lee's narrative about Malcolm X, are we led to believe that these scenes share in that documentary reality and all its empowering attributes? Lee's juxtaposition (of documentary and feature footage) creates a montage effect: we carry our highly charged emotional reaction to the King video with us into the story of Malcolm X—as if King's experience were part of the backstory to X's life.

Just as the film begins with an excerpt of single-source documentary footage, it ends with a massive assembly of documentary footage. And not just that, but it ends with a variant of strictly (empirical) documentary film that might be called "choreographed documentary," where the subjects are not part of the narrative film but are still being told what to do and what to say. Candidates for choreographed documentary include footage of present-day South Africa and Harlem and a classroom of students exclaiming, "I am Malcolm X," their teacher Nelson Mandela standing nearby. Another inflection of this kind of documentary approach—something like reenactment—occurs when we hear Ossie Davis read his eulogy for Malcolm X: Davis originally presented the eulogy on February 27, 1965, and now, for Lee's film, he reads his words again as a voice-over. Davis, who also contributed to *The Autobiography of Malcolm X* (in fact, he has the last word in the book), creates a tremendous emotional energy in the film's denouement. And again, that power seems to derive from juxtaposing narrative elements (such as the choreographed documentary) beside historically grounded empirical elements (such as Davis's eulogy and even Davis himself, who is part of the nonfiction story of X's life and death).

Of all the documentary pieces assembled at the end of Lee's film, perhaps the most difficult to understand is the only film and audio of Malcolm X himself—a few seconds in the midst of the 202-minute running time. Immediately following the image and voice of Nelson Mandela, we hear and see Malcolm X say, "By any means necessary"—as if finishing Mandela's sentence. Just as Lee began with the provocative Rodney King footage, he ends with X speaking angrily and exclusively. What does Lee mean by this intervention of documentary footage? A viewer who has just seen Malcolm X return from Mecca with a new outlook may wonder whether Lee is giving the last word to a version of Malcolm X that X himself eventually denounced.

Does Lee believe that the militant X is the *real* X or the most important version of X in terms of his legacy? If so, is Lee suppressing the end of X's life—returning to an earlier time, before the protagonist's redemption, insight, or change of heart? As Ossie Davis writes in the final paragraphs of the *Autobiography:*

> But in explaining Malcolm, let me take care not to explain him away. He had been a criminal, an addict, a pimp, and a prisoner; a racist, and a hater, he had really believed the white man was a devil. But all this had changed. Two days before his death, in commenting to Gordon Parks about his past life he said: "That was a mad scene. The sickness and madness of those days! I'm glad to be free of them."
>
> And Malcolm was free. No one who knew him before and after his trip to Mecca could doubt that he had completely abandoned racism, separatism, and hatred.

Davis's sentiment is countered by Armond White, who says, "It is misleading—but typically Hollywood—to pretend that Malcolm X matters because of his late ecumenism."[43] If Hollywood is prone to emphasize redemption over deviance and turmoil, making it the logical and necessary part of our understanding of individual identity, does the presence and placement of the documentary footage of X saying "by any means necessary" imply that Lee has missed the point of X's conversion—and thus is not guilty of making a movie typical of Hollywood? Since the viewer is shown a range of documentary photographs of X—from angry stump speech to a smiling handshake with Dr. Martin Luther King Jr.—he may wonder what Lee wants him to think about X. The tone and allusive qualities of the phrase "by any means necessary" seem to be a natural fit for the anger and violence sustained in the aftermath of the Rodney King beating. Upon news of the police officers' acquittal on April 29, 1992, riots erupted in Los Angeles. At the time of the release of *Malcolm X,* Lee knew the outcome of the case. Did Lee mean for his film biography of *Malcolm X* to stand as his own contribution to the protest against such injustice? Lee ends with the agitated X, not the enlightened X.

Only a few years before *Malcolm X* appeared, Lee directed *Do the Right Thing,* which ends with scenes resembling the attack on Rodney King and the riot that erupted as a response to the police officers' acquittal. In that film, white New York City policemen apprehend Radio Raheem (Bill Nunn), place him in a choke hold, and suffocate him to death. (At the time, the dramatization referenced a 1983 incident in which Michael Stewart, a graffiti artist, had been beaten during his arrest and died following a lengthy coma.)

Lee appears to be using the Rodney King footage as a way of illustrating, in a very literal way, that white-on-black violence really happens and keeps happening—not just in his movies. As a result, Lee shows support for a correspondence theory of truth, in this case, where events outside the film are used to offer legitimacy to what happens in the film. For an activist or a politician, this theory of truth may be useful to effect change, but for an artist, it seems misplaced. Lee makes it seem that things are legitimate only when they really happen in the world; the viewer is encouraged to believe that he glimpses truth in art only when he recognizes its grounding in the affairs beyond it, when imagined things measure up to real things. On this view, art is "truer" the more it aligns with actual events. Inadvertently, Lee creates the conditions in which his fictional re-creation of X's life is dependent on empirical biography: in short, he eviscerates the authority of art by linking it to what lies beyond it. As many thinkers from Plato to Shakespeare have emphasized, truth comes from art, not directly from the world. By putting the Rodney King footage at the beginning of his film, Lee seems to be saying that Malcolm X's story is important because white men are still beating black men. But that reduces, narrows, and simplifies X's life and his contributions to culture. And even as the dependency on an extrafilmic reality diminishes the coherency of X's life, it also undermines the authority of art, including Lee's dramatic representation of that life. As one gets more invested in making a point, making art slips away.[44]

Identity and Inscription

In philosophical discussions of the self, invariably a debate emerges about whether we can refer to the identity of the self as fixed or whether it is something deeply mutable, incapable of being harmonized into anything coherent or consistent. The controversy has been around since the pre-Socratics, and it endures in contemporary discussions in the field of neuroscience.[45] How exactly are we to understand what we are referring to when we refer to a *self*? Does my name signify my self, and insofar as I have the same name, am I the same self? What if I change my name? Or what if I feel I've changed, but my name stays the same? These questions are not exhaustive, but they indicate the kinds of questions asked in relation to the persistence or transformation of personal identity.[46] Closely linked with the philosophical debate over identity is the way writing informs or even creates identity. For instance, does it make sense to say that by writing something an identity emerges? What is the relationship between the self of autobiography (the subject of the book) and the self who writes the autobiography (the author of the book)?

With *Malcolm X,* Spike Lee participates in this lengthy and ongoing debate; his film dramatizes scenes that emblematize the above questions. For example, when X learns to read by studying the dictionary, Lee places the discovery in the context of the etymological uses and cultural histories of the words *black* and *white.* As it invariably must be, the contrast between these definitions is affecting and succinctly gives credence to the sense that X is undergoing a kind of double illumination: at once learning a language and the occasional horrors it encodes. In the *Autobiography,* we learn of X's motivation to commence a disciplined study. As Haley writes in X's voice:

> I did write to Elijah Muhammad. He lived in Chicago at that time, at 6116 South Michigan Avenue. At least twenty-five times I must have written that first one-page letter to him, over and over. I was trying to make it both legible and understandable. I practically couldn't read my handwriting myself: it shames me even to remember it. My spelling and my grammar were as bad, if not worse. . . .
>
> It was because of my letters that I happened to stumble upon starting to acquire some kind of homemade education.
>
> I became increasingly frustrated at not being able to express what I wanted to convey in letters that I wrote, especially those to Mr. Elijah Muhammad. In the street, I had been the most articulate hustler out there—I had commanded attention when I said something. But now, trying to write simple English, I not only wasn't articulate, I wasn't even functional.[47]

Shame, confusion, and a sense of powerlessness lead X to commence his "prison studies."[48] He wanted to "command attention" through what he wrote, but more crucially, he wanted to make himself intelligible to another human being. He wanted what he wrote to reflect what he thought and felt; in short, he aimed to use his writing as a surrogate self, a representative that could speak for him freely, beyond the walls of his prison cell. "I saw that the best thing I could do," X recalls, "was get hold of a dictionary—to study, to learn some words."[49] Both Haley and Lee depict these "prison studies" as the process of Malcolm Little's transformation into Malcolm X. The compression of the story, in both cases, possesses the quality of a legend: X copied the dictionary, word by word, starting with *aardvark.* His writing was understood initially as a form of imitation that would eventually evolve into literacy, with its power to facilitate self-understanding and self-expression.

"I knew right there in prison that reading had changed forever the course of my life."[50] And eventually, the letters he wrote to Elijah Muhammad would be part of a process that culminated in his taking a new name.

By dramatizing X's account of copying the dictionary, Lee perpetuates a philosophy of language central to the *Autobiography*, one that does not make a lot of sense. As Mikhail Bakhtin writes: "It is not, after all, out of a dictionary that the speaker gets his words!"[51] To counter this fantasy, Lee could have offered a competing account, such as X in the process of drafting a speech, allowing the viewer to see X learning the logic of writing sentences, the difficult art of writing aphoristically. And through such a scene, Lee could have offered a theory of personal identity more consistent with the idea that literacy creates self-understanding: that for X, writing and speaking define him anew with each subsequent sentence and speech. Instead, Lee reinforces X's myth of language acquisition, a view not unlike the one with which Wittgenstein begins *The Philosophical Investigations:* a story Augustine tells in his autobiographical work, *The Confessions*, about how he learned language.[52]

In conversation with Haley, X said: "When you study the science of philology, you learn the laws governing how a consonant can lose its shape, but it keeps its identity from language to language."[53] But it is not at all clear that X himself believed that his identity persisted from name to name, from self to self. This seemed especially so in the final months of his life, after he traveled to the Middle East and adopted yet another name: El-Hajj Malik El-Shabazz. "My trip to Mecca has opened my eyes. I no longer subscribe to racism."[54] Since so many of the beliefs that had shaped his life as Malcolm X were now contradicted and overturned, it didn't seem plausible to say that he continued to be or think as Malcolm X. Just as "Detroit Red" and "Satan" and "Homeboy" were all proud and familiar names he claimed and was called during his years of criminality (but disparaged once he became Malcolm X), at the end of his life he didn't believe in what Malcolm X believed in. He had moved on to become some further self, succeeding himself. And this is what he achieved in taking a new name: a sign to mark his new worldview.

X's practice of naming and renaming himself—something Lee traces carefully throughout the film—raises anew the connection between one's name and one's identity. Especially after he leaves prison, when his naming seems part of a self-conscious decision meant to reflect a new outlook, X reconfigures identity to mean something other than a preexisting, subjective self. And yet, X himself struggled to keep things straight. With all these names, how does one refer to oneself? Does each name bespeak a different self? Or should all the names reference a single self, but from a different aspect or in a different mode of being? X was dogged by these very questions, and at one point far into their collaboration he asked Haley: "How is it possible to write one's autobiography in a world so fast-changing as this?"[55]—meaning a world in which *he* was changing so fast. How, though, would a fast-changing world—or one's fast changes in it—create an urgency about writing an autobiography? Is one's identity dependent on the identity of the world? Isn't accounting for one's changes part of any autobiographical project? After his return from Mecca in 1964, Malcolm X wrote to Haley: "I hope the book is proceeding rapidly, for events concerning my life happen so swiftly, much of what has already been written can easily be outdated from month to month. . . . So I would advise you to rush it on out as fast as possible."[56] The rush is necessitated not merely by his internal changes but also by his sense that time is running out. "If I'm alive when this book comes out it will be a miracle."[57] Only fifty weeks lie between the rupture with Elijah Muhammad and X's death; he spent twenty-five of those weeks abroad in the Middle East and Africa. Certainly X feels the urgency of living under the threat of death, but an awareness of living in danger displaces another substantive anxiety. His life story is changing too quickly for him to comprehend it, leaving him disoriented, unable to fathom what to say next. He worries about his story becoming "outdated" and containing internal contradictions that will render it unintelligible.[58] That would be the view taken by someone who believes different versions or stages of his life invalidate others; for example, that the self of Malcolm Little is incommensurable with the self of Detroit Red, and the self of El-Hajj Malik El-Shabazz is at odds with Malcolm X, and so on.

Lee uses X's continual transformations of self, naming, and identity to structure the film, and he dwells on the tensions and conflicts that arise at these moments of transition. By framing the narrative on the axis of X's experiments in personal identity, Lee proposes one of the most sympathetic aspects of X's personality and temperament: that he undergoes these changes reluctantly, almost involuntarily and accidentally. X does not shift frivolously from one identity to another, from one set of beliefs and activities to another; rather, X suffers—agonistically—each subsequent version of himself. He rends himself from place to place, awkwardly, with sweat on his brow and a quickened heartbeat. Lee does not hide or smooth over these crucial moments of transition; he slows down to give us time to appreciate these trials. In doing so, Lee ably highlights one of the core contributions of X's life to a philosophical understanding of autobiography and, subsequently, to film biography: the ability and humility to fathom identity as indefinite and perpetually unfinished. Paul John Eakin acknowledges this innovation by saying: "The disparity between the traditional autobiographical fiction of the completed self and the biographical fact of Malcolm X's ceaselessly evolving identity may lead us, as it did Malcolm X himself, to enlarge our understanding of the limits and the possibilities of autobiography."[59] One of those possibilities, as we have seen, is that writing one's autobiography need not be a solitary exercise; a second point is that, when writing, one ought not believe that the act of writing is somehow outside of one's life experience. With regard to the second point, Eakin notes that at the end of his life, "Malcolm X came to reject the traditional autobiographical fiction that the life comes first, and then the writing of the life; that the life is in some sense complete and that the autobiographical process simply records the final achieved shape."[60] X's perception that the world is too "fast-changing" and that Haley ought to "rush" the book is at odds with his calmer, deeper insight that he must sustain the effect of having successive selves—identities that follow and even contradict one another.

As he collaborated with Haley, especially in the final months of his life, X continued to make significant discoveries about the meaning and shape of his life, and it is at such times "during the writing of one's story that an autobiographer may be forced to recognize the presence and nature of the fictions on which his narrative is based."[61] Such discoveries are both liberating and terrifying, depending on one's mood, and Lee shows patience and discipline when he lets both aspects emerge in scenes of X's convulsions and contestations of identity. With each subsequent change, we are reminded of the absence of definitiveness in self-creation. Even at the very end, as X substantiates his new identity as El-Hajj Malik El-Shabazz, the viewer may legitimately wonder what innovations lie ahead. Indeed, four days before his death, X said: "I'm man enough to tell you that I can't put my finger on exactly what my philosophy is now, but I'm flexible."[62]

What would have happened to X's *Autobiography* if Haley wasn't there? Finding a response to this question goes a long way toward replying to the opening question of whether a person can write another's autobiography—and why it is important that he can. As Haley fields X's nervous questions about the possibility of writing an autobiography and his pleas to "rush" things, we find in Haley a writer with a clear sense of how the book should be written. In his epilogue, Haley gives the reader a glimpse into another reality, a world in which *The Autobiography of Malcolm X* is redacted—and rewritten—according to the beliefs of his late and last self, El-Hajj Malik El-Shabazz:

> I had become worried that Malcolm X, bitter, would want to go back through the chapters in which he had told of his Black Muslim days and re-edit them in some way. . . . I raised my concern. . . . "I have thought about that," he said. "There are a lot of things I could say that passed through my mind at times even then, things I saw and heard, but threw them out of my mind. I'm going to let it stand the way I've told it. I want the book to be the way it was."[63]

Haley was being protective of Malcolm X's story and, in particular, of the literary quality of the book he was writing. He recognized that if the reader knew at the outset that Elijah Muhammad was eventually rebuked, "the book would automatically be robbed of some of its building suspense and drama."[64] Haley pleaded with X to let Haley's account stand, the logic being that none of us knows what we will think or do in the future, so why let a future self impose insight and knowledge onto a prior self that was never privy to it?[65] Haley says, "I only made the objection" to X's threat of emendation "in my position as a writer."[66] But what other position is there? Based on this exchange and our experience of both the *Autobiography* and *Malcolm X*, the author is the creator of the selves we come to know.[67] The variety of selves in Haley's book and reflected in Lee's film are literary and cinematic inventions. This is philosophically significant, because readers and viewers are reminded that the self is not something "out there" in the world that needs to be isolated and accounted for once and for all; it is an idea that is under continual negotiation by means of writing and other modes of representation, such as film. Lee illustrates this dramatically by ending his film with documentary footage of Malcolm X saying, "By any means necessary." In doing so, Lee subverts claims that in X's "late ecumenism," his life finds its true and enduring significance (a view shared by Haley, Davis, and many others), and that the anger and violence reflected in the phrase "by any means necessary" is anachronistic.[68] In this discrete but highly consequential example, we glean how authorship creates a forum for the contested self. At last, who is writing whose autobiography?

Many things have been written about *The Autobiography of Malcolm X* as it features and functions in the American tradition of autobiographical writing—often with reference to works by Benjamin Franklin, Frederick Douglass, Henry Adams, Richard Wright, and James Baldwin, among others—and considerable attention has been paid to the special and enduring characteristics of X's autobiography.[69] It is worth exploring how *Malcolm X* figures in this tradition. I conclude by noting a point of continuity between Lee's work and the tradition: Lee uses film biography the way earlier generations used autobiography—as a means of articulating philosophical and artistic principles, while registering a protest against abuses of political power, social injustice, and racial hegemony. Lee appears to develop the genre of film biography to accord with what Roger Rosenblatt has identified as "two elements in black autobiography that are constant": "the expressed desire to live as one would choose, as far as possible; and the tacit or explicit criticism of external national conditions that, also as far as possible, work to ensure that one's freedom of choice is delimited or nonexistent."[70] Lee continually reminds us that Malcolm X, like his own film, appears in the flow of a lengthy history of tumultuous events that have often disparaged or compromised the status of African Americans. When X says, "We didn't land on Plymouth Rock, Plymouth Rock landed on us," he references 400 years of African American experience. Part of that extended experience involves the crucial role that writing played in creating political existence. As Henry Louis Gates Jr. suggests:

> Ironically, Anglo-African writing arose as a response to allegations of its absence. Black people responded to these profoundly serious allegations about their "nature" as directly as they could: they wrote books, poetry, autobiographical narratives. Political and philosophical discourse were the predominant forms of writing. Among these, autobiographical "deliverance" narratives were the most common and the most accomplished. . . . Text created author; and black authors, it was hoped, would create, re-create, the image of the race in European discourse.[71]

By framing Malcolm X's mid-twentieth-century life story amid the fraught racial climate of the late twentieth century in Los Angeles, South Africa, and Harlem, Lee continues a tradition in which black writers link the act/performance/production of writing with a defense of humanity, black humanity. Lee, using the medium of film, "writes" (and rewrites) X's autobiography, but he is also deeply—and evidently—engaged in writing his own autobiography by registering what is happening for him, making a film that summons X's life for his own ideological uses and political purposes. Even though Lee casts himself in the film—playing X's hoodlum friend Shorty—it is in other places that we discover how Lee has written himself into the film, such as the framing devices of Rodney King's beating and Nelson Mandela's soliloquy (given soon after being released from twenty-seven years of politically motivated imprisonment). Spike Lee, like Alex Haley, has contributed to the ongoing project of creating the autobiography of Malcolm X, even as he has implicated his own autobiography in that story. Lee appears to acknowledge this at the end of the film when he shows Mandela and a series of children saying, "I am Malcolm X." By claiming X's identity for oneself, one says that Malcolm X is part of *one's own* autobiography. As in Stanley Kubrick's *Spartacus* (1960), the claim of another's identity—"I am Spartacus"—functions here to create both a sense of shared humanity and a protective anonymity, which, in the end, come to the same thing. We are all Malcolm X, and we all participate in writing his autobiography insofar as we make his life part of our own.

Notes

I thank K. L. Evans (Yeshiva University) for critical remarks that proved crucial to the logic and theory of this essay, and Mark Conard for attentive editing.

1. See Kenneth Dauber, *The Idea of Authorship in America: Democratic Poetics from Franklin to Melville* (Madison: University of Wisconsin Press, 1990).

2. See *Malcolm X,* end credits sequence.

3. Plato, *Complete Works,* ed. John M. Cooper and D. S. Hutchinson (Indianapolis: Hackett, 1997).

4. Boethius, *Theological Tractates, The Consolations of Philosophy,* trans. H. F. Stewart, E. K. Rand, and S. J. Tester (Cambridge, Mass.: Harvard University Press, 1973).

5. Michel de Montaigne, *The Complete Essays of Montaigne,* trans. Donald Frame (Stanford, Calif.: Stanford University Press, 1958), xxvi.

6. John Locke, *An Essay Concerning Human Understanding* (1689) (Indianapolis: Hackett, 1996), chap. 27, sec. 9, p. 138.

7. René Descartes, *Discourse on Method* (1637), pt. IV.

8. David Hume, *Treatise of Human Nature: Being an Attempt to Introduce the Experimental Method of Reasoning into Moral Subjects* (1739).

9. Ludwig Wittgenstein, *Tractatus Logico-Philosophicus,* trans. D. F. Pears and B. F. McGuinness (London: Routledge, 1974), §5.631, p. 57.

10. *The Žižek Reader,* ed. Elizabeth Wright and Edmond Wright (Oxford: Blackwell, 1999), viii–ix.

11. Scientific developments that impact our accounts of the self include quantum mechanics, bioinformatics, and a range of materialist theories (for instance, where consciousness is understood to be an epiphenomenon—or effect—of the changes in purely physical arrangements).

12. *Žižek Reader,* ix.

13. William C. Spengemann and L. R. Lundquist, "Autobiography and the American Myth," *American Quarterly* 17, 3 (autumn 1965): 516.

14. A meronym is a literal semantic relationship between words or concepts. A

gunshot is part of the total attributes of a real gun; thus the sound signals a relationship to the object. The gunshot may also be read figuratively as a synecdoche—a part of a whole that can stand as its representative; using a meronym to refer to its holonym is a synecdoche.

15. *Malcolm X* DVD (1992), 18:43 (disc 1).

16. Ibid., 44:11.

17. Ibid., 1:03:24 (disc 2).

18. Ibid., 1:04:13.

19. Ibid., 1:10:20. For further discussion of Lee's use of this technique, see Jerold J. Abrams's essay in this volume.

20. Ralph Waldo Emerson, "Experience," in *Essays, Lectures, and Addresses,* ed. Joel Porte (New York: Library of America, 1983), 471.

21. In his Greenwich Village apartment, Alex Haley found the following aphorism by an unknown Persian poet written by Malcolm X on a napkin: "Learn wisdom from the pupil of the eye that looks upon all things and yet to self is blind."

22. *The Autobiography of Malcolm X as Told to Alex Haley* (New York: Ballantine Books, 1992), 460; hereafter cited as *Autobiography.*

23. Stanley Cavell, *The World Viewed: Reflections on the Ontology of Film,* enlarged ed. (Cambridge, Mass.: Harvard University Press, 1979), esp. chap. 4.

24. *Autobiography,* 447.

25. Ibid., 444.

26. Ibid., 447–49.

27. Ibid., 472.

28. Ibid., 449.

29. Ibid., 523.

30. Ibid., 445.

31. Ibid., 448.

32. Leaving Haley out of *Malcolm X* ignores a significant part of X's late life. One can imagine a film biography that employs Haley as a central character, finding in his relationship with X and their meetings in Greenwich Village an opportunity to explore not only the intimate revelations of X's life but also the issues at stake in filming scenes of metaphilosophical discovery, such as occur in the *Autobiography.*

33. Consider an inversion between Alex Haley and Samuel Taylor Coleridge: Haley wrote as a biographer who fashioned an autobiography, and Coleridge claimed to be writing an autobiography but ended up calling it *Biographia Literaria.* Haley, then, became someone else's autobiographer, while Coleridge became his own biographer.

34. "The term 'autobiography' implies only that the author is writing specifically about himself; it has nothing to do with factual truth. Autobiography does not communicate raw experience, for that is uncommunicable. It presents, rather, a metaphor for the raw experience. The language of autobiography stands in symbolic relation to both author and subject." Spengemann and Lundquist, "Autobiography and the American Myth," 501–2. The controversy surrounding James Frey's admission that some of the things in his memoir *A Million Little Pieces* (New York: Doubleday, 2003) did not happen

as he describes them provides an occasion to consider the implications of Spengemann and Lundquist's claim, including an understanding of the truth one expects to find in an autobiography, for example, as opposed to a novel. Frey says his memoir is "a combination of facts about my life and certain embellishments. It is a subjective truth." In a new preface saturated with contrition that was added to post-controversy copies of the book, Frey characterizes his error as "writing about the person I created in my mind to help me cope, and not the person who went through the experience." For more on Frey, see Ben Yagoda, *Memoir: A History* (New York: Riverhead Books, 2009), and a review of Yagoda's book by Daniel Mendelsohn, "But Enough about Me," *New Yorker*, January 25, 2010, 68–74.

35. Stephen Davies, *Empiricism and History* (New York: Palgrave, 2003), 45.

36. Ibid., 49.

37. Ibid.

38. Ibid., 50.

39. Ibid.

40. Ibid., 52.

41. Ibid., 57.

42. For more on the King incident in the context of cultural, judicial, and media history, see Linda Williams, *Playing the Race Card: Melodramas of Black and White from Uncle Tom to O. J. Simpson* (Princeton, N.J.: Princeton University Press, 2001), 252–95.

43. Armond White, "Malcolm X'd Again," in *American Movie Critics: An Anthology from the Silents until Now*, ed. Phillip Lopate (New York: Library of America, 2006), 578.

44. Didacticism, though not always appealing, seems to function better in documentary film than in features. Given Lee's demonstrated talent for documentary, exhibited at the conclusion of *Malcolm X*, it is gratifying to see that after finishing the film Lee went on to make several acclaimed documentaries. Lee's first feature-length documentary as director was *4 Little Girls* (1997), about the 1963 church bombing in Birmingham, Alabama. Others include *The Original Kings of Comedy* (2000), *Jim Brown: All American* (2002), *We Was Robbed* (2002), *When the Levees Broke: A Requiem in Four Acts* (2006), *Passing Strange* (2008), and *Kobe Doing Work* (2009).

45. For reflections on personal identity among the pre-Socratics—especially Pythagoras and Epicharmus—see Jonathan Barnes, *The Presocratic Philosophers: From Thales to Zeno* (London: Routledge, 1979), 1:106–16. For works in neuroscience, see Anthony Damasio, *Descartes' Error: Emotion, Reason, and the Human Brain* (New York: Avon Books, 1994); A. R. Luria, *The Man with a Shattered World: The History of a Brain Wound* (Cambridge, Mass.: Harvard University Press, 1997), and *The Mind of a Mnemonist: A Little Book about a Vast Memory* (New York: Basic Books, 1998); Steven Pinker, *How the Mind Works* (New York: W. W. Norton, 1999), and *The Blank Slate: The Modern Denial of Human Nature* (New York: Viking, 2002); and Oliver Sacks, *The Man Who Mistook His Wife for a Hat* (1970; reprint, New York: Touchstone, 1998). For an account with a wider historical scope, consult Raymond Martin and John Barresi, *The Rise and Fall of the Soul and Self: An Intellectual History of Personal Identity* (New York: Columbia University Press, 2006).

46. The idea of persistence, as it relates to personal identity, raises the question of the extent to which one can speak of being the same person over time. Also related is the question of whether one continues to exist, as it were, out of time—either prior to or after earthly existence. Plato's *Phaedo* is a historically early engagement with the nature of identity persistence after life has expired.

47. *Autobiography,* 195, 197.

48. Ibid., 198.

49. Ibid.

50. Ibid., 206.

51. "[The word] becomes 'one's own' only when the speaker populates it with his own intention, his own accent, when he appropriates the word, adapting it to his own semantic and expressive intention. Prior to this moment of appropriation, the word does not exist in a neutral and impersonal language (it is not, after all, out of a dictionary that the speaker gets his words!), but rather it exists in other people's mouths, in other people's contexts, serving other people's intentions: it is from there that one must take the word, and make it one's own." Mikhail Bakhtin, "Discourse in the Novel," in *The Dialogic Imagination,* ed. Michael Holquist, trans. Caryl Emerson and Michael Holquist (Austin: University of Texas Press, 1981), 293–94.

52. Ludwig Wittgenstein, *The Philosophical Investigations,* trans. G. E. M. Anscombe (Englewood Cliffs, N.J.: Prentice Hall, 1958).

53. *Autobiography,* 478.

54. Ibid., 474.

55. Ibid., 469.

56. Ibid., 475.

57. Ibid., 471. "Every autobiography, black and white, is an extended suicide note; both announcement and vindication of the event." Roger Rosenblatt, "Black Autobiography: Life as the Death Weapon," in *Autobiography: Essays Theoretical and Critical,* ed. James Olney (Princeton, N.J.: Princeton University Press, 1980), 178.

58. "The autobiographer has always had to consider how to manage, and whether to dramatize, the discontinuities inherent in autobiographical recreation." Frances R. Hart, "Notes for an Anatomy of Modern Autobiography," *New Literary History* 1 (1970): 489, 501.

59. Paul John Eakin, "Malcolm X and the Limits of Autobiography," in *Autobiography: Essays Theoretical and Critical,* 183. Although he quotes from this essay by Eakin, Bashir M. El-Beshti claims that the *Autobiography* offers "the authorial speaking voice, the one telling us about this string of provisional identities that finally culminate with the autobiographical self, one that is seen to be final and complete." "The Semiotics of Salvation: Malcolm X and the Autobiographical Self," *Journal of Negro History* 82, 4 (autumn 1997): 359.

60. Eakin, "Malcolm X and the Limits of Autobiography," 192. The commonness of this belief, which Eakin describes as a "fiction," shows people subscribing to "the natural and seemingly inevitable inference that the individual first discovers the shape of his life and then writes the life on the basis of this discovery." Ibid., 183.

61. Ibid., 184.

62. Ibid., 182.

63. *Autobiography,* 473. "The problem of establishing a subject and form gives special interest to the rewriting of autobiographies. . . . For whether the restlessness that brings a man back to recast his image and form be psychic or critical, the stages of his self-presentation have to be tied up with a question of identity; the autobiographer loses clarity and authority even as he multiplies himself. One's autobiograph*ies* constitute an anomaly, though autobiography, as Wordsworth and Malcolm X in different ways have shown, may be generated out of a subject's knowing struggle for identity, by stages, or his undergoing a conscious evolution of self-conception." M. G. Cooke, "Modern Black Autobiography in the Tradition," in *Romanticism: Vistas, Instances, Continuities,* ed. David Thorburn and Geoffrey Hartman (Ithaca, N.Y.: Cornell University Press, 1973), 259.

64. *Autobiography,* 476.

65. "The distinctive feature of the *Autobiography* is its naturalistic use of time, the willingness to let the past stand as it was, in its own season, even when later developments, of intellect or intuition or event, give it a different quality." Cooke, "Modern Black Autobiography," 274.

66. *Autobiography,* 476.

67. James Baldwin spent two years writing a screenplay adaptation of Haley's *Autobiography,* completing it only after the death of his cowriter, Arnold Perl, in 1971. James Baldwin's estate would not give permission for him to be listed as a screenwriter on *Malcolm X,* so Lee shares screenwriting credit with Perl.

68. X continued to use the phrase "by any means necessary"—with a clear promise of physical violence, initiated or reactive—until just weeks before his death. At a public rally in Harlem on January 24, 1965, X read from a telegram he had sent to the head of the American Nazi Party: "This is to warn you that I am no longer held in check from fighting white supremacists by Elijah Muhammad's separatist Black Muslin movement, and that if your present racist agitation against our people there in Alabama causes physical harm to Reverend King or any other black Americans who are only attempting to enjoy their rights as free human beings, that you and your Ku Klux Klan friends will be met with maximum physical retaliation from those of us who are not hand-cuffed by the disarming philosophy of nonviolence, and who believe in asserting our right of self-defense—by any means necessary." *Malcolm X Speaks: Selected Speeches and Statements,* ed. George Breitman (New York: Grove Press, 1965), 201.

69. Werner Berthoff, "Witness and Testament: Two Contemporary Classics," *New Literary History* 2 (1971): 318, 320; Eakin, "Malcolm X and the Limits of Autobiography"; Barrett John Mandel, "The Didactic Achievement of Malcolm X's Autobiography," *Afro-American Studies* 2 (1972): 269–74; Carol Ohmann, "*The Autobiography of Malcolm X:* A Revolutionary Use of the Franklin Tradition," *American Quarterly* 22 (1970): 131–49. See also *Malcolm X: The Man and His Times,* ed. John Henrik Clarke (New York: Macamillan, 1969). For work on autobiography, including American autobiography, see William C. Spengemann, *The Forms of Autobiography: Episodes in the History of a Literary Genre*

(New Haven, Conn.: Yale University Press, 1980); and Elizabeth W. Bruss, *Autobiographical Acts: The Changing Situation of a Literary Genre* (Baltimore: Johns Hopkins University Press, 1976), and *American Autobiography: Retrospect and Prospect*, ed. Paul John Eakin (Madison: University of Wisconsin Press, 1991).

70. Rosenblatt, "Black Autobiography," 170.

71. Henry Louis Gates Jr., "Writing, 'Race' and the Difference It Makes," in *"Race," Writing and Difference*, ed. Henry Louis Gates Jr. (Chicago: University of Chicago Press, 1985), 11.

Contributors

JEROLD J. ABRAMS is associate professor of philosophy at Creighton University in Omaha, Nebraska, where he teaches and writes on pragmatism, bioethics, and the philosophy of film. His essays have appeared in several volumes on film and popular culture, and he is the editor of *The Philosophy of Stanley Kubrick*.

GABRIELLA BECKLES-RAYMOND is currently completing her PhD dissertation, which explores questions of liberal theory and mixed-race identity. She has worked as a freelance writer, and her research interests include social and political philosophy, critical race theory, moral psychology, and culture.

MARK T. CONARD is associate professor of philosophy and chair of the Philosophy and Religious Studies Department at Marymount Manhattan College in New York City. He's the coeditor of *The Simpsons and Philosophy* and *Woody Allen and Philosophy* and the editor of *The Philosophy of Film Noir*, *The Philosophy of Neo-Noir*, *The Philosophy of Martin Scorsese*, and *The Philosophy of the Coen Brothers*.

ELIZABETH HOPE FINNEGAN is assistant professor of English at D'Youville College in Buffalo, New York. She is a filmmaker and painter whose works have been exhibited internationally. Her films, which combine narrative, experimental, and documentary forms to both expand and challenge traditional notions of narrative and narrativity, have won awards at festivals in the United States, Canada, and Germany.

DAN FLORY is associate professor of philosophy at Montana State University, Bozeman. His publications include several essays on philosophy, film, and critical race theory, and he is the author of *Philosophy, Black Film, Film*

Noir. He has served twice as guest editor for the journal *Film and Philosophy* and is currently working on a book about empathy, race, and philosophical reflection.

Richard Gilmore is associate professor of philosophy at Concordia College in Moorhead, Minnesota. He is the author of *Philosophical Health: Wittgenstein's Method in "Philosophical Investigations"* and *Doing Philosophy at the Movies.*

Karen D. Hoffman is associate professor of philosophy at Hood College in Frederick, Maryland. She has authored essays on philosophy and film for *The Philosophy of Stanley Kubrick, The Philosophy of Martin Scorsese,* and *The Philosophy of the Coen Brothers.*

Jason Holt is associate professor in the School of Recreation Management and Kinesiology at Acadia University, where he teaches communication and philosophy of sport. His books include *Flexibility: A Concise Guide* (with L. E. Holt and T. W. Pelham), *The Daily Show and Philosophy* (editor), and *Blindsight and the Nature of Consciousness,* which was shortlisted for the 2005 Canadian Philosophical Association Book Prize.

David LaRocca is coordinating producer and consulting editor of the documentary film project *The Intellectual Portrait Series.* He is the author of *On Emerson* and the editor of Stanley Cavell's book *Emerson's Transcendental Etudes* and *The Philosophy of Charlie Kaufman.* His articles on film, autobiography, and aesthetic theory have appeared in *Epoché, Film and Philosophy, Afterimage,* and *The Journal of Aesthetics and Art Criticism.*

Douglas McFarland is professor of liberal studies and director of the General Education Program at Flagler College in St. Augustine, Florida, where he teaches classics and film studies. He has published works on Alfred Hitchcock, the Coen brothers, and John Frankenheimer and is currently at work on a book-length study of the early films of Peter Bogdanovich.

R. Barton Palmer is Calhoun Lemon Professor of Literature at Clemson University, where he also directs the Film Studies Program and serves as interim chair of the Department of English. He is the author, editor, or general editor of more than forty books on various film and literary subjects. His books include *Hollywood's Dark Cinema: The American Film Noir* and *Joel and Ethan Coen.* He has edited *Perspectives on Film Noir, After Hitchcock:*

Imitation, Influence, Intertextuality (with David Boyd), and *Nineteenth and Twentieth Century American Fiction on Screen.* With Steven Sanders, he recently edited *The Philosophy of Steven Soderbergh.*

CHARLES F. PETERSON is associate professor of Africana studies and chair of the Cultural Area Studies Program at The College of Wooster in Ohio. He is the author of *DuBois, Fanon, Cabral: The Margins of Elite Anti-Colonial Leadership.*

ROBERT PITTER is associate professor in the School of Recreation Management and Kinesiology at Acadia University, where he teaches courses on sport, physical culture, and media. His research focuses on topics concerning sport and society, and his articles have appeared in *Quest, Sociology of Sport Journal, International Review for Sociology of Sport, Industrial and Environmental Crises Quarterly,* and *Technology Studies.*

MICHAEL SILBERSTEIN is professor of philosophy at Elizabethtown College and permanent adjunct professor at the University of Maryland–College Park, where he is also a faculty member in the Foundations of Physics Program. His primary research interests are foundations of physics and foundations of cognitive science, as well as how these branches of philosophy and science bear on more general questions of reduction, emergence, and explanation. He also writes about film whenever possible and is writing a book on film and interpretation.

RONALD R. SUNDSTROM is associate professor of philosophy at the University of San Francisco. His areas of research include race theory, political and social theory, and African and Asian American philosophy. He has published several essays in these areas and is the author of *The Browning of America and the Evasion of Social Justice.*

Index